GALA

HEALT[...]
YOUR [...]

D0725738

VOLUME 2

Parts 1 & 2
(Instant Diagnosis &
Cure of Serious Diseases)

DEVENDRA VORA, M.D. (Honorary)

(Honorary Degrees bestowed upon by International
University for Complementary Medicines, Colombo, Sri Lanka)

Thirteenth Edition

NAVNEET ®

Knowledge is wealth

years of

1959 2009

imparting
knowledge

NAVNEET PUBLICATIONS (INDIA) LIMITED

Navneet House	**Navneet Bhavan**
Gurukul Road, Memnagar, Ahmadabad – 380 052.	Bhavani Shankar Road, Dadar, Mumbai – 400 028.
Phone : 6630 5000	Phone : 6662 6565

DHANLAL BROTHERS DISTRIBUTORS

70, Princess Street, Mumbai – 400 002.
Phone : 2201 7027 / 2205 3716

G 4501

Visit us at : www.navneet.com | e-mail : npil@navneet.com

Price : Rs. 85.00

(Concessional rate for India only)

Dedicated
to
Mother Nature

Write to: **Dr. Devendra VORA**   Phone: 2649 1564
(Only in Hindi or English or Gujarati)   Only between 8.00 to 10.00 A.M.
C/7, Vasant Kunj, North Avenue,   & 5.00 to 8.00 P.M.
Santacruz (W), Mumbai – 400 054.   E-mail: doctordevendra@vsnl.net

For Personal Guidance Contact Dr. Devendra Vora at

ACUPRESSURE CENTRES

1) SANTACRUZ (West):
SMT B C J HOSPITAL ACUP. CENTRE
(Asha Parekh S & M Ward), S. V. Rd.,
Santacruz (W), Mumbai – 400 054.

Days/Timings:
Wednesdays   9.00 a.m. to 10.30 a.m.
Saturdays   4.30 p.m. to 6.00 p.m.

2) KHAR (West):
THE KHAR RESIDENTS' ASSOCN. (Regd.)
Kamalabai Nimbkar Library,
Nr. Madhu Park, Khar (West),
Mumbai – 400 052.

Days/Timings:
Sundays   9.00 a.m. to. 11.00 a.m.
Thursdays 4.00 p.m. to 6.00 p.m.

3) GHATKOPAR (West):
SARVODAYA HOSP. ACUP. CENTRE
LBS Marg, Ghatkopar (W),
Mumbai – 400 086

Days/Timings:
Saturdays 9.00 a.m. to 10.30 a.m.
Tuesdays 9.00 a.m. to 10.30 a.m.

4) CHEMBUR:
MEDICAL RELIEF CENTRE
Shree Chembur Jain Sangh,
Opp. Jain Mandir, Chembur,
Mumbai – 400 071.

Days/Timings:
Mondays 4.00 p.m. to 6.00 p.m.
Fridays 4.00 p.m. to 6.00 p.m.

Dr. Devendra Vora conducts Training Course of
"BE A DOCTOR IN 12 HOURS" Based on his Bestseller
books "HEALTH IN YOUR HANDS – VOLUME I & II".
Any Organization/University who desire to arrange such
Training Seminar may contact at the above address.

ACUPRESSURE

Acupressure is a great boon given to mankind by the Creator/Nature.

Baby, just one day old, can take treatment of Acupressure – No side effects.

CANCER, can also be prevented, diagnosed and cured at home.

Diagnosis made with Acupressure is equal to M.R.I. test-which can be done by oneself and without any cost.

Easy-most easy-even a child of 10 years can practise it and so it is excellent.

FREEDOM from fears about all types of diseases, even Cancer and HIV/AIDS.

"FANTASTIC IS ACUPRESSURE"

These books – Health in Your Hands : Volume 1 & 2
will bring REVOLUTION
in Medical World &
Health & Happiness to ALL ....

PROUD PUBLISHERS
are

 NAVNEET PUBLICATIONS (INDIA) LIMITED

Mumbai : 1. Bhavani Shankar Road, Dadar, **Mumbai – 400 028.**
(Tel. 6662 6565 • Fax : 6662 6470)

2. **Navyug Distributors :** Road No. 8, M. I. D. C., Next to Indian Institute of Packaging, Marol, Andheri (East), **Mumbai – 400 093.** (Tel. 2821 4186 • Fax : 2835 2758)

Ahmadabad : Navneet House, Gurukul Road, Memnagar, **Ahmadabad – 380 052.**
(Tel. 6630 5000)

Bengalooru : Sri Balaji's, No. 12, 2nd Floor, 3rd Cross, Malleswaram, **Bengalooru – 560 003.**
(Tel. 2346 5740)

Chennai : 30, Sriram Nagar, North Street, Alwarpet, **Chennai – 600 018.** (Tel. 2434 6404)

Delhi : 2-E/23, Orion Plaza, 2nd Floor, Jhandewalan Extn., **New Delhi – 110 055.**
(Tel. 2361 0170)

Hyderabad : Kalki Plaza, Plot No. 67, Krishnapuri Colony, West Maredpalley,
Secunderabad – 500 026. (Tel. 2780 0146)

Kolkata : 1st Floor, 7, Suren Tagore Road, **Kolkata – 700 019.** (Tel. 2460 4178)

Nagpur : 63, Opp. Shivaji Science College, Congress Nagar, **Nagpur – 440 012.** (Tel. 242 1522)

Nashik : Dharmaraj Plaza, Old Gangapur Naka, Gangapur Road, **Nashik – 422 005.**
(Tel. 231 0627)

Navsari : 3/C, Arvind Nagar Society, Lunsikui Road, **Navsari – 396 445.** (Tel. 244 186)

Patna : 205, Jagdamba Tower, 2nd Floor, Sahdeo Mahto Marg, Srikrishnapuri,
Patna – 800 001. (Tel. 254 0321)

Pune : Navneet Bhavan, 1302, Shukrawar Peth, Near Sanas Plaza, Bajirao Road,
Pune – 411 002. (Tel. 2443 1007)

Rajkot : 20-21, Jagnath Corner, B/h Dhanrajani Builiding, Yagnik Road,
Rajkot – 360 001.

Surat : 1, Ground Floor, Sri Vallabh Complex, Kotwal Street, Nanpara, **Surat – 395 001.**
(Tel. 246 3927)

Vadodara : Near Hanuman Wadi, Sardar Bhuvan Khancho, **Vadodara – 390 001.**

Printed & Published by Navneet Publications (India) Ltd., Dantali, Gujarat.

ABOUT THE AUTHOR

Sri Devendra Vora hails from a noble, religious Jain family of Bhavnagar (Gujarat), India. He is a Commerce Graduate and as an exporter of Rayon fabrics, he has been awarded the National Award twice, for having the highest export from India.

Since 1977, he has dedicated his life to give health and happiness to mankind through Nature's own health science of Acupressure of ancient India. Open International University bestowed on him degrees of D.Sc., M.D. and F.R.C.P. a Merit Medal for his Research about Cancer. He has made several outstanding RESEARCHES in this medical field and put ACUPRESSURE on top of all the therapies; so that Cancer has become one of the easiest diseases to be cured. He has shown an easy way to Instant Diagnosis and Cure for almost all diseases from common cold to HIV/AIDS.

His achievements during the last 23 years have been phenomenal. He has personally examined over 2,00,000 patients, which include 2500 Medical Practitioners. He has given training to over 30,000 students of Acupressure in India and abroad.

More than 50 million patients have benefited from this therapy. His desire is to eradicate cancer and cataract from the world and give health and happiness to all.

He is also a poet and has written poems in Gujarati, Hindi and English since the age of 18. Out of his five collections of poems, the first one – 'Priti Bhavo Bhavni' – in Gujarati, a saga about conjugal eternal love is published.

He has great interest in religion and his book 'Glimpses of Jainism and Lord Mahavir' is published.

He loves sports, music and mankind.

FOREWORD

It is my pleasure and privilege to write foreword to this book, "Health In Your Hands : Volume 2 – Part – 1". Most of my time has been spent in medical studies and practices all these years. To be honest I was not aware that Science of Acupressure did exist. For this I am grateful to my friend Raji who introduced me to Shri Devendra Vora, Pioneer of Acupressure in India and who has already published two most popular books, "HEALTH IN YOUR HANDS : Volume 1 & 2", of which more than 2 million copies are sold out.

My friend Raji had appendicitis five years ago. She had gone through all the necessary tests in a famous hospital. She was advised to undergo operation the very next day. But she had to look after her bedridden mother, therefore she backed out of the operation. The surgeon even threatened her, "If you come 24 hours late, peritonitis will set in and I will not touch you." The brave lady accepted the challenge and with a common friend went to seek Shri Vora's advice. Within 8 days her pain subsided and in 60 days she was completely cured. This was a great revelation to me.

After a year or so, I had pain in both lower extremities. Being a patient of peptic ulcer it was not possible to take too many painkillers. At that point of time, my friend coaxed me to visit the Santacruz Centre to meet Shri Vora. He immediately diagnosed that I had a problem of the Sciatic nerve. As per his advice I started the treatment. Lo and behold, within 8 days my pain was gone. Since then, I am a firm believer in Acupressure Therapy. I joined his classes and worked with him for three months. Since then, I consider him as my Guru.

I have gone through all the chapters of this book. They have been written with great care and affection. Even the dreaded diseases have been clearly discussed and advice has been given in simple ways. The way he arrives at diagnosis is simply marvellous. This has not come to him easily. There is lot of hard work and a research-oriented mind behind this. In this book, he has explained how he arrives at a diagnosis. I have observed that not only the diagnosis made by him is instant and costless but it is equal to any diagnosis arrived at through X-Rays, Sonography and M.R.I. Tests. The most important aspect of medical treatment is proper diagnosis as early as possible. By just reading this book, the patient will be able to diagnose his/her problem and start treatment immediately. **Thus, this book is a great boon to mankind.**

In my day to day practice, I too preach Acupressure methods. Many of my colleagues have been informed about this. We have even met the higher authorities of Mumbai University and requested them to include Acupressure Science as a subject for college students.

Prevention is always better than cure. So far only a few people have heeded our requests. But a day will soon come when all will turn their attention to such a safe alternative method of medicine.

Shri Devendra Vora's dream is to reach this book to all people who will benefit from it. I pray all homes have this book and utilise the knowledge given to maintain good health. Perhaps our busy lifestyle prevents us from taking interest in the care of our body. If we devote at least 10 minutes daily for ourselves, it will do a lot of good.

I congratulate Shri Vora for writing this book in simple language so that it is understood by laypersons irrespective of their educational qualifications. I am confident that this book will be widely read and appreciated not only in India but also all over the World.

– Dr. (Smt.) Chandra M. Shanbag
M.D., D.G.O, D.F.P., F.C.P.S.

101, Nagree Terraces,
Soonawala Agiary Road,
Mahim,
Mumbai – 400 016.

PREFACE

During the last twenty years, I have examined more than 2,00,000 patients, who have come to me as a last resort. After trying out other therapies and not having been cured; these patients come without much knowledge about Acupressure. I have made it a point to go to the root cause of their problems. I am not carried away by complaints or medical reports brought by the patients. The science of Acupressure has enabled me to arrive at a correct diagnosis. In the first meeting with the patient about 90% of the root causes are found out; and the remaining 10%, of the root cause is found out in the second or third meetings. Since I am pressed for time, having to examine about 40 to 50 patients in an hour, I hardly get about 75 seconds to arrive at the correct diagnosis. In spite of that, with the grace of the Great Supreme Power, which controls the cosmos, the diagnosis made uptil now have been correct. The treatment suggested on the basis of the diagnosis has proved to be effective showing a marked improvement within 10 days.

Many a time, I have given a totally different diagnosis than that made by the doctors, who treated the patients previously. In more than 85% of the cases of continued cold, sinusitis and even Asthma, the root cause has been found to be 'excess heat in the body'. In several cases of Asthma exceeding 20/25 years, it has been found out that it was not Asthma, but 'excess heat in the body', along with side effects of the drugs/treatment taken on the basis of wrong diagnosis.

Even in cases of Cancer in the elementary stages, it can be detected and even its location in the body can also be detected. Later on all types of Cancer can be easily cured. During the last 10 years, I have traced such Cancer, which I call as 'degeneration' in over 10,000 patients and only in 15 days, with immediate treatment, there has been marked improvement. Even in cases, where patients are aware of his/her problem I ask them not to tell me. Just by pressing certain points, I am able to pinpoint the location of such Cancer and its degree.

During the last ten years, more than three hundred patients suffering from trouble of kidneys and advised transplantation have come to me. Transplantation is not only a costly affair, but also it is difficult to find a suitable kidney. Since this is time-consuming, patients prefer to try other therapies as a last recourse. On thorough examination of such patients, the damage to the kidneys was found to be less than 50%. In the case of female patients, it was found out that there was degeneration in the uterus. In the case of male patients, in most of the cases, the root cause was found to be degeneration in prostate. In few cases, these patients also had venereal disease. All these patients were put on proper treatment in their homes. Every 15 to 20 days they came to our free centre for check-up and as improvement was noticed, they were asked to continue treatment. And surprisingly, within five to eight weeks, these patients were cured of their problems. Dialysis was stopped from the very beginning. Later on, the same experts who had recommended kidney transplantation agreed that there was no necessity of such operations.

This health therapy of Acupressure has enabled me to go to the deepest root cause of any disease. A five-year-old girl was brought to me with a complaint that she did not feel hungry, had cough and cold very often and was very pale–anaemic. On examination, she was found to have worms in intestines, her spleen, liver, pancreas, adrenal, thyroid and parathyroid were found not working properly. This indicated Thalassaemia minor. Immediately I examined her seven-year-old brother, who had accompanied her for check-up. He was also found to have Thalassaemia minor. Such problems are inherited from parents, so I checked them. The father was found to be suffering from venereal disease which he confirmed; whereas, the mother from infection of uterus, i.e. degeneration in uterus. The medical check-up took me only 6 minutes and the family was guided to take proper treatment.

During the last twenty years, more than 2,500 medical practitioners have come to me for check-up and guidance. The root cause of the problem in many of these doctors was different than what they believed. They were impressed with this instant quick diagnosis and took treatment and later on reported being cured. In fact, this has increased my faith in the efficacy of Nature's health science of Acupressure.

The above facts prove the utmost importance of correct diagnosis. Sometimes, many of my patients and even my colleagues suspect that I have some hidden knowledge, which enables me to come to a proper diagnosis in a short time. Although I am totally dedicated to Acupressure, I do not have any special power or extra knowledge. Whatever I have learnt from experience and from insight, I am explaining in this book.

It is true that for doing all these diagnoses, I have used my thumb and fingers and I have examined the palms of the patients, and there has been no necessity to use any other instruments nor do any tests. The costs of instruments and machines which are used for the tests of E.C.G., Sonography, M.R.I., etc. are exhorbitant, and therefore they cannot be imported by poor developing countries. And so most people of these countries do not get the benefits of this advanced technology. Only a few wealthy patients of these poor nations can afford to go to the U.S.A. or U.K. for medical check-up and treatment. For instance, a 39-year-old patient, after three years of unsuccessful treatment in Bangkok, Thailand, went to London, U.K. He was informed that he had Leukaemia, i.e. blood cancer and there was no guaranteed cure for the same. He saw my book in one bookstore in London, bought it and got inspired. He requested me to come to Bangkok, but as I do not go anywhere to see patients, I asked him to come to our free Centre at Santacruz, Mumbai. He was surprised with the correct diagnosis made without any tests and instruments or without seeing his medical reports. He was happy to learn that his disease could be cured and so asked his wife to come to Mumbai for medical check-up. She was found to have Cancer of the uterus. The couple left Mumbai with great satisfaction and confidence and after three months, he reported that they were cured.

Now, with my latest research, it is possible to detect HIV in its elementary stage. In such cases, I call the husband, wife and their children below fifteen years. And uptil now, in more than 6000 families my doubt has been found correct. All these patients are guided to take treatment at home and within 45 to 60 days, I am happy to see that their HIV has become negative.

Thus it can be observed that the diagnosis made by Acupressure is equal to or even better than that of M.R.I. test, because the report is instant. Any medical practitioner or for that matter even a patient can diagnose the problem without any test or cost.

As M.R.I. test is not free even in advanced countries, so in most of the cases M.R.I. test is not done. A method of trial and emission is followed. I have conducted such health camps in Canada, U.S.A., U.K. and Germany and found that the patients were suffering from a long time and had many side effects because proper diagnosis was not done. A medical practitioner may practise any branch of therapy but in order to start proper treatment immediately it is most necessary to come to a proper diagnosis at the earliest.

I am not a Medical Doctor and I am not aware of the names of various diseases. But my desire has been to be useful to mankind and so whatever knowledge, experience and insight I have acquired from examining over 2,00,000 patients, I have put in this book. Further, thousands of my students, medical practitioners and millions of readers have confirmed the efficacy of Acupressure. This has inspired me to write this book for the benefit of all the medical practitioners and Mankind.

– **Devendra Vora**

30th December, 2001

HEALTH IN YOUR HANDS

Part 1

Instant
Diagnosis

DEVENDRA VORA M.D.

CONTENTS

LEGAL NOTICE

CHAPTER 1

IMPORTANCE OF PROPER DIAGNOSIS

In an advanced country like the U.S.A., where people are aware of the side effects of drugs, the average medical cost in 1992 was about $1300 per man, woman and child. The cost of medical services was over 10 % of the Gross National Product (Income). In their best-seller book, 'Take Care Of Yourself', Donald M. Vickery, M.D. and James F. Fries, M.D. say, "Among the billions of different medical services used each year, some are life saving, some result in great medical improvement and some give great comfort. But there are some that are totally unnecessary and harmful. You can even suffer physical harm if you receive a drug that you don't need or a test that you don't require."

"Drugs obviously have many beneficial effects and so they are consumed. However from time to time it can have undesirable effects–called the side effects or adverse reactions." Some of them are simply annoyances, some are more serious, though not dangerous. Finally, some are dangerous leading to severe diarrhoea, erratic heartbeats and palpitations, throbbing headaches, kidney problems, etc. **"Such adverse reactions are serious and capable of causing death and so outweigh the benefits of drugs."**

"There are basically two types of side effects–those that are obvious to the patient and other that can be detected only through laboratory tests."

"There are about 40 drugs which may cause diarrhoea. About more than 20 drugs which may cause fluid retention. About 40 drugs which may damage nervous system. And more than 20 drugs which may cause blood diseases. All these drugs are commonly and immensely consumed." These quotations are taken from "Family Medical Guide" by the editors of Consumer Guide (having a sale of over 30 million copies in the U.S.A.) – Ila J. Chansnoff M.D., Jeffery W. Ellis, M.D. and Zachary S. Finnman, M.D.

"The patients may take the drug improperly or at a wrong time or too frequently. They may continue drinking alcohol or taking other drugs perhaps not realising that such things as pills for cold, oral contraceptives and vitamins could affect the action of the prescribed drug. The end result may be that the patients do not get better; perhaps they may suffer a dangerous overdose." Editors of Consumer Guide for Prescription Drugs – 1991 edition.

"People over the age of 50, constitute about a quarter of the general population, consume more than half of the prescription drugs and that most adverse drug reactions and interactions take place in the older people. Drugs work by causing subtle changes in the body's chemistry. However, the effects of drugs are not always localised and this is one of the reasons that drugs have side effects."

"With increasing age, there is small blood flow to the liver. (The amount of blood your heart can pump in a minute's time decreases by 1% per year.) In addition the liver gets smaller with age. As a result your liver becomes less efficient in metabolising some drugs. The kidneys also become less efficient with age. Drugs that are not inactivated by the liver usually depend upon kidneys for termination of their effect."

The list of possible adverse side effects attributed to each drug is almost always long.

Many adverse drug reactions are the result of drug interaction. The more drugs you take, the more likely, there will be interaction in someway. "Diseases can modify your response to Drugs," quotes Brian S. Katcher, Pharma D in his book, 'Prescription Drugs'.

In the API Textbook of Medicines, where the chief editor is Dr. Shantilal J. Shah, M.D., it is mentioned by Dr. Ashok B. Vaidya, M.D., in his article, "Drug Interactions in Clinical

Practices" about the side effects and interactions which are not known.

Thus, even assuming that the diagnosis was correct and proper drugs were taken at the proper time, the serious side effects of prescription drugs have been admitted by the doctors in the U.S.A. and India.

As such one can imagine the dangers of side effects if the diagnosis, in the first place, is not correct or if proper medication is not given to counter the reaction of the drug. In a country like India, (it may be the same or worse; in other developing countries) drugs to remove worms from the intestines of the children is freely given. Such drugs are advertised and available without prescription. Parents are not aware of the fact that these drugs could adversely affect the liver and so further medication to improve the function of liver and change in diet are necessary. Moreover, the doctors also do not warn the parents about such drugs. Consequently, nothing is done to activate the liver or have necessary changes made in the child's diet. So gradually, the digestive system of the child gets damaged and he becomes a long-term patient.

Often fast acting pain relievers are taken without restraint, which later on damages the heart and which could develop into Rheumatoid Arthritis. In the same way heavy dosages of antibiotics should be given only after urine culture and finding out which drug is more effective and least harmful. However, in most cases, such antibiotics are administered without doing urine culture. While doing so, there is great possibility of severe side effects, if the drug does not suit the patient.

In advanced countries, several books are available, wherein detailed information about the side effects of different drugs is given and people are conscious. Moreover, in view of the legal action which a patient can take, the doctors there, take precaution while prescribing such drugs.

Even then there are side effects. In most of the cases, such side effects – adverse reaction to such drugs are slow, but go on accumulating in the body. And only when it is concentrated in excess and upsets the patient with some other disease, then its side effects, are found out.

Furthermore, in the advanced countries, there is a strict drug control policy which, prevents production of drugs of a sub-standard quality. In spite of this, there are still cases, where drugs have caused severe side effects. Sometimes, these side effects are found after a generation and such drugs are banned and the manufacturers are forced to withdraw such drugs from circulation. In the meanwhile, thousands of patients and their children are adversely affected, e.g. Thalidomide, a drug formerly used as a sedative, was withdrawn from use in 1961, as it was found to cause fetal abnormalities involving limb malformation when taken by pregnant women. Such things will happen even in future because, in this fast moving world, the scientists do not have sufficient time to test the drugs on human bodies for a longer period. At this juncture, credit should be given to Ayurveda, in which deep study about the interaction and side effects of not only drugs but also eatables was being made over a period of two generations by a group of research medical practitioners. And that is why Ayurveda is becoming popular in Western countries.

If this sorry state of affairs persists in advanced countries, one shudders to think about the extent and gravity of side effects in other developing countries, where there are no laws to protect patients, and as such the medical practitioners take less precaution. Moreover, there is little or no proper drug control. Often the medical practitioners do not have enough time to go through the patient's medical history and **so to the root cause,** and treatment is given on the basis of symptoms narrated by the patients.

Such a grave condition worsens when the proper diagnosis is not made. The patient is in a hurry to get rid of whatever symptoms he is suffering from and the medical practitioner does not have time to discuss the effects of the drugs he is prescribing. Moreover, many patients do not have enough time and money to undertake several tests if necessary, and they do not ask the doctor to give slow acting drugs which have least side effects.

Now, one can imagine the dangers of severe serious side effects if the diagnosis itself is not correct, and heavy dosages of high power drugs are given to the patient. The side effects are of such grave nature that they sometimes impair the whole life of the patient and sometimes they prove fatal.

Recently, two cases came to me of about five-year-old boys. In both the cases, it was informed that these boys had high fever after taking triple injections and fever was brought down by heavy dosages of antibiotics.

In the case of one boy, the speech was so damaged that he could not even stammer to be understood. The damage was found to be in the brain. This happened because of excess heat created by the drugs. Parents gave him treatment as prescribed by me in their home and to their great surprise the boy got his speech to normal within a month.

And in the case of another boy, the movement of legs was impaired. On examination his Pituitary, Pineal, Adrenal, Thyroid – Parathyroid glands were found to be damaged along with point nos. 1-2-5 of the brain. On further inquiry, the parents informed that since 18 months, the boy had difficulty in walking. It was a case of Muscular Dystrophy. Treatment was given accordingly and within 90 days there was remarkable improvement.

Thousands of such cases can be mentioned about the side effects of drugs under the popular therapy of Allopathy.

Let us look at the way of diagnoses in various other therapies that are practised in India. In Allopathy, several tests, many of them quite costly, are required to come to the exact diagnosis. Even then many a time, the problems created by the malfunctioning of endocrine glands are not located. A few months back, two eminent, qualified doctors from the U.S.A. came to our centre. They were allowed to sit by me and watch how diagnosis was done. After an hour, they admitted that it was really amazing to come to such correct diagnosis within two minutes. They mentioned that to come to such a diagnosis in the U.S.A., they would require several tests over a minimum period of seven days and people who were not covered under the Health Insurance would not be able to afford such tests and consultations.

Where Homoeopathy is concerned, long sittings between the patient and the Homoeopathic consultant are necessary for the latter to understand the tendency of the patient and to find out the root cause of the disease. Sometimes, the symptoms are so similar that the homoeopath is not able to find out the proper root cause and has to refer to the "trial and elimination" method. This takes a long time.

In the case of Ayurveda, India's ancient health science, nowadays, there are very few practitioners available who are capable of finding out the root cause just by examining certain pulse situated at the base of palms. Such examination is called Nadi Pariksha.

In the case of Nature Cure, a useful health science, it is practised on the Western concept that all the people are alike and so the same treatment is prescribed for all the types of patients without going deep into the root cause. Sometimes, therefore, such treatment is not suitable. According to Ayurveda, all the people are divided in three categories of 'VAT-PITT-KAPHA' PRAKRUTI and require different treatment according to the type to which the patient belongs. Moreover, they do not correct the Solar Plexus, and so such treatment of Nature Cure may suit one type of people, but may not suit other types.

The worst is that most clinical tests are lengthy, costly and sometimes not necessary. And in spite of undergoing numerous tests, the root cause is not found out. For example, in most cases of cold and Asthma, the root cause is 'Cold due to heat'. However, treatment is given to increase the heat in the body and suppress the cold. But such cold is not cleared from the system, of course it is temporarily suppressed, but as soon as the body becomes powerful, it again tries to throw out the suppressed cold. This cold then becomes chronic and ultimately develops into Allergy and Asthma, and becomes the root cause of Arthritis and Rheumatism.

Further it has been admitted by the Western experts that very little is known about the complex working of the endocrine glands and it has been difficult for most of the therapies to diagnose problems connected with the malfunctioning of these endocrine glands, e.g. migraine.

During the last twenty years, I have observed that the root cause is malfunctioning of one or more endocrine glands, e.g. when Thyroid/Parathyroid glands are overworking, calcium in our food is turned into solids, i.e. calcified and called 'stones' and in spite of operations to remove the stones, new stones go on forming till these glands are corrected. In cases of retention of water, which is considered to be a kidney failure, and the patient is kept on dialysis; the root cause is found to be malfunctioning of the Pineal gland. In some cases of heart problem, the root cause is malfunctioning of the Thyroid/Parathyroid gland. In psychological cases, it is observed that these problems are due to malfunctioning of one or more endocrine glands. Therefore, in this book Chapter 2 is devoted to these endocrine glands.

Proper diagnosis has great importance when treating young children, who cannot speak or explain their problems. Child specialists have admitted that in many such cases they take 'a shot in the dark'. Because these children require immediate treatment and they cannot be exposed to certain tests like X-ray, instant and proper diagnosis is most vital and can be made with Acupressure. And so this 'Do It Yourself' therapy is a MUST in every home, children's clinics and hospitals.

Today, society and nations of the world are more worried about increasing cases of Retardation, Thalassemia, Deafness and Dumbness, even Blindness and Muscular Diastrophy among children. One of the root cause is the damage to the sex glands of the parents. Now HIV is spreading like wildfire and innocent wives and children are the victims. All these problems can be PREVENTED.

During my studies about HIV/AIDS in the U.S.A. in 1994, I was surprised to learn that HIV virus gets directly into the blood and damages the spleen. Generally, HIV infection is not suspected even during 10 to 15 years. However, the affected patient can transmit this disease to his/her life partner and children born after such infection. And so in free and easy society of Western countries and Africa it is spreading in a big way.

In countries like India and other developing countries, where little care is taken about the hygiene of women engaged in sex business, the problem of HIV is spreading like wildfire. During my health camps in various parts of India, I am surprised to observe the high number of HIV cases. In case of doubt, I have made it a point to call the husband, his wife and all the children below the age of 15 years and I am shocked to find HIV in most of such cases. Such detection is made even in the elementary stage of HIV, while in advanced stages of HIV and AIDS, the detection is very simple and instant.

It is now high time, when not only W.H.O. and all those engaged in the noble profession of medical service but also all the health conscious people of the World should put Acupressure to a drastic Test and only when satisfied with the results should accept it. Acupressure is the health science of Nature and the only therapy capable of **prevention, instant proper diagnosis and cure of most of the diseases without cost and side effects.** If mankind desires to lead healthy life free from dreaded diseases like Cancer, Heart problems, Muscular Dystrophy, Brain problems and HIV / AIDS, it will have to terminate its prejudices and vested interests and unite to give Health to all by the year 2005, so that man can be more happy and healthy in the 21st century and thereafter.

Before we refer to Diagnosis, it is important and necessary to know our body. The more we try to understand its organs, its endocrine glands and the complex system of their functioning, the more we will realise how our body is really the most wonderful and compact creation of nature. Therefore, it is advisalde to study "Health in Your Hands : Volume 1."

CHAPTER 2

ENDOCRINE GLANDS

Nature has provided our body with proper regulators and protectors. These are known as endocrine (ductless) glands. The knowledge so far available in the West about these endocrine glands is very limited. However, yogis in India were aware of their great importance and working even before Ayurveda and have described them as *chakras*.

Names of Chakras	Equivalent endocrine glands	Function
1. Sahastrar	Pineal (Point no. 4)	Regulates water balance. Acts as a manager of all glands; controls cerebrospinal fluid and sex desires; stimulates growth of nerves.
2. Ajna	Pituitary (Point no. 3)	Controls air and space. It is like a king of all glands; controls growth of body and brain power and also memory.
3. Vishudha	Thyroid / Parathyroid (Point no. 8)	Controls air—so lungs and heart; controls temperature regulation; governs energy production through control of calcium.
4. Anahat	Thymus (Point no. 38)	Acts as a godmother till the child reaches puberty, i.e. 12 to 15 years.
5. Manipur	Adrenal and Pancreas (Point nos. 25 & 28)	Controls fire and production of digestive juices; Regulates blood and sugar level; controls stress, activeness and character building, controls sodium and water balance.
6. Swadhisthan	Solar Plexus (Point no. 29)	Controls Apan Vayu '(अपान वायु)' and so movement of stools and urine; also controls all organs below diaphragm.
7. Mooladhar	Sex / Gonads (Point nos. 14 & 15)	Controls water and phosphorus content, produces sex hormones.

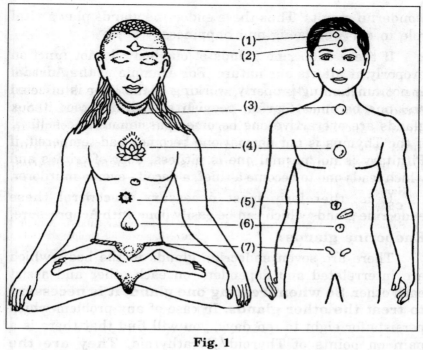

Fig. 1

These main endocrine glands produce 140 types of internal secretions which on getting mixed with blood go to build up the body and maintain it in a healthy condition. Yogis have shown that these endocrine glands also mould the mind and character. The main functions of these glands are to maintain the metabolism-control of five basic elements of the body, to regulate the functions of all the organs and the brain and to adjust the body against changing environment and thus protect it against any illness. These glands play a very important role not only in the development of our body and mind, but also in the development of our looks and even character.

Psychological effect of Endocrine glands :

From my experience, I have found that even psychological problems are connected with one or the other endocrine glands and the treatment of the same has given wonderful results. Thus these endocrine glands play a vital role in our well-being and happiness.*

If these endocrine glands of our body do not function properly, it affects our nature. For example, if the Adrenal is not functioning properly, working of the liver is affected and one becomes fearful, peevish and ill-natured; if Sex glands are overactive one becomes passionate and selfish; if the Thymus is not normal one becomes bad-tempered; if Pituitary is not normal one is pitiless, doer of crimes and which leads one to become a thief, a dacoit—even a murderer.

It is, therefore, most necessary to control these endocrine glands which can be easily done with Acupressure.

Endocrine glands :

There are seven endocrine glands in the body, which are interrelated and dependent on each other and assist each other. **So when treating one gland, it is necessary to treat the other glands.** In case of any problem which persists for eight to ten days, you will find that there is a pain on points of Thyroid / Parathyroid. **They are the barometers of the body.** In case of chronic problems, you will observe that points of more than one endocrine gland would be hurting when pressed.

Thymus Gland (Point no. 38) :

This is a very important gland and can be considered as a godmother for a child. It protects the growing child against any disease. The child will develop properly in body and mind, if treatment for two minutes is given twice a day on the point of this gland in the soles till the child is one year and also in the two palms till the age of 12/15 along with treatment on points of all the other endocrine glands and organs.

Once the body is fully developed, this gland gradually shrinks and stops its activities, its functional tissue being replaced by fatty tissue. However, if for some reason, it

---

* It was discovered by urologist J. Edwin Blackwell in 1979, that all the systems of our body could be kept functioning properly by activating the exocrine and endocrine glands.

becomes active, it produces dullness and general fatigue leading to total inactiveness of selected muscles (known as Myasthenia). The point of this gland is situated under point no. 30 and as such deeper pressure is to be applied on point no. 30 to reach the point no. 38 of Thymus gland.

Thyroid / Parathyroid Glands (Point no. 8) :

These glands play an important role in the development of the child's body. As it digests calcium and eliminates poison, toxins, they assist in controlling the heat of the body and thus maintains its health. If these glands do not function properly, it leads to weakness, disease – even twisting of muscles – rickets and convulsions and so the development of a child is retarded – the child becomes fat and dull. Similarly, the overworking of this gland leads to over-growth – bulging eyes, goitre, protruding Adam's apple and tendency to become a bully. Even after puberty if this gland does not function properly, it leads to problem of calcification – stone. These glands control the element of air and so the lungs and the heart.

It also helps build human qualities like affection – love – capacity for high thinking and concentration, leading to self control – balanced temperament, purity of heart and unselfishness. When it is deranged, a person becomes mentally unstable – too talkative and ungrateful. When these glands are damaged along with Sex glands, women during pregnancy and or after child birth or removal of ovaries, tend to become plumpy and put on weight around the abdomen and waist.

'Mr. V' reports about two patients discharged from a reputed hospital in Mumbai for being afflicted with incurable disease. They were found to be suffering from toxic Thyroid and were given Acupressure treatment. On the 4th day both the patients showed signs of improvement and within 40 days they were completely cured.'

As these glands are barometers of the body, there is a hurting on their point no. 8 when there is a complaint that persists over 8/10 days. When these glands are not functioning adequately there is a deficiency of calcium, so it is also necessary to make up the deficiency of the body by taking calcium-cal. phos + cal. flour − 12 or 30 power (biochemic medicines) 3 pills in the morning and 3 pills in the evening for 45 days.

Ovaries-Testes-Sex-Gonad Glands (Point nos. 14 & 15) :

These glands maintain the unbroken chain of procreation and also regulate the water element and also nerves, cells, flesh, bones, bone marrow and semen.

Malfunctioning of these glands is noticeable only when the children start getting mature at the age of 12 to 14. Girls have problems of menstruation−late or painful or too little−leading to pimples and excess heat in the body, or sometimes too much bleeding leading to anaemia. This leads to underdevelopment of the body.

As for the boys, they turn to masturbation, start getting erotic dreams, become shy−often disturbing the growth of the body and beard. Moreover, this creates psychological problems, which if not solved immediately, often become the root cause of unhappiness in newly married couples.

A regular and proper functioning of these glands helps in maintaining the heat of the body and plays an important role in contributing to the attractiveness of a boy or a girl. Moreover, their nature becomes amiable, they become charming with good manners and agreeable words, and they enjoy good health. Their disorder, makes one selfish, envious, lustful and of an angry disposition.

After delivery or sterilisation if these glands function less, fat starts accumulating in the body. So to maintain a proper figure, women are advised to take treatment on point nos. 14 and 15 during and after pregnancy. Further, these glands secrete sex hormones. Insufficient working creates rigidity and problems during menopause. Sometimes, the root cause of infertility can be traced to the damaged condition of sex glands of the couple.

'A doctor couple had no issue even after 14 years of their marriage. Both of them started treatment on the points of these glands and within 15 months, they became proud parents of a baby girl.'

Pancreas Glands (Point no. 25):

These glands regulate digestion of sugar-glucose in the body by creating insulin. In modern times due to excessive use of sugar (not the natural sugar found in cereals, fruits, milk, honey, which is easily digestable) it has become essential to look after the proper functioning of this gland.

Furthermore, as per the latest research, it has been observed that overfunctioning of this gland leads to low Blood Pressure, Migraine headache, and at times creates more desire for sweet foods and sweet drinks leading to diabetes and sometimes to Alcoholism.

'Mrs. G.' wife of an Income tax officer, had severe migraine since many years. She started taking Acupressure treatment and within 15 days she was completely cured.'

"Mr. P, an Acupressurist, observed that this pancreas gland was overworking in all sixty workers who were feared to be alcoholics. He showed them how to take treatment. More than 70 % of the workers stopped drinking alcohol."

Adrenal Glands (Point no. 28):

These glands control and regulate the fire element of the body and so control the spleen, liver and gall bladder and assist in the creation of biles and digestive juices. Qualities like keenness of perception, untiring activity, the drive to action, inner energy and courage are due to proper functioning of these glands. They also intensify the flow of blood, help proper oxygenation and develop organising power—inspire to leadership. They play an important part in the character building of a child.

In the case of disorder of these glands, persons abuse their natural vigour to satisfy their lust or antisocial activities. They suffer from a sense of vain glory and are conceited – become extremely restless – impatient and short-tempered. They cannot have control on diet and suffer from stomach problems and blood pressure.

Case Study :

"A Prince had lost interest in life from the age of 16. He stopped studies in the final year of University and had no interest even in sex. So, he did not marry. At the age of 31, after he unsuccessfully tried treatment under various therapies, he consulted an acupressurist. On examination, his thyroid and adrenal glands were found to be damaged. The acupressurist told that the cause of all his troubles was some type of deep fear, a severe shock which had damaged his adrenal gland. The King admitted that the Prince had at the age of 16 joined him on a hunt and had fallen down from the horse and was miraculously saved from a tiger. Since then he had halucinations and lost interest in life. The prince was given Acupressure treatment and gold-silver-copper charged water to drink. Within 30 days he became normal and started taking interest in his hobby of painting and also in his usual chores."

"A young professor came to our Free Centre on one Wednesday morning and informed me that he was so badly depressed that he desired to commit suicide. I agreed that he should commit suicide on the next Wednesday at 3.00 P.M. But meanwhile, he should take treatment on all endocrine glands and drink charged water during the week and report me on the next Wednesday morning. Thereon that day he came with a smiling face only to inform me that he wanted to live long and enjoy life." His desire to commit suicide had disappeared, Similarly, thousands of such cases can be quoted.

Pituitary Gland (Point no. 3) :

This gland controls air and space in the body. This gland is like a master of all glands and sends orders to all the other glands. It controls will-power, sight, hearing, memory and discrimination. It also rectifies the faults of the other glands.

In the case of its predominance, it helps people become great geniuses, eminent literary men, poets, scientists, philosophers and lovers of mankind.

As this gland controls the growth of the body, so its over-working leads people to become physically large in size. While its insufficient functioning may result in making them into dwarfs.

This gland also governs the growth of the hindbrain. This gland may be damaged due to fear or injury or sometimes due to tension during pregnancy. This also leads to the malfunctioning of other glands. And that results in mental retardation in children. So if the problem of mentally retarded children is to be solved, the pregnant women should take treatment on all endocrine glands and avoid damage to the fetus. Further, it is observed that in those glands and sends orders to all the others. It controls the will-power, sight, hearing, memory and discrimination. It also rectifies the faults of the other glands.

In case of its predominance, it helps people to become great geniuses, eminent literary men, poets, scientists, philosophers and lovers of mankind.

As this gland controls the growth of the body, its over-working leads people to become physically large in size, while its insufficient functioning may result in their becoming dwarfs.

This gland also governs the growth of the mind and brain. This gland may be damaged due to fear or injury or sometimes, due to tension during pregnancy. This also leads to the malfunctioning of the other glands. And that results in mentally retarded children. The pregnant women should take treatment on all the endocrine glands. This will avoid damage to the fetus. Further, those children whose gland is not working sufficiently, tend to become mean, heartless, mischievous and bullies, liars and disobedient. They are even led to steal. With the proper treatment of this gland, in most cases the parents and teachers will get amazing results. As this gland and the pineal gland are situated in the head, it is harmful to hit the children on the head.

This gland could be damaged during pregnancy and childbirth, which can lead to malfunctioning of the other glands especially sex glands which in turn can lead to obesity after childbirth. All these prove the great importance of maintaining this gland in proper working order.

Case Study :

"A 16-year-old girl from a well-to-do family was reported to be stealing petty things from her classmates and no amount of persuasion, scolding or even corporal punishment had any effect on her. An acupressurist found that the point of her pituitary gland was tender and on further examination her sex glands were also found to be damaged. On enquiry she admitted that she had scanty as well as painful menses which was the root cause of her habit of stealing. She started taking Acupressure treatment and within 15 days, she stopped stealing and within 45 days, her menses became normal."

If the growth of the body and brain is not normal, give treatment on point no. 3 in the middle of the thumbs and big toes, to give necessary stimulation.

Pineal Gland (Point no. 4) :

It acts as an organiser and controller of all the glands. It controls the development of the glands and regulates them. Malfunctioning of this gland leads to high blood pressure and also premature awakening of sex glands resulting in sexual delinquency. Moreover, it controls the potassium/sodium balance in the body and so its malfunctioning leads to excessive retention of fluids in the body which can be mistaken for a serious kidney problem. Its less working leads to sweating of palms/soles even in cold weather. It controls the flow of cerebrospinal fluid and thus keeps all the glands and body vitalised, strong and healthy.

It is also known as the primitive third eye. The predominance of this gland generates a sense of sublimity –helping men grow into sainthood, endowed with divine qualities. These people have great wisdom and tenderness of heart, and also strong will-power and so are not affected by physical sufferings or sorrow.

Lymph glands (Point no. 16) :

Although they are not endocrine glands, because of their importance, they have been included here. The point of these glands is under point no. 16 in the middle of the wrists. They control the immune defence system of our body, prevent the formation of pus on any cut or boil on the body and quickly heal the wounds.

These glands help clear the toxins from the body – clear the dead cells from the system. But when such toxins and dead cells are in excess, these glands have to overwork and they become weak and tender. At that time, when you press on the point of these glands, it pains. If such pain continues, it means that these glands are not able to stop the malignant growth forming from toxins and dead cells. As such the first symptom to detect Cancer even at a very early stage is to find out whether there is any pain on this gland. Moreover, it has also been found that if there is a pain on these glands and also on the point of pancreas, it indicates diabetes, increase of glucose in the blood. Thus, you will observe that to prevent Cancer and sugar in the blood, it is most necessary to keep these glands in active condition. Further hurting on this point no. 18 donotes possibility of HIV/AIDS.

Increasing Will-Power :

Our mind has a great effect on these glands. For example, continuous fear damages the pituitary gland and makes one timid. Similarly, tension and worry disturb the pineal gland and so lead to high blood pressure and as pineal gland controls the other glands, it disturbs other glands and the digestive system. In modern times, stress, tension or worry have increased and often they disturb these endocrine glands. If these endocrine glands are not treated immediately, it might lead to malfunctioning of the other glands in the body. As these glands are interrelated, whenever one gland is disturbed, the other glands are also disturbed. When you press on the points of these endocrine glands, you will observe pain on the points of more than one gland – especially in case of chronic diseases. Therefore, it is very important to give treatment on all the endocrine glands and keep them under proper control.

Since these glands also control the mind, the will-power, so in order to get rid of bad habits like smoking, drinking alcohol, drug addiction or even over-eating, it is necessary to give treatment on all the endocrine glands for at least 15 days. Because, these people lack the necessary will-power to refrain from such bad habits, they often break their vows to stop such bad habits and are considered unreliable. However, a treatment of 15 days will give them the necessary will-power to stop these bad habits on the sixteenth day. And they will be free from the evil effects of these bad habits.

"A Government officer had the habit of drinking alcohol every evening. He started Acupressure treatment and drank hot water in the evening. Surprisingly enough he succeeded in getting rid of his habit of drinking."

"A young man was addicted to drugs. In spite of many persuasions by his mother and brother, he continued breaking vows and taking drugs. He was advised Acupressure treatment and so after one month he got himself fred not only from drugs but also from smoking and even masturbation."

It has been observed that if children are taught to take this treatment from an early age of 8-10; not only will their physical growth be normal but they will have no problems at the time of puberty and inclination towards delinquency and they will become attractive and will develop a well-balanced outlook on life and will be able to live happily as good citizens.

If the police department tries this treatment on the juveniles and criminals, it will be possible to reduce the crime rate.

Psychological Problems :

Many problems which are considered to be psychological are the result of improper functioning of these endocrine glands. So, with the proper treatment on these glands, such problems can be easily solved, e.g.

"A girl with a bright record in school, had at the age of 17, a typical problem. About 45 days before her examinations, her hands would start shivering a few minutes after she started studying and the book would fall down. So, she was not able to prepare for the examination and day by day she became more nervous. An Acupressurist was consulted. He found her adrenal gland to be tender-damaged. On further examination her sex glands were also found to have been disturbed. She admitted that she had profuse bleeding before this complaint started. She started taking Acupressure treatment and in due course passed the examination creditably."

It has been admitted by allopathic practitioners that by taking unnatural hormones like oestrogen to counter the effects of menopause and osteo porosis, the possibility of developing cancer in the body greatly increases. The best way to control hormonal balance, is to take treatment on point nos. 11 to 15 at least twice a day. That will ensure that this natural phenomenon of menopause passes away without any side effects. Moreover, when sex glands are disturbed, thyroid and parathyroid glands are also disturbed, leading to decalcification – leading to fracture or forming of stones. As such, treatment on point no. 8 and other endocrine glands is necessary.

It has been observed that in the case of the cancer, as the disease progresses, these endocrine glands become increasingly tender, and because of overworking, they become tired and eventually stop secreting the most vital hormones in the body and damage the very metabolism of the body and at this stage this disease is considered malignant, and if proper treatment is not taken, it develops rapidly and becomes deadly. Hence, the great importance of controlling all these endocrine glands must be properly realised. If all these endocrine glands are controlled properly and thereby all the organs, the possibility of cancer becomes remote.

In case of severe damage due to overworking/
underworking of any of the endocrine glands i.e.
hypothyroid, the same treatment as mentioned for
cancer is to be taken.

It is only Acupressure which shows the proper
way to control these vital glands in the easiest way.
As these endocrine glands are interrelated, in order
to correct the defects of one gland, it is necessary to
give treatment on all the endocrine glands. These
glands are situated deep inside the body and so a
little more pressure preferably with the thumb in a
vertical position or unsharpened pencil or harder
massage on the glands will be necessary.

FUNCTIONS AND EFFECTS OF THE MALFUNCTIONING OF ENDOCRINE GLANDS

Name of Gland	Effect of Malfunctioning
1. Thymus Gland (Point no. 38) Protects child up to the age of 15.	Child gets sick. In case this gland becomes active later on, it brings dullness.
2. Pineal Gland (Point no. 4) Controls sex system and water of body and is a primitive eye.	Premature sex development, increase in water content, high blood pressure.
3. Pituitary Gland (Point no. 3) It is the master of glands and controls the other glands, governs the brain and the development of the body.	Body becomes dwarfish or bulging, produces mental retardation. Child becomes a bully or a liar and tends to be disobedient.
4. Thyroid / Parathyroid Glands (Point no. 8). These glands control the supply of calcium and phosphorus in the body. Also controls the development of the body.	Underworking leads to rickets, convulsions, teeth problems, twisting of muscles, fatness and dullness. Overworking leads to overgrowth, bulging eyes, protruding Adam's apple, etc.
5. Adrenal Glands (Point no. 28) Control production of biles and controls liver and flow of blood, blood pressure and also moulds character.	Underworking leads to dullness, timidity, less energy, less oxygenation. Overworking leads to high B.P. Less bile leads to acidity and vomiting and severe headache and even increase in cholesterol level.
6. Pancreas Glands (Point no. 25) Controls digestion of sugar in the body and digestive juices.	Underworking leads to diabetes and overworking leads to low B.P., dizziness and even to alcoholism through hypoglycaemia, i.e. deficiency of glucose.
7. Ovaries, Testes & Sex Glands (Point nos. 14 & 15) Controls digestion of phosphorous and heat of the body, attractiveness and reproduction.	Reproductive organs are damaged, problems of less or more menses, masturbation, loss of heat leading to development of fat, unattractiveness of the body, less/more sex desire follow.
8. Lymph Glands (Point no. 16) Stops formation of pus and prevents germs.	Disease called lymphocytosis cancer. Leads to increase in blood sugar.

CHAPTER 3

HOW TO BEGIN DIAGNOSIS

Qualification :

First and foremost qualification of a medical practitioner is his fitness and health of not only body but also of mind. He / She must be cheerful and free from any prejudices. He / She should be following the same therapy which he / she will preach for others. He / She must remember that the patient is a human being and has come to get rid of his / her problems and clear doubts about his ailment.

First Clue :

A warm smile and welcoming handshake is what a patient expects. When you shake the patient's hand, you get a clue about the problem. If the patient is younger than yourself, his palm should be warmer than yours, however, if the palm is cooler, you will know that the energy flow in the patient's body is less. Similarly, if the patient is older than you, the palm should be cooler. But if the palm is warmer, it indicates that there is excess heat in the body or the patient has fever.

Solar Plexus :

Methods to confirm whether the solar plexus is in order or not :

(1) In the morning, on an empty stomach, when you lie down on any hard surface on your back and if you press your finger or thumb in the navel, you will feel a throbbing sound just like the thumping of the heart, it means that the system is O.K.

(2) Lie down on your back, arms straight by your sides. Keep legs straight and the toes upright. The two big toes should be in level with each other. If they are not, it indicates a disturbance in the solar plexus.

(3) Join the two palms as shown in fig. 2 and match the lines 1 and 4. These lines will match with each other if the solar plexus is in order. If the solar plexus has shifted, line no. 4 will not match.

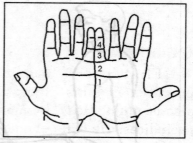

Fig. 2

(4) However, if there is not enough space for the examination table on which the patient can lie down, then the following method can be used :

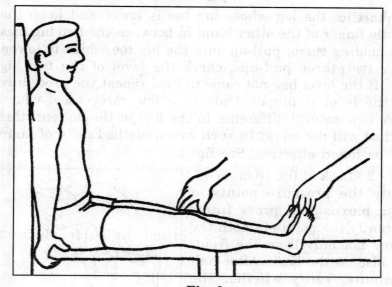

Fig. 3

Take two chairs of equal height. Ask the patient to sit down erect on one chair as tightly and backward as possible. Then ask the patient to keep both legs (without shoes and socks) on the other chair. Examine the level of the two big toes. If the solar plexus is not in order, the big toes will not be in a straight line, i.e. at the same level, which means that the solar plexus is not in order.

To Set Solar Plexus in Order :

(1) Correct the solar plexus by pressing with one hand

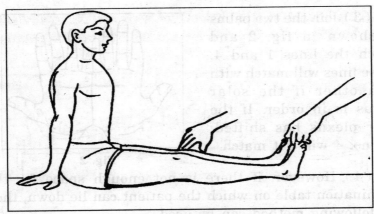

Fig. 4

the knee of the leg whose big toe is lower and keep the middle finger of the other hand in between the two big toes and holding them, pull-up only the big toe which is lower. After two / three pull-ups; check the level of the two big toes. If the level has not come in line, repeat the procedure till the level is proper. Only in a few rare cases, where there is a natural difference in the feet of the patient, this method will not work. In such cases, method no. 4 of lamp will be found effective. See fig. 6.

(2) Look at fig. 16 (a) & (b), locate the pressure points of solar plexus and press intermittently the points in both the palms not only from the front, but also on the back. After half a minute, verify whether the solar plexus has come in order.

The following method can also be tried :

(3) Keep your right palm vertically on the joint of elbow of the left hand and try to touch the left shoulder with the thumb

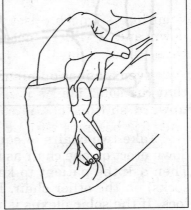

Fig. 5 : Picture showing how to correct the solar plexus

with a jerk. Repeat five times. In the same way do with the right hand and verify as in fig. 2.

This is one of the easiest ways. Hence it is advisable to do this exercise every morning whether solar plexus is in order or not.

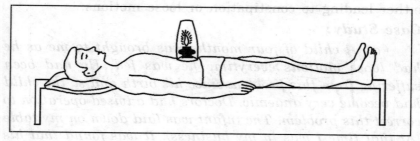

Fig. 6

(4) Put a small oil lamp / candle on the navel (a coin or something can be kept on the navel as a base to hold the candle), cover it with a metal glass and press it for a minute (see fig. 6). The air inside will burn out and a vaccum will be created. This vaccum will bring the solar plexus to the centre. Then lift glass from one side after one minute. Repeat this three to four times till throbbing is felt at the centre.

After correcting solar plexus, drink water or milk adding dry ginger in it.

In the case of a chronic problem like diarrhoea / vomiting / stomach upset, the solar plexus may shift up or down and it will be necessary to correct it at least two / three times a day.

Even a minor difference in the level of big toes indicates that the solar plexus is not in order. It may be noted that upward shifting of the solar plexus leads to constipation and if it becomes chronic, this can lead to piles and even Cancer of the colon. The muscle above the navel becomes stiff and this problem is many times termed as Hiatus Hernia. Similarly, when the solar plexus has shifted downwards it leads to loose motion. This often is wrongly diagnosed as Diarrhoea and prescribed treatment ends up by damaging the whole digestive system. The drugs taken to control such Diarrhoea can lead to acidity and ulcers, and long term Diarrhoea leads to colic pain, anaemia and serious consequences like Cancer.

In the case of children too, the correction of solar plexus is very important. For a breastfed baby, if the mother has gastric problem, the baby's solar plexus also gets damaged either leading to constipation or loose motions.

Case Study :

(a) A child of four months was brought to me as he had loose motions everytime he was fed. He had been suffering from this problem since his birth and so the child had become very anaemic. Doctors had advised operation to correct this problem. The infant was laid down on my table (At that time I was in my business). It was found that his two big toes were not in level. It was duly corrected. On the third day, his father came and informed me that loose motions had stopped since then and the child was passing properly stools twice a day. Thus just by correcting solar plexus, the operation was averted.

(b) In a similar case, during my visit to the U.S.A. in 1991, a child of 4 years was brought to me. Since birth she was not passing stools for up to three days and would only pass stools when suppository was inserted into her anus. Her solar plexus was corrected and her mother was taught how to correct it. Since then, that child now a young lady, has regular motions and is having good health to the satisfaction of her parents.

(c) During my visit to Katni (Madhya Pradesh, India), I met a surgeon, who was giving his services free in a clinic. He was open minded and so on observing the Acupressure camp, he asked me to see one of his patient, who had an 'Hiatus Hernia' and was advised operation. I found that the solar plexus of the patient was not in order. I corrected it and the patient had great relief.

During the treatment the patient felt as if a lock was opening in his stomach. After 3 such sittings of one minute each, the hard lump above the stomach softened. The patient was taught to do such treatment at home. After four days, the Doctor examined the patient and he declared that the operation was not necessary any more. **Where 'Hiatus**

Hernia' is diagnosed, correction of the **solar plexus will give good results,** and operation can be averted.

(d) Similarly, a patient came to me four days before the operation of piles was fixed. I corrected his solar plexus and taught him how to do so at home. On the fourth day, when he went to the hospital, after examining him, he was told by the doctors that there was considerable improvement and operation was not necessary.

Several such instances can be quoted. In the case of any pain around navel or even in chest, just check up the solar plexus. In most of the cases, you will find that the solar plexus is not in order, and hence **correct the solar plexus before suggesting any other treatment.**

What should be done in cases of frequent shifting of the Solar Plexus :

Due to frequent gas trouble, weakness of intestines, lifting of heavy articles, sometimes, there is a shifting of the solar plexus. In case of such frequent shifting of the solar plexus (sometimes it gets shifted in the afternoon even though it was corrected in the morning) the following treatment should be followed :

First correct the solar plexus. Take a little string (thicker than a sewing thread) and tie eight to nine rounds of this thread around the base of a big toe. It should not be very tight, then make a knot (See fig. 7). Do the same with the other big toe. Ask the patient to keep it on for a minimum of three days. During this period, this thread may be removed only, if there is unbearable pain in the big toes. Later on, the patient can check up the solar plexus every alternate days and correct it if necessary. For a complete cure, the patient should have a diet of green juice, fruit juices and light food and also do some exercises, asanas to strengthen the muscles of the digestive system. Since the solar plexus is like the mainspring of a watch, it must always be kept in order.

Explain to the patient to find out himself about whether his solar plexus is in order or not as per method on pages

36–37 and also teach him how to correct the solar plexus as shown on pages 37–39.

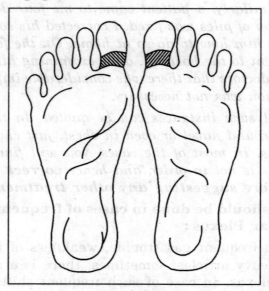

Fig. 7

Barometer of the body :

Next, check up point no. 8 of the Thyroid / Parathyroid gland. This is the barometer of the body. In case of any complaint anywhere in the main functioning organs of the body, for more than eight days there will be a hurting pain on this point when pressed. It is no surprise, that its points on palms and soles are the biggest which indicates its importance. In case there is no pain on these points, when pressed, it indicates that the patient is healthy and the problem is minor and there is nothing to worry about. Inform the patient accordingly. Many a time, the patient has a little doubt of having something wrong in his/her body. And so when the patient is assured that there is nothing to worry about, he/she is relieved from unnecessary worry and tension.

However, in all the patients who have come to me for check-up, I have found this point to be tender in their palms.

The degree of pain on this point denotes the severity and the extent of problem in the body. Such seriousness can be measured from the following illustration :

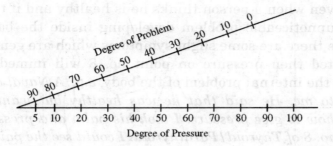

Fig. 8

This means that when you press this point even slightly, i.e. 5 degree of pressure and the patient cries in agony, it denotes that degreewise the problem is very serious. In the same way, when you press very hard say 100 degree of pressure, and there is no pain or flicker in the eyes of patient, it denotes that there is no problem. From experience one would be able to know the exact degree of such seriousness.

Similarly, the degree of damage to any organ, can be found out by the above illustration chart, i.e. when pressed slightly on point no. 6 of throat and if there is severe pain, it denotes inflammation of the tonsils due to bacterial or viral infection, causing a sore throat, fever and difficulty in swallowing.

This method is very useful in cases of chronic and serious disease, e.g. if there is pain on point no. 16 of Lymph gland and also on point nos. 11 to 15 of Sex gland, it denotes 'degeneration in Uterus' in the case of a female patient and 'degeneration in Prostate' in the case of a male patient.

Unless the patient is under great agony and there is severe pain on vital points of 36-37-26 and 30, the degree of problem cannot be more than 90%. As such in all the problems even in the case of Cancer of blood or in the case of HIV/AIDS, treatment of 45 to 60 days is enough to cure the disease. And so the practitioner can be confident of curing almost all the diseases.

Even when a person thinks he is healthy and if there's some unnoticeable problem developing inside the body or may be there are some slight symptoms which are generally neglected then pressure on point no. 8 will immediately reveal the internal problem of the body, e.g. *'A Naval officer came to me. He said that he was healthy but wanted to know how to give pressure. I took his palm and pressed on point no. 8 of Thyroid / Parathyroid. I could see the pain and agony on his face. Slowly, I went on pressing different points and he went on confessing about hurting pain on various points. The nature of disorder was identified as the beginning of a brain tumour. Later on, the officer got himself thoroughly checked in a Naval Hospital, which had the best equipment. And my diagnosis was confirmed. The officer, then, started taking treatment as suggested in my book and cured himself and saved his well-paid job.'*

While in Athens, I was invited by the Open International University for Complimentary Medicines, Colombo, Sri Lanka to attend their 19th World Health Conference in 1989 to accept the Honorary Degree of M.D. for my book and Merit Medal for my Research about Cancer. When I was conducting a workshop, I told the large gathering of eminent doctors who had gathered from different countries of the World that, "Acupressure has advanced so much that without knowing the past history of the patient and without any tests, just by pressing on the palms, diagnosis is possible." I was asked by the chairman, Dr. Batliwala, an eminent accupuncturist of India, to prove my statement. I asked the doctors to come on stage one by one. I pressed their palms and told each of them what was wrong with them. In the case of three doctors, I had to tell them that they were suffering from Cancer and that too of a particular organ. Not surprisingly, all of them agreed with my diagnosis made within 60 seconds. However, in the case of a German lady doctor, when I informed her that she had lots of tension and was on the verge of collapse, she laughed it off. But within 15 minutes, she collapsed in the hall.

All the doctors present were greatly impressed by the efficacy of instant diagnosis and immediately bought copies of my book 'Health in your Hands'.

Several such instances can be quoted. On many occasions, I have been challenged. I will narrate only one instance. Once I was invited by former Finance Minister of India, Mr. Narayan Dutt Tiwari to his hotel room in Mumbai. His wife is a qualified gynaecologist and had studied my book thoroughly. When I reached there, Mrs. Tiwari discussed about this therapy and when she was convinced that Acupressure is a Health Science she called her husband from the next room. Mr. Tiwari is a tall, well-built, strong man. I was told that they will not inform me about any complaint and I have to diagnose and tell them about the problem. I started pressing point no. 8, there was flicker of pain in Mr. Tiwari's eyes, then one by one I went on pressing other points and told them about five different problems he was having. When I told them he was suffering from severe piles Dr. (Mrs.) Tiwari jumped up in great astonishment, greatly impressed by the efficacy and exactness of this therapy. Then I scolded her for not curing her husband of his constipation which he was suffering from a long time. I corrected the Solar Plexus and guided them about the treatment, which he had to take himself. After a week, Mr. Tiwari thanked me because his problem of constipation and piles had been cured.

Exactness of Diagnosis :

Once I was invited by an eminent eye specialist at his residence. He asked me to examine his 27-year-old healthy looking son. After examination of both the palms in three minutes, I told them that there were tonsils on the right side and only reddishness on the left side of the throat and the root cause was 'cold due to heat'. The doctor could not accept such a diagnosis, so he called for a torch and a spoon and examined his son's throat. Later, he was glad to admit that my diagnosis was perfectly correct.

How to reach the root cause :

After you have checked the solar plexus and corrected it, if necessary, you press on point no. 8 and when you find pain on the same, proceed further and ask the patient about his / her complaints and go on pressing on corresponding points. **However, never come to any conclusion about diagnosis till you are satisfied about the root cause.**

'A female patient of about 35 years, complained about backache. Her eyes were pale and hands were cold. This symptom of pale eyes indicates the possibility of worms in intestines and cold hands denote less energy. On further examination, it was found that there was pain on point no. 11 to 15 of Sex glands. On inquiry, she admitted that she had whitish or yellowish discharge – Leucorrhoea since the last ten years. She never had regular menstruation since the beginning of the cycle. Her husband had come with her and was strong and healthy. He confessed of his demands for sex even when his wife was not willing. The root causes were found out and proper treatment was advised. Now, after two months they are a happy couple'.

'A young man of 19 years, came to me complaining about less appetite and less concentration during his studies. I went on pressing points no. 8 and then 11 to 15 (after observing white spots on the nails and that the white moons were very negligible – these symptoms denote possibility of masturbation); also point nos. 23-27 & 28 and then no. 16. On all these points, there was pain indicating degeneration in prostate-Sex glands and problem in the digestive system. Slowly, the boy revealed that since last five years he had lost his mother, he was doing masturbation. He was unhappy and so depressed that he was thinking of committing suicide. All these problems had developed into degeneration of –

cancer of Gonads–Sex glands. He and his father, who had accompanied him and who was totally ignorant about the masturbation of his son, were explained about the seriousness of the case. The boy was convinced about the futility of suicide and confidence was given about cure. They agreed to give co-operation, treatment was given at home. Of course, along with acupressure treatment, a change was made in Diet–more of green juices + health drink + honey and more of fruits and fruit juices and concentrated gold / silver / copper iron charged water were prescribed. Within just two months, the boy was alright. Now he is an ardent practitioner of Acupressure and studying hard to be a professor'.

It is a fact that in India and other less advanced countries, patients are not willing to discuss their sex and menstrual problems. But Acupressure can lead you to the root cause. For proper diagnosis, it is most important to study fig. 16 and fig. 17 in this book and about the functioning of all the endocrine glands and lymph glands narrated in Chapter 2 of this book. When any of the main functioning organs are damaged or not functioning properly, carbon gathers around the corresponding points, which are found to be tender and when pressed there is pain. This pain is unpleasant and totally different from the experience of pressure given on that point. And when there is pain there will be flicker in the patient's eyes. Thus even without any information from the patient or without any physical examination or any other tests, diagnosis can be made just by pressing different points located in both the palms/soles.

Our body is really a great wonder. It reveals any small problem on these points of palms and soles.

It may be noted that the diagnosis made by Acupressure is so accurate that on several occasions, I have challenged the diagnosis made with X-rays and other tests like Sonography. I quote three such instances :

(1) *An athlete suffering from severe backache was asked to have his spinal cord operated upon on the basis of diagnosis made by X-rays. He approached me and on examination, I found out that there was no pain on point no. 9 of the spinal cord. So I told him that there was no damage to the spinal cord, and as such the operation was not necessary. However, in order to find out the root cause of his severe backache, I pressed the point of the sciatic nerve (See fig. 9). These points were found to be tender which indicated damage to sciatic nerve. He admitted that it was true. Being an athlete, during his daily exercises, he was doing Halasana.*

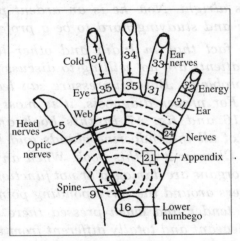

Fig. 9 : Back of right hand

He had to go out on tour for about 12 days and there he could not do his daily exercises. After he returned, he tried to do Halasana. But his legs would not touch the ground. So he asked his son to bring down the legs slowly. However, his son brought down the legs fast with a jerk and damaged his sciatic nerve. The patient was told how to follow the treatment at home and within ten days he was totally cured of his backache.

(2) A gentleman was suffering from Jaundice. On the basis of X-ray and Sonography, he was prescribed to remove stone from gall bladder by operation. I was called three days prior to the operation for check-up. On examination,

I found his heart to be in sound condition, there was little tenderness on point no. 22 of the gall bladder; but the points no. 23 of liver and no. 26 of kidney and no. 28 of Adrenal gland were found to be tender and point no. 8 was the most tender. I told the patient that there was no stone in gall bladder (because of excess heat in the body as indicated by pain on point no. 28 of Adrenal gland, liver is damaged. Because of excess heat the liquid of bile stored in the gall bladder had dried up and became like crystals and looked like stone in Sonography and this prevented free flow of bile into intestines and which caused Jaundice). I told the patient that there was no necessity of operation of gall bladder. But as there was pain on point no. 8 and no. 26 there was a possibility of stone in kidney.

*However the operation was done and gall bladder was removed and even on minute bisection **no stone** was found; as the small pieces of gall bladder which were removed during the operation, could not be stitched together, they were thrown away. After four hours of operation, the patient's X-ray was taken and a big stone was found near the right kidney. This stone was removed by further operation of four hours. Fortunately, the condition of the patient's heart was good and so he survived. But as his gall bladder has been removed, he has got a life long problem of digestion.*

*(3) A patient was told on the basis of X-ray ınd medical investigation that he had cancer in the mouth and operation was necessary. He consulted me and I told him, within two minutes of examination of point nos. 16, 6 and 8, that there was **No Cancer**. All he suffered was from soreness in the throat and the lump was due to cold. However, on the insistence of relatives, operation was carried out and it was found that there was no malignancy.*

Acupressure practitioners, thus, need not be carried away by the diagnosis made by other tests and other medical practitioners of other therapies. In most of the cases, the patient will come to you as a last resort and bring with him the reports of all his tests. He will also argue with you when your diagnosis differs from the earlier diagnosis. But you rely only on the observation you make from the hurting points on palms / soles of the patient.

Self-Diagnosis :

The wonderful part of this therapy is that the patient himself can find out his problem with self-diagnosis.

'One gentleman had pain in his chest. Fearing a heart attack, he went to a hospital. A cardiogram was taken and as there were no irregularities, he was discharged after four days. Later on, every time he had pain in the chest, he would call for a doctor, get his cardiogram done and be satisfied to know that it was normal. Then, he was presented with my book. Afterwards, whenever he had any chest pain, he himself would press his point no. 36 of the heart, and since there would be no pain he would be relieved of anxiety just in a minute. During one year alone, he saved not only more than Rs. 30,000 but also a great deal of tension. When I had a chance to meet him, on examination, the root cause of his chest pain was found to be the shifting of the solar plexus, which was then corrected'.

The method of self-diagnosis is a unique feature of Acupressure. It helps to locate a developing disease before outward symptoms appear. For example, you are practising Acupressure daily and you do not feel pain on any point. But one day, when pressed on point no. 36, there is a slight pain. Do not neglect. This slight pain denotes that something is wrong with the heart. Perhaps a heart attack is in the offing. Immediately take bed rest and correct the Solar Plexus for treatment of the heart.

For instance, one officer in the bank felt uneasiness. He pressed his point no. 36 and felt a slight pain. He immediately took leave, went home and took bedrest for 72 hours and took the treatment. Then he went to a cardiologist. The cardiologist told the officer that he had survived a heart attack. The officer thanked me and I thanked the Great Supreme Power.

For cure of any disease, an early detection or diagnosis is always the most important factor. **Now, if you have the habit of pressing your two palms daily or at least three times a week, you come to know immediately about what is wrong with you without any visit to a doctor or any other tests. And so you can start treatment immediately and cure/curb the developing disease at the earliest.** Such an early detection is possible not only in the case of ordinary diseases but also in the case of serious dreaded diseases like Heart-attack, Stroke, Cancer, Brain problems and even HIV/AIDS.

Diagnosis of Child :

When any child is brought to me and looks pale, I examine him for worms and also press point no. 37 of spleen. If pain is observed on this point, I examine point nos. 22-23-25-27 and 28 as well. If pain is observed on these points, it denotes Thalassemia. In order to find out why the child has got Thalassemia, I call for the child's parents, sisters and brothers and also examine them. In many cases, I have been shocked to find the father suffering from HIV infection, which is transmitted to the mother and all the children born thereafter. These other children also are found to have same symptoms of Thalassemia, which denotes the early stage of HIV. Even though it may be negative at the time, but there are chances later on of it developing into HIV positive. So I recommend immediate treatment for the family. I am glad to tell that due to such immediate treatment, such Thalassemia and HIV gets cured. (Read Part 2 of this book)

Acupressure is very useful for infants or even children of 3 years or more, who are not able to tell or explain their problems. Just by pressing on different points of the soles in case of small children, or on palms, the exact root cause can be found. Because when you press the different points, the child will cry out or pull away its leg or palm, when that point is hurting. That gives a clear indication about the problem without exposing the young patients to tests which can sometimes be hazardous. Instant diagnosis being an unique feature of this therapy, a chapter has been devoted for children's diagnosis.

Diagnosis of Dreaded Diseases :

You will be surprised to note that proper Diagnosis of any dreaded diseases like common cold, Asthma, Cancer, Brain problems and even HIV/AIDS, is possible in just two minutes without any test. Not only can you find out whether the patient has Cancer or not, but you can detect the exact location of Cancer. Once I was asked by a lady, who had just returned from the U.S.A., to tell about her problem. After examining her palms for less than two minutes, I told her that she was suffering from Cancer of the right breast. She admitted that it was true and informed that because of Cancer her right breast had been removed. I told her that in spite of the operation, the effect of Cancer was still there and had started damaging her liver. She started taking treatment as mentioned in my book and got completely cured. Now even after fifteen years, she enjoys good health.

A lady was put on dialysis, thrice a week. Later on, as there was no improvement, she was told that as both her kidneys had almost failed, she should go in for transplantation of kidneys. In India, it would cost about Rs 4,80,000 (equivalent to US $ 10,000). She got scared and came to me. Thorough examination of point nos. 11 to 15, 16 & 26 revealed that the root cause was Cancer of the uterus and her kidneys were not more than 50% damaged. She was advised treatment which she took at home. Just within 15 days, the swelling on her legs disappeared and she started passing clear urine quite regularly. She also felt energetic and became confident. Within 45 days of treatment, she was cured. The total cost of her treatment came to hardly Rs 200, i.e., less than 5 US $.

That is why it is very important not to be carried away by what the patient narrates or by the previous report. In my practice, I have never seen such reports. Very frankly,

I know very little about the terms of these reports as I am not a medical student. And upto now, there has never been any necessity to call for such reports. Pay attention to the symptoms the patient narrates and just think about what the root cause could be and within a minute you will be able to locate the exact root cause of his/her problem.

In case of common cold, tonsilitis, sinusitis, asthma etc., in most of the cases, the root cause is 'excess heat in the body.' *And it is most important to find out the root cause,* because if the patient is suffering from 'cold due to excess heat', popular treatment may be effective for a short period, and it will not cure the problem. On the contrary, such treatment worsens the problem and leads to allergy, asthma, etc. and disturbance in the digestive system. This in turn leads to acidity, etc. Because of its importance a chapter has been devoted to the common cold.

I have to advise the practitioners or readers that if any point is pressed very hard there is bound to be pain. But such hard pressure is not to be given. It is a wrong and unethical method on the part of some professionals to impress upon the patient that he/she is suffering from a serious disorder and so requires a long term treatment. On all points, except that of the endocrine glands nos. 3-4-8, 11 to 15, 25-28 & 38 enough pressure is to be given only to feel the pressure, i.e. 3 to 5 lbs. pressure.

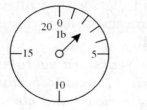 

Fig. 10

How to use the scales-weighing machine :

With zero on the scales, give pressure on it with your thumb till the scales show between 3 to 5 lbs. It is a normal pressure to be given on all points.

And only on the points of the endocrine glands, little deeper pressure of about 12 to 15 lbs. on the scale is to be given. Since Acupressure is a 'Do-It-Yourself' therapy, one can easily do it without an expert's guidance. Only in chronic cases, where the root cause has not been traced, an expert's guidance is required. Moreover, I have to advise new practitioners that unless they have tried this therapy on at least 100 patients under the supervision of some expert or at a reputed Acupressure centre, they should not advise treatment. Moreover, the practitioners should never reveal to a patient the seriousness of the disease in the very first meeting. Instead tell the patient that too much toxins have gathered in the body, which have damaged many organs and endocrine glands, and weakened the life battery. It is therefore, necessary to take a longer treatment and make a change in the diet. If possible, give the patient literature-pamphlet or book on Acupressure to read. The patient will be able to locate the problem and in the next sitting will ask you to confirm the root cause.

Moreover, never commit the mistake of telling a lady patient about her serious problem if she is alone. In such cases ask her to bring her husband or senior member of the family (preferably male in less developed countries) and then discuss the seriousness of the problem. But give them an assurance that as the root cause is found out, with proper treatment and change in diet, within fifteen days there will be a remarkable improvement and within 45/60 days the disease will get cured.

A lady teacher, aged 40 years, came to me. On examination of her point nos. 11 to 15 (because she complained about irregularity of periods) and point no. 16 it was found that there was a beginning of Cancer– degeneration in Uterus. On her insistence, I told her about this problem. Then for 15 minutes, I had to see her weeping and sobbing. With great difficulty, I managed to assure her that she need not worry and that Cancer did not mean *retirement from life and that it was most easy to cure it at home. She calmed down enough to understand the treatment. After a month, she happily reported that she was feeling much better, gaining vitality and strength and that her confidence in this therapy had greatly increased. Within 2 months of this treatment, she was perfectly well. The total cost of her treatment was hardly Rs 200; i.e. less than 5 US $.*

It is also necessary to tell the patient **that his/her symptoms may get aggravated in the beginning of the treatment and that he/she should not worry, as it is a good sign that this therapy is working properly.**

Our body is so unique, that any minor disturbance is reflected on the corresponding point on palms/soles as tenderness and so when that point is pressed, you will experience pain. Therefore, till you are satisfied that you have detected the root cause, go on checking and finding out the tender points. Use your common sense, understanding and observation. Think twice before jumping to any conclusions about Diagnosis. Slowly and steadily you will get the insight. With experience your own brain computer will start functioning in such a way that your thumb will automatically find the exact points of tenderness and your diagnosis will be correct.

CHAPTER 4

SOME OBVIOUS HINTS

Our body is the most wonderful creation of the Great Supreme Power or the Creator. Not only it cures itself but also it creates antibodies and its own medicine in the form of urine which we throw away. In the same way it reveals any problem that may exist anywhere in the body by way of pain, when pressed· on the corresponding points on the palms/soles.

Similarly, before you start pressing different points, you should observe certain external clues, which give you indication of the problem in the body.

(1) **Hand :** When you take the palm of the patient in your hand, it reveals the degree of vitality present in the patient. This has already been mentioned in Chapter 3.

(2) **Eyes :** If the eyes of the patient are whitish and there is no redness in the corners of the eyes, it denotes anaemic condition, which could be due to worms and so you should press the middle of the outside part of nails of the small finger/toes as shown here in fig. 11. And when you observe pain on that point, it indicates that there are worms in the intestine of the patient.

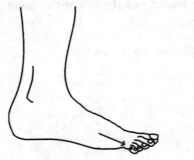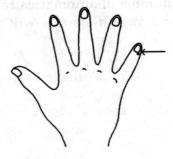

Fig. 11

Similarly, the eyes reveal the vitality of the body. In the case of a healthy person, the eyes would be shining, radiating health and happiness.

Then carefully observe the eyes. If there are dark circles and swelling below them, it denotes that the kidneys of the patient are not functioning properly and so you should check up point no. 26 of the kidneys in both the palms.

(3) Face : If you observe black pigmentation mixing with the original skin colour of the face, it could be due to excess heat in the body or some skin problem or even an indication of HIV.

(4) Males : If you observe that the growth of the beard has not been all over the face and there are patches where the beard has not grown, then it indicates sex problem in males. It could be excessive masturbation and for that just check the nails for half-moons.

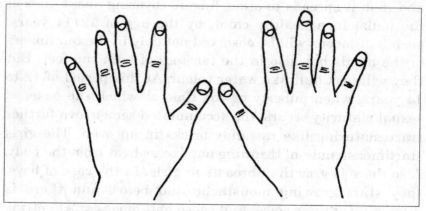

Fig. 12 Picture showing half-moons in nails

(5) Females : If you observe hair growth above the upper lips or on the face of a lady, it indicates that the Sex glands are not functioning properly.

Fig. 13

(6) **Nails :** When you hold the hand of the patient in your hand, observe carefully the nails of the patient and you will be able to find out the level of syndrome-virility, i.e. the level of the immune system of the patient.

Because from the day, a baby is born, the body starts manufacturing semen/ova from the food. The details about this process has already been mentioned in Volume I. Now there is no place where this semen/ova is stored in the body. Till the age of 12/14 years, it goes on increasing—multiplying in the body. It is like raw clay. The storage level in the body is revealed in the nails and seen as half-moons in the thumb and other fingers. These half-moons, if observed in the growing child, appear first in the thumb and then it spreads to other fingers covering about 40 % of the nails. In a healthy child, by the age of 12/14 years, such half-moons will be observed not only in the ten fingers of the hands but also in the ten toes of both the feet. But they will look dull like water colour. At this period of 12 to 14 years, when puberty or the time at which the onset of sexual maturity occurs, the accumulated semen/ova further start maturing like raw clay bricks in an oven. The girls start menstruation, throwing out excess heat from the body. Also there is growth of breasts in girls. In the case of boys, they start growing moustache and beard and there is deepening of their voice. And these half-moons start getting whiter and deeper. This process is like the ripening of fruit-becoming sweet and sweeter. These half-moons become milky white and so prominent that they look as though they are pasted on the nails, and sparkling, new light comes in the eyes, reflecting virile, vibrant health. These youngsters look attractive and their manners become pleasant. The syndrome of the body becomes powerful and the immune system becomes sound and strong enough to prevent any disease. It is like spring for the youth. The boy and the girl get attracted to each other like north and south poles resulting in marriage. And if they remain faithful to each other and do not disturb their health by unnatural ways, they can enjoy good health and blissful sex throughout life. Such virile boys and girls develop an excellent resistance to cold and heat and the change in weather does not upset them. **A happy, healthy couple is the best asset of a nation. They are good citizens and also become good parents.**

Unfortunately, due attention has not been paid to this important aspect of growth in the body. While studying about HIV/AIDS, I was shocked to observe that western doctors have not understood about the immune system of the human body and so have not understood about its syndrome, while 10,000 years ago, Indian yogis in India knew about same and they have named the Sex glands, which creates vital hormones, semen and ova, as the basis of the body—Mooladhar Chakra (मूलाधार चक्र).

The above study became possible because during the last 19/20 years, while examining all types of patients, I have made it a practice to observe my patient's nails from infants to old people. Whenever many youths-between the age of 15 to 30 years have complained about loss of appetite, weaker memory, general weakness (debility), weak eyes, the root cause has been found to be disturbance in their Sex glands (Gonads), Thyroid/Parathyroid glands. On further inquiry all these young men admitted doing masturbation for the last few years.

Similarly, whenever young women between the age 14 to 30 years, have complained to me about loss of appetite, dullness, depression, pimples, etc. the cause has been damage to their sex glands, Thyroid/Parathyroid and sometimes to their Adrenal glands. They admitted having whitish or yellowish discharge and irregular periods.

If this damage to the sex glands is not halted in time, then it leads to degeneration in the body; and a hurting pain will be observed on point no. 16 of the Lymph gland. Further, the patient feels depressed (point no. 28) and even thinks of committing suicide. The face and eyes become dull and listless. With a little experience, a look at such patient reveals the inside story. If the nails of such patient are examined they will reveal small tiny white spots coming out of the half-moons in the nails, denoting that the vital life force is being discharged in an unnatural way. As a practitioner your thumb should go to the sides of wrists, press on points no. 11 to 15 and the patient will admit about hurting pain. Then ask the male patient frankly, "Since how long have you been masturbating ?"

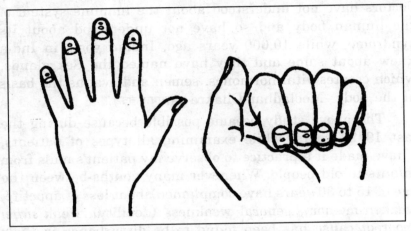

Fig. 14 Showing white spots coming out of half-moons

In the case of female patients, such white tiny spots in their nails, denote white discharge and when asked, they will also admit to irregularity in periods and having whitish or yellowish discharge called Leucorrhoea.

Even though masturbation and white discharge may have stopped, the white spots in half-moons, if any, would be smaller and that indicates weakness of sex glands both in men and women.

When you tell your patients about their sex problems, the patients get more confident about you because you have found about their secrets, which they were shy to tell. The patients require an assurance and proper guidance to their health problems. Even if they are too much depressed and have suicidal tendency, do not worry. **Boost their confidence level. Give them hope and courage.** As their Adrenal gland is not functioning properly, these patients do not have the necessary courage to cut short their life.

'A professor aged 35 years came to me and told me that he was so much depressed that he wanted to commit suicide. On examination, I found no half-moons on his nails and points of Sex glands. Thyroid/Parathyroid and Adrenal glands were paining when pressed. I told the professor to go ahead with his plan of suicide but delay it for sometime. It was fixed up after eight days in the afternoon. In the meanwhile he was asked to start the treatment as shown by me and report after eight days in the morning. The next week, he came and told me that he had changed his mind and wanted to live. Later on, he was completely cured and lived life to the fullest.

In another case, a professor wrote to me that he had become very shy and nervous. He used to shut himself in his room and was not interested in marriage or life. As he had shown courage to admit his situation, I called him to see me. His point nos. 11 to 15 were found to be very tender. He admitted of masturbating regularly which made him suffer from an inferior complex. But with proper treatment for three months, he had his confidence back and he started mixing with the opposite sex and in less than two years, he got married and lives a happy life.

A young girl of 21 years came to me. She complained that her skin was becoming dark and she was getting pimples and even had traces of hair on the upper lip. Her nails revealed the real story. She was having irregular menstruation from its beginning, then had white discharge. Consumption of drugs added excess heat in her body which turned her face and skin darker. She was assured of complete cure. In less than six months, the girl turned into an attractive lady, got married within a year and as she followed Acupressure religiously, became a proud mother of a healthy son, whom she calls an Acupressure baby.

A young modern couple, who were engaged came to me. They had physical relations during their engagement period. The girl admitted that she was not happy and did not wish to marry the boy. The boy's nails disclosed that he indulged in excessive masturbation. Even the pale girl admitted of having to much bleeding about five / seven days every month. Both were given proper guidance and asked to postpone their marriage plans for at least a year and abstain from sex play. After about fifteen months, I received an invitation to attend their marriage. The happy couple thanked me and I thanked Acupressure and the Great Supreme Power for preventing a disaster.

Infertility :

In about 80% of the cases, where a couple comes to me after an issueless marriage of over 3 to 15 years, I have found that the root cause is the husband. His indulgence in masturbation before marriage creates excess heat leading to premature ejaculation. On inquiry the husbands admitted of self-abuse and wet dreams, i.e. semen being discharged during night's erotic dreams. With proper treatment, these couples, have become happy parents after 10-15 years of marriage.

During the examination, when I hold the palms of these patients in my hand, observation of their nails reveal the facts. Moreover, I have also observed that even though they are very much younger than me, their palms were cooler. As mentioned earlier in this chapter, these half-moons denote the quantity and quality of semen (in males) and ova (in females). I have been invited to many high schools and colleges to give talks and demonstrations. I request the teachers and professors not to enter the room, and talk freely with these youngsters. These talks bring to light many pitiful facts. The doctors who visited these institutions, encouraged masturbation and neglected complaints about irregular menses. These youngsters had no proper knowledge about their sex organs.

White spots in nails of children under 12 years :

Moreover, it was observed that in the case of youngsters of less than 12 years that they were having tiny white spots coming out of half-moons on their nails. The root cause was discharge of saliva – a life force from the mouth during night. In most of such cases, it was observed that they had worms in intestines and their solar plexus had shifted. It may be noted that such discharge of saliva is a serious matter and immediate steps should be taken to correct the same.

Moreover, in few cases of sinus these young patients breathe through the mouths and are not able to control or prevent discharge of saliva from their mouths.

It should be noted that such discharge of saliva is very harmful to the body. It is almost equal to the discharge of semen from the body. And as such when such white spots are noticed on the nails of young patients, it is most necessary to check further and find out the root cause and treat the same.

Debility in married life :

Now in the case of natural ejaculation of semen/ova during sexual intercourse, these half-moons go on diminishing very slowly as the discharge is replaced by doubling of semen/ova as mentioned in volume 1. Only in the case of over-indulgence in sex; these half-moons reduce fast and there is weakness in Sex glands, which in turn can be verified by pressing the point nos. 11 to 15. Moreover, it is observed that due to excess heat in the body, the semen/ova becomes thinner and easily pass out in wet dreams (in men) or as leucorrhoea (in women). In such cases, the male patient will admit of having premature ejaculation. This can be found out by pressing these point nos. 11 to 15 of Sex glands, which will be found to be tender and hurting.

Important Root Cause of Heart Attack :

Another startling fact is found out from the observation of nails. I have found out that in more than 85 % to 90 % cases of heart problem in male patients between the age of 35 and 50, these half-moons were not properly visible. On pressing, there was hurting on point nos. 11 to 15 denoting damage to Sex glands. On inquiry, these patients have confided in me as doing masturbation – having discharge in wet dreams and indulging in more sex resulting in premature ejaculation. Thus the syndrome of the body was found to be damaged which in turn led to the problems of heart. Even the World Health Organisation has admitted that the problems of heart are more in males than in females. I urge people engaged in medical field to make more investigation and research in this direction, and reveal their findings for the benefit of mankind.

Root cause of unhappy married life – hysteria :

Moreover, incidences of unhappy married life are on the rise resulting some times in divorce or separation. Less satisfaction in married life and absence of sex play, leads many women to depression, emotional instability, hysteria and even suicide. The root cause in all these cases, will be observed in the male partner who has indulged in masturbation before marriage and so has premature ejaculation leaving his female partner sexually dissatisfied. It may be noted that having children does not prove proper virile manhood. Now, this can be prevented very easily.

Important precaution before engagement/marriage :

When the parents of a girl are serious about her marriage, they should not be carried away by the looks, smartness and wealth/education of the boy. During meeting, the girl should hold the hand of the boy/suitor in her hands and observe the nails – which will reveal the real facts. Even the girl's parent should observe the nails. Unless the girl or her parents are satisfied with virility of the boy; they should not proceed with engagement and marriage. If otherwise, boy is acceptable, the boy should be advised to take the treatment for at least 8 to 12 months. It may be noted that in Nature, there is no short cut. Moreover, after marriage it is difficult to abstain from sex and so it is most advisable to all the prospective brides and bridegrooms to take the treatment before marriage. In case engagement is already entered into, marriage should be postponed till proper treatment is carried out. In the same way, if the girl has no proper white moons, she will not be in a proper health to undertake the added responsibility of married life. She may suffer from lack of sexual desire or inability to achieve orgasm. In some cases, she may feel repulsion towards sexual activity. Moreover, she may have difficulty in conceiving, have miscarriage or may give birth to weaker offsprings.

Red signal about HIV :

It is a well-known fact that many youths indulge in sex before marriage or even indulge in addictive drugs and so they catch HIV infection. They look virile and can have properly developed white half-moons. But in case of such HIV infection, when you press their point no. 37 of Spleen, it is found to be hurting which denotes HIV infection. Now at that time if pain is also observed on point nos. 11 to 15 & 16; it denotes suffering from venereal disease. **So for best precaution against disaster after marriage, it is absolutely necessary to check up not only the nails but also point no. 37 and point nos. 11 to 15 before getting engaged or getting married.** This will prevent disasters after marriage. The details about HIV and AIDS are given in this book.

The following precautions will save the couples, their parents and the future generation in particular and the society at large in general from many undesirable, unwanted, preventable, physical and psychological problems.

Precautions :

(a) From the age of 8 onwards, the children must be taught to press their two palms for 5 minutes each. This will ensure their normal growth and prevent problems at the time of puberty.

(b) At the age of 12, these children should be taught to sit on the ball. This will prevent sexual delinquency and even leucorrhoea. See fig. 15.

Fig. 15

(c) Regular medical check-up should be made for worms in the intestine and necessary treatment should be taken.

(d) Parents should see that their children's problem of sinus is cured at the earliest and see that they breathe through their nose during the sleep.

(e) The children have the habit of sucking their thumb or fingers resulting in their saliva getting discharged. Such bad habits should be curbed at the earliest.

Thus precautions under (c), (d) and (e) will prevent the discharge of saliva which is a vital life force in the case of children.

(f) Proper treatment, wherever necessary, should be taken by young men and women who wish to marry, for at least six to ten months, to correct hormonal imbalance before the marriage.

(g) Married couples should have trust in each other and they should be faithful in marriage. They should not indulge in casual, indiscriminate sexual intercourse. Different methods of contraception should be practised for birth control. This will also prevent them from getting infected with HIV/AIDS.

(h) At least from the sixth month of pregnancy, husbands should abstain from sex till the baby is breastfed and take treatment to increase hormones-spermatoza as mentioned in my book "Health in Your Hands : Volume 1", under the Chapter "Men's Problems". This will ensure blissful, married life.

Thus, observation of nails, hands, eyes and face is very important for medical practitioners. They will be able to get clues from their examination-diagnosis of their patients.

———

CHAPTER 5

HOW TO FIND OUT ABOUT THE TYPE OF FEVER

The chief, most notable thing about fever is that it is a very good friend. He comes in your body to burn down the toxins and clean the body system and so instead of fighting against him, he should be assisted in his work. The best way to assist him is to –

(1) Drink 3 to 4 glasses of lukewarm to hot, gold / silver / copper / iron charged water reduced from 6 to 8 glasses, which will empower the battery of the body. Gold is a very efficient antibiotic, so further medicine of anti-biotics will not be necessary.

(2) If charged water is not possible, then drink only one glass of hot water every $1\frac{1}{2}$ hour.

(3) If possible, do fasting, i.e. abstain from food.

(4) Otherwise, drink green juices and fruit juices.

(5) If possible, take enema preferably of lukewarm water by adding 2 teaspoons of coffee powder + 1 tablespoon of castor oil and observe the amount of toxins that is thrown out of the body.

(6) If the temperature rises above 102 degrees, keep ice packs on the head and stomach.

In the case of high fever crossing 103 degree :

(7) Cover-up the body with a wet bedsheet and then woollen blanket and allow perspiration to flow profusely. Then wipe it out and keep the body dry.

(8) Have complete bedrest.

In order to have further proper treatment, it is necessary to find out about the type of fever. So press different points on the palms / soles and if there is hurting on –

Point no.	It denotes / symptoms
6	Throat – could be tonsillitis.
30	Congestion – could be bronchitis
37	Malaria (It is obvious as the patient gets fever after a short bout of shivering, fever upshoots and comes on alternate days. There is sweating, and the loss of healthy red cells results in anaemia.)
19	Could be typhoid, causing general weakness, high fever, chills, sweating, inflammation of the spleen and bones.
23	Jaundice-liver is badly damaged.
16	Some infection in the body.
16 + 26	Infection in kidneys.
16 + 37	Advanced infection in blood – could be due to degeneration (Cancer) in blood or advanced case of AIDS.
16 + 1 to 5	Could be Meningitis, causing an intense headache, fever, loss of appetite, convulsions, vomiting and delirium.
16 + 6	Fever due to Cancer in mouth – could be in gums, teeth, cheeks or throat.
16 + 11 to 15	Due to infection – cancerous effect in prostate (in males) and in uterus, vagina (in females).
16 + 30	T.B., Pneumonia. There is fever, feeling of uneasiness, headaches, etc. together with cough and chest pain.

In any of these fevers, ask the patient not to worry, but to take proper treatment as mentioned in my book "Health in Your Hands : Volume 1 & 2."

CHAPTER 6

COMMON DISEASES

In Acupressure therapy, it is an accepted fact that our body is so wonderful, it reveals all its problems. There is no need to study the symptoms or names of the diseases. Even it is not necessary to go in long details about the past history. Because, any problem even though it may be just in the beginning stage, the corresponding point on the palms/soles become tender and so when you press there, you feel pain.

It is easy to find out which organ has been damaged. In fig. 16 (a) & 16 (b), 38 points, which are related to different working organs, are shown. In my book "Health in Your Hands : Volume 1". cure of all different diseases is mentioned, i.e. in the case of problem of liver, point no. 23 has to be pressed. While in the case of trouble in the right eye, point no. 35 on the right palm has to be pressed. For easy diagnosis, this process has to be reversed. That is, for example, for any eye problem like watering, redness or pain, etc. will be diagnosed when you press on point no. 35 and observe hurting on it. So whether a patient tells you about his eye problem or not while checking his/her palms, if you observe any hurting, even a flicker in the eyes, when you press on point no. 35 of right palm, you can tell the patient that he/she has problem in the right eye. At the same time, also press point no. 35 on the left palm, and if there is hurting, such problem also exists in the left eye. To go further, also press on points of the optic nerve on the back of both the palms, and if it is hurting there it denotes that the patient has a problem in retina of his/her eyes. Now, you are aware that the optic nerve is controlled by the Pituitary gland. So to get confirmation about the damage to the retina, you are supposed to press on point no. 3 on

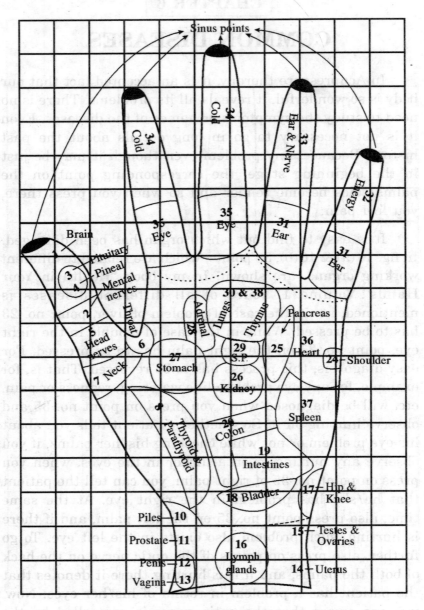

Fig. 16 (a) : Left hand
Location and Number of points connected with
different organs and endocrine glands

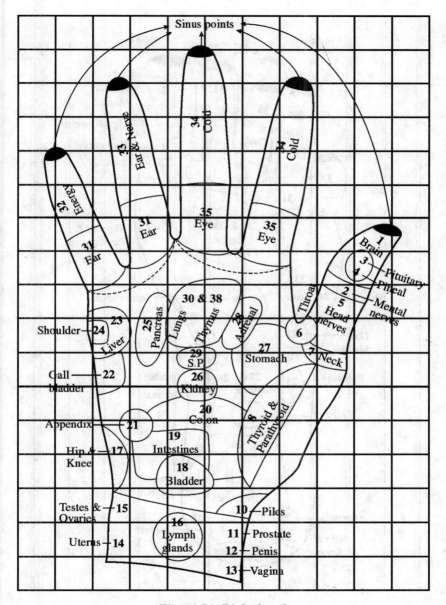

Fig. 16 (b) : Right hand
For treatment : Pressure is to be applied on and
around these points of palms

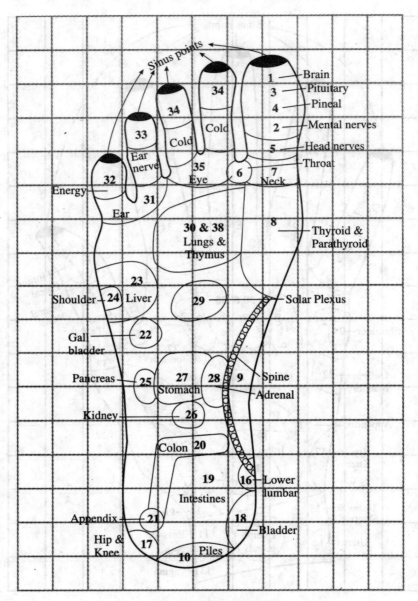

Fig. 17 (a) : Right Sole

Location and Number of points connected with

different organs and endocrine glands

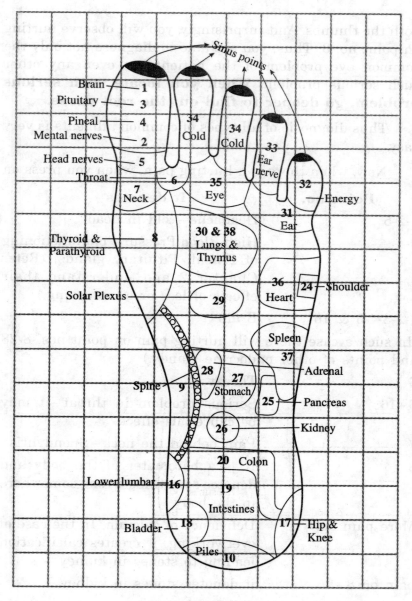

Fig. 17 (b) : Left Sole

**For treatment : Pressure is to be applied on and
around these points of soles**

both the thumbs. And surprisingly, you will observe hurting on point no. 3. Thus, you are able to diagnose not only the common eye problem of the patient but even any other such serious problem. **When you locate such serious problem, go deeper to find out the root cause.**

Thus diagnosis of all types of common ailments is very easy.

Now, when there is a hurting pain, when you press on

Point no.	It denotes
1-2-5	Headache – cold in head.
3-4	High Blood Pressure/malfunctioning of Pineal, Pituitary glands. (Refer Chapter 2 and understand their effects of less or overworking.)
1-2-3-4-5 & 16	Brain

(In such a case there will hurting pain on point nos. 8-28 and points of other endocrine glands.)

6	Throat
6+16	Serious problem in throat – it may be cancerous effect.
7	Pain behind the neck – Spondylitis
8	It is a barometer of the body and denotes something wrong somewhere in the body.
More pain on 8	Deficiency of calcium. In the case of overworking, it creates calcification leading to stones in kidney – so
pain on 8+26	it denotes stones in kidney.

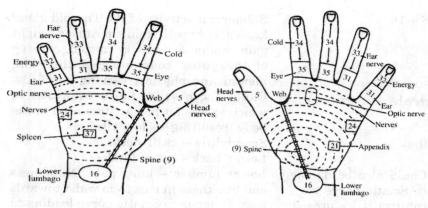

Fig. 18 (a) :
Back Side of Left Hand

Fig. 18 (b) :
Back Side of Right Hand

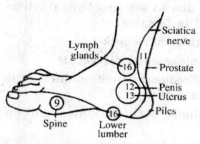

Fig. 19 (a) : Inside of Foot

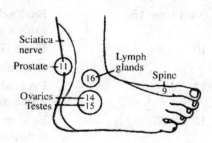

Fig. 19 (b) : Outside of Foot

8 + 16	Subnormal activity of the Thyroid gland known as hypothyroidism causes weight gain, undue sensitivity to cold, slowing of the pulse, coarsening of the skin, mental and physical slowing
8 + 11	Cause for obesity, i.e. a condition in which excess fat has accumulated in the body, resulting in low vitality
9	Spondylitis – Stiff neck. Lower back – lower lumbar.
Could also be damage to Sciatic nerve so confirm it by pressing on the point of Sciatic nerve on legs. See fig. 19 (a) & (b).	Lower lumbar – knee pain. Numbness and weakness in legs from waist towards toes. Damage to Sciatic nerve leading to loss of sensation, muscle weakness – slipped disc.
9 + 37 + 16	Degeneration of bones.
9 + 11 to 15	Backache due to sex problems (both in males and in females)
10	Piles (In this case check the solar plexus and correct it)
11	Prostate. Frequent urination during the day and or night.
11 to 15	Sex problems both in males and in females. (Pimples, less or more menses, painful menses, irregular menses, timidity, loss of libido, less virility (Check the nails).)
11 to 15 + 16	Degeneration of prostate (in males) even V.D., Degeneration of Uterus (in females)
17	Pain in hips and knees.
18	Problem in bladder or trouble in passing urine or excess storage of urine.
19	Problems of intestines.
19 + 22 + 23 + 28	Ulcers-acidity-gas trouble, if pain persists, check the mouth as there could be ulcers.
20	Problem about colon, the main part of the large intestine.

20 + 16	Degeneration of colon.
21 (inner part of the hand)	Appendix (It also indicates early development of this problem.)
21 (back of palm)	Allergy.
21 + 8	Allergy + deficiency of calcium.
22 – 23	Problem in Gall bladder + liver, an early indication of jaundice.
More pain on 22 – 23	Jaundice – indication of crystallisation of biles in gall bladder (considered to be stone in gall bladder)
23 + 16	Degeneration of liver.
24	Stiffness in shoulder.
9 + 24	Frozen shoulder.
25	Malfunctioning of Pancreas, overworking leads to migraine, desire to eat-drink sweets and later on to alcoholism.
25 + 28	Underworking of Pancreas
25 + 28 + 16	Diabetes.
26	All problems related to kidneys –
26 + 25	Skin problem.
26 + 4	Retention of fluid.
26 + 8	Stone in kidney.
27	Stomach – loss of appetite, digestion problem, gas trouble.
27 + 16	Degeneration of stomach
28	Problem related to Adrenal gland, excess heat in the body. Depression, fear of more pain, severe depression indicates desire to commit suicide (suicidal tendency), less circulation of blood and so less oxygenisation.
29	Solar plexus if shifted upwards leads to constipation, Hiatus hernia-piles-fistula; if shifted downwards, leads to loose motion. Colitis, i.e. inflammation of the colon, leading to diarrhoea and lower abdominal pain.

30	Lung problems.
30 + 6	Bronchitis, even fever due to it.
30 + 16 + 8	T.B.
31	Ear problems – less hearing, etc.
31 + 28	Cold around ears due to excess heat.
31 + points for worms + 16	Ear infection due to worms.
31 + 16 + 33	Frequent noise in the Ears – even Vertigo.
32	Less energy, low vitality.
34	Cold
34 + 27	Common cold affecting the nose, throat and bronchial tubes
34 + 28	Cold due to excess heat
34 + 8 + 6	Tonsils.
35	Problems of redness of eyes, watering of eyes, etc.
35 + (point of optic nerve) + 3 & 4	Beginning of damage to retina.
+ pain in eyes	Advanced stage of damage to retina, could be glaucoma, a condition in which the pressure within the eyeball causes dimness and ultimately loss of vision.
36	Problems relating to heart.
36 + 28	Less circulation of blood.
36 + 8	Could be heart attack
36 + 8 + breathlessness	Varicose veins, blockade in arteries.
37	Problem of spleen, anaemia. (Check the point of worms.)
37 + 16	Degeneration of blood
37 + 16 + 9 (Back of palm)	Degeneration of blood and bones.
37	Patient otherwise looking healthy could be HIV-affected, therefore, call for partner and children below 15 and if such pain found in partner it could be HIV.
37 + 11 to 15	HIV due to sex abuse, multiple sex partners and unnatural sex, could also be Venereal Disease or any disease

	transmitted by sexual intercourse (In that case of V.D., there may be burning sensation while urinating & hurting on point no. 16.)
37 + 22 + 23 + 28	In children, Thalassemia. Call the parents other children and check them to find out the root cause.
38	Problems relating to Thymus in the case of children – Weakened defence system. In the case of adults; overworking of Thymus – leading to Myasthenia gravis, a condition causing loss of muscle power.

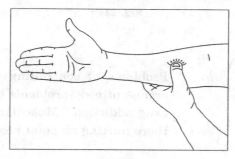

Fig. 20

In the middle circle in right hand (See fig. 20)	Weakened valve of energy flow leading to decaying and old age.
16 (Front side)	Diabetes – infection – boils, etc.
16 + 25	Diabetes over 2 % – 200 in blood + sugar in Urine leading to thirst, loss of weight and the excessive production of urine.
16 + 31	Infection of the Ears.
16 + 26	Infection of the Kidney.
16 + 11 to 15	Infection of the sex organs – Prostate, Penis or Uterus leading to degeneration + V.D.
16 + 11 to 15 + on back of right palm (middle)	Degeneration of prostate (in males) Degeneration of Uterus (in females) Degeneration of Uterus + right breast
16 + 11 to 15 + on back of left palm (middle) (See fig. 21)	Degeneration of Uterus + left breast

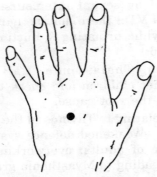 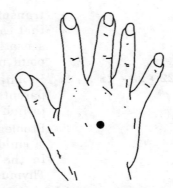

Back of Left Palm   **Back of Right Palm**

Fig. 21

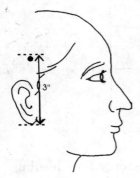

Problems of controlling the different organs of body-problems of the brain + drug addiction + Muscular Distrophy if there hurting on point nos. 1 to 5 & 16.

Fig. 22

Point 3" above the earlobes

16 + 6	Degeneration of Teeth, Tongue and Throat.
16 + point between 6 & 27	Degeneration of Windpipe (causing difficulty in swallowing)
16 + 27	Degeneration of Stomach.
16 + 19	Degeneration of Small intestine.
16 + 20	Degeneration of Large intestine.
16 + 22 + 23	Degeneration of Gall Bladder & Liver
16 + 30	Degeneration of Lungs (T.B.)
16 + 1 to 5	Destruction of healthy Brain cells (could be tumour of the brain)
16 + 37	Degeneration of Blood.
16 + 37 + 9	Degeneration of Blood + Bones

(In the case of pain of point no. 37, first check-up if there are any boils, pus formation in cuts/ear infection, etc. before coming to the above conclusion about degeneration.)

If not, get the medical check-up done of urine and blood sugar. If no sugar is found in the urine or blood, i.e. if there is no diabetes, then it is a clear indication about degeneration. But the practitioner/patient need not worry. Assure the patient that all types of degenerations are curable.

In the same way even in the case of V.D. and HIV or Thalassemia, assure the patient that if proper treatment (as mentioned in this book "Health in Your Hands : Volume 2 – Part 2") is taken for 60/75 days, it is curable.

CHAPTER 7

CHILDREN'S PROBLEMS

Acupressure is unique in the diagnosis of children, because young children are incapable of speaking about their problems and many times, they cannot explain their problems. Moreover, children should not be exposed to certain tests – like X-ray, Sonography, etc.

While examining a child, give a smile and hold his/her palm in your hands and lovingly, press it lightly. The child will then allow you to examine him/her.

First look into the eyes. If they are found to be whitish, check for worms. (See fig. 23)

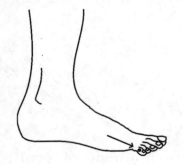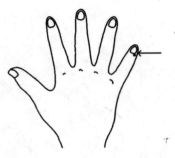

Fig. 23

In the case of any complaint about constipation, loose motion, pain in stomach, etc. check up the solar plexus as given in method (2) on page 36 and correct it as given in fig. 3 (for children below 8 years; otherwise as mentioned in fig. 5).

For Constipation or Loose motion :

Check up point no. 8. If it is not paining then, the minor problem may be due to the shifting of the solar plexus. And so when you adjust it, problem of constipation, pain around stomach or loose motion will get automatically corrected.

For Ear Infection :

Many breastfed children or those feeding on milk, generally get ear infection, which you can find out by pressing on point no. 31 of the ears and no. 16 of the lymph glands.

Observe flickering in the eyes :

Afterwards, you can proceed as per the indications obvious to you or as may be hinted by the parents. Accordingly press different points. In case of hurting or pain on the points you press, the child will immediately, withdraw his/her hands, or may even cry. While pressing different points on palm/sole of the child, always look into his/her eyes. Some children are stubborn and they resist, so you may not get any indication about pain, when pressing the points. But when you watch their eyes, you will observe a flicker of pain when they feel it. That gives you a clear indication about the problem.

For Heart :

In the case of any minor or major problem of the heart, such as a hole in the heart, or septal defect, you will observe pain when you press on point no. 36 of the heart.

For Diabetes that sets about in childhood (Juvenile Diabetes) :

Press on point no. 16 of the Lymph gland + point no. 25 of Pancreas.

Diptheria :

Press on point nos. 8 – 11 to 15 + 6 + 30.

Thalassemia :

Press on point nos. 37 + 27 + 28 + 22 – 23. The child will be looking pale – anaemic. In case of any doubt, call the parents and check them also. You will get the root cause. Those symptoms could be hereditary or due to HIV acquired from the mother and so when you examine the parents and other brothers and sisters under 15 years, your doubt would be confirmed.

Retardation and hereditary problems :

In case there is serious damage to more than three endocrine glands including Pineal, i.e. Thyroid/Parathyroid, Adrenal and Pineal and/or Pituitary endocrine gland, it indicates that the child could be retarded and would develop into a patient of Multiple Sclerosis, a chronic disease causing paralysis, speech and visual defects, etc. It is an accepted fact that this retardation is due to harm to the brain during pregnancy. Another accepted fact is that the brain goes on developing up to six to nine months after the birth of a child. Now in the case of any harm to the brain of the child, it can be diagnosed at the earliest after the birth and immediate treatment can be started. The result will be that there will be a better chance of curing such retardation, deafness, even Muscular Dystrophy. Every newborn child cannot be exposed to X-rays, Sonography and Catscanning. But Acupressure test can be done without any harm. Therefore, I earnestly urge all the parents and medical practitioners, especially the child specialists connected with maternity homes to carry out this Acupressure Test – to find out harm to the brain and the vital endocrine glands.

I have got wonderful results in problems with children under 10 years and over. Even in the case of Muscular Dystrophy, the results have been fantastic. And so if such harm to the vital endocrine glands and the brain could be diagnosed within one to three months of the birth of a baby, we shall be able to control the mega problem of retarded children, Multiple Sclerosis and Muscular Dystrophy.

In the case of children, do not hastily come to any conclusion in the first visit. Give guidance about treatment to be given at home. Ask the mother to reduce the quantity of milk or food. Give the child 1 to 2 glasses of lukewarm charged water reduced from 2 to 4 glasses and call the patient after 3 to 5 days. In the next sitting, you will be able to make the correct diagnosis of the serious problem.

————

CHAPTER 8

MEN'S PROBLEMS

Acupressure plays a very useful part in solving men's problems. Because in most of the cases, young patients between the age 13 to 20 or even mature adults do not talk about their sex problems like masturbation, emission of semen in erotic dreams, i.e. wet dreams, premature ejaculation or general disease, and HIV/AIDS. They try to mislead the practitioner regarding symptoms like loss of appetite, memory loss, early tiredness, general debility, etc. or burning sensation in the body.

Now, in all such cases, the root cause could be disturbance in the Sex glands called Gonads. It can be detected very easily in the following manner.

Early Detection :

(1) **Feel the palms :** If they are cooler, then they denote less vitality.

(2) Check the nails for the white moons. If white spots are noticed on these moons, it indicates emission of vital life force, i.e. semen from the body. (In case of children, if you observe such white spots, it denotes discharge of saliva from the mouth during sleep or sucking of their thumb or fingers.) Now, these white spots also indicate emission of semen in an unnatural way, i.e. masturbation or emission in erotic wet dreams. (See fig. 12 & 14)

Sex Problems : In case there are no such white spots on the nails, but the moons have reduced and are looking pale like water, it denotes emission in a natural way but clearly indicate excessive sex. The patient may have practised masturbation earlier, came out of that bad habit, but have oversex in married life or has physical relations outside marriage. In advanced stage, such water-like moon will be observed in the thumb or only in the thumb and the first finger and not in other fingers. (See fig. 12)

(3) In such cases, press point nos. 11 to 15. Pain on these points will confirm problems regarding sex, like improper functioning of the Sex glands and imbalance of hormones.

In all these cases, when pressed on point no. 8 of Thyroid/Parathyroid, there will be pain—which indicates deficiency which indicates deficiency of calcium and weakened will-power.

(4) **Venereal Diseases** : Now, in the case of patients above 16/18 years of age, when you observe pain on point no. 13 of penis and point no. 16, it indicates venereal disease, the cause of having unprotected sex with prostitutes and degeneration of prostate gland, due to bacterial infection and can be either acute or chronic. In case of Venereal Disease, the patient would have regular or casual burning sensation while urinating. Take the patient in confidence and he will admit his mistakes. Assure him that the disease is also curable.

(5) **HIV/AIDS** : Sometimes when you hold such patient's hands you will find them warm and will observe the nails with big white moons. There may be hurting pain on point nos. 37 and 11 to 15. This is an indication of HIV infection, because such infection affects the blood and damages the spleen. In such cases, call all the members of his family. Surprisingly, the patient's wife will have pain, when pressed on point nos. 37 and 11 to 15 and in advanced cases, even on point nos. 11 to 15 and 16. Over and above such indications of disease or disorder there will also be symptoms of Thalassemia which will be observed in all their children (up to the age of 15) who may have been born after such HIV infection.

Case Studies :

I will quote here a few incidents :

(a) *A patient came to me at our Centre and complained about burning sensation while passing urine. On examination, point nos. 8, 11 to 15, 16 and 28 were found to be tender. And negligible white moons only on thumbs and first finger were observed. When asked, he confessed having regular sexual relations with prostitutes and also confessed of having a deep scar on the penis. So without any physical examination, diagnosis of venereal disease was possible.*

(b) A young man came to me and complained about having loss of appetite. I held his palms in my hand and they were cold, white spots were observed on his nails and on further examination, he felt pain on point nos. 11 to 15 when pressed. When asked, he admitted of having been masturbating since last four years and now had emissions in wet dreams.

(c) A young lady of about 24 years brought her 2-year-old baby, for having frequent colds. On examination the baby was found to have symptoms of Thalassemia. There was feeling of pain on point nos. 37-22-23-27 & 28 and 8. In order to find out the root cause, I examined the baby's mother who was looking healthy, but I observed that there was greater pain on point no. 37 and slight pain on point no. 16. I called her husband and on examining him found that he had pain on point nos. 37-16-11 to 15. He had acquired HIV infection from sexual relations with prostitutes and unwittingly passed it on to his wife and the result was such that both mother and the baby were infected with HIV.

It may be noted that the creation of semen and its storage continues in the body till the age of 12/14 and then its fermentation-heat-process develops into syndrome of the body, more white and prominent milky half moons on the finger nails indicate virile-strong syndrome. The ejaculation of semen before marriage at the age of 24 years or more, through masturbation, leads to damage to Gonads, which in turn leads to excess heat in the body and thins the vital semen. Later on, the semen is ejaculated during erotic wet dreams and in advanced stage, it starts coming out and is known as passing of Albumin in urine.

Moreover, such emission in an unnatural manner gives pleasure or relief of tension in the beginning but turns into a guilty feeling and this in turn damages the vital organs of the digestive system. Loss of appetite, less assimilation of food and less creation of new blood – all this in turn leads to Anaemia and disturbance to Adrenal and other endocrine glands which leads to depression and negative thinking, even that of committing suicide. It may be noted that damage to the Adrenal gland leads to inferiority complex.

(d) A young patient complained about continuous stammering especially at the time of interview. His point nos. 11 to 15 and also 8 and 28 were found to be tender. He had developed an inferiority complex–which was due to occasional stammering. The root cause was masturbation, a habit he had developed since his teenage days. He knew well that he should not waste his semen but, he could not control the emission. This fear damaged his Adrenal gland which led to occasional and later turned to continuous stammering. He started proper treatment and he gained confidence – after which there was no more stammering and stuttering. Later, he was selected for an important high-salaried job.

Root cause of Thalassaemia-weak children :

Recently, I am startled to observe increasing number in cases of Thalassemia minor. The root cause of this problem is a hereditary disorder of the blood due to defects in the synthesis of haemoglobin, which is sometimes fatal in children. The affected red cells cannot function normally, leading to anaemia. Moreover, I have found that the root cause is HIV infection inherited by the husband and then passed on to his wife and children.

Moreover, many couples have admitted that as they were having hormonal trouble before and after marriage, they were advised total restraint from sex for 2/3 years. But they could not control themselves and as a result weak children with Thalassemia minor were born.

In cases where the wife is also suffering from sex problems-more bleeding, leucorrhoea, i.e. a whitish or yellowish discharge, infection of the lower reproductive tract, the chances of getting weak children increases manifold when the husband is also afflicted with sex problems.

CHAPTER 9

WOMEN'S PROBLEMS

The difference between a female and a male is about their sex and tenderness of mind. It is observed that most of the problems in women start from the irregularity about menses, which denotes hormonal imbalance. By nature females are gentle and tender in mind, more emotional and sentimental. So during the childhood and till the start of menstruation, they could have hurt feelings, damaging their endocrine glands. Now, due to ignorance about the same, and as the endocrine glands being not corrected, there is an hormonal imbalance which becomes obvious at the time of the start of menses.

Irregularity about menses means (a) early or late cycle with pain, (b) less or more flow, (c) The flow may not be red in colour and could be easily washable. It may be noted that regular cycle means regularity of menstruation without pain on 28th/29th days as it is connected with the monthly cycle of the moon. There should be even menstrual flow for 3/4 days and this flow should be red in colour and easily washable. It is also important to know that the monthly cycle varies from individual to individual. The disturbance of hormonal imbalance leads to many physical as well as psychological problems for women.

In India and many less advanced countries, women are shy to talk about the irregularity of menses and problems connected with sex. Therefore, when any female patient comes to you, you have to :

(1) First observe her nails and the white half-moons in the nails.

(2) In case, these females have nail polish, carefully observe around the mouth. The disturbance in hormonal imbalance, in a little advanced stage, is very obvious. You will observe growth of hair around the mouth, above the upper lip. (See fig. 13)

(3) Hold the palms of the patient in your hands. If you feel that the palms are cool, then it denotes more bleeding and less vitality.

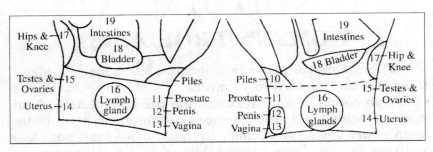

Fig. 24

(4) These observations will be confirmed, when you press the wrists on point nos. 11 to 15. There will be hurting pain on these points. Thus you are very easily able to diagnose about the hormonal imbalance in such patients.

(5) In the case of excessive bleeding during menses, the face and eyes will be pale and the palms cooler. There may be fluffiness in the body.

(6) In cases of advanced stage the patient could be very anaemic. This will be confirmed by pressing on point no. 37 of the spleen. Moreover, check for worms.

(7) In the case the patient is suffering from Leucorrhoea, you will observe white spots on the half-moons of the nails.

(8) In the case of scanty or less menses there may be pimples on the face and the palms may be warm. Press on point no. 28 of Adrenal gland. You will find pain which denotes excess heat in the body.

It may be noted that less menstrual flow leads to problems of excess heat in the body, which in turn leads to pimples, constipation, chronic cold due to heat, and even skin problems. While more menstrual flow or excessive bleeding leads to lessening of heat from the blood, lower vitality, loss of appetite, timidness, less desire in sex, anaemia and is one of the root cause of obesity and could lead to leucorrhoea, i.e. abnormal whitish discharge. And if this is not controlled, later on it could lead to wasting of body−even infection of the lower reproductive tract−uterus.

Backache:

Many a times, the root cause of backache is irregularity of menses. Press on point nos. 9–11 to 15.

Hormonal Imbalance:

Moreover, disturbance in hormonal balance of Sex glands creates difficulty in conceiving a child, and even leads to miscarriage. So in all these problems, the root cause is the disturbance of Sex glands and also the excess heat in the body. (Check point nos. 28-22-23)

Mammography:

In acupressure, such test of Mammography is very easy and simple but SURE.

Now, when you observe painful hurting on point nos. 11 to 15 of the Sex glands, other endocrine glands and lymph glands, check up the circle in the middle of the back of palms as shown in fig. 25.

Pain on the back of the right palm denotes problem in the right breast. In the same way pain on the back of left palm denotes problem in the left breast. At this time, check up point no. 16 of the lymph gland. If there is acute pain, it indicates degeneration. This can be confirmed by Biopsy, if you so desire.

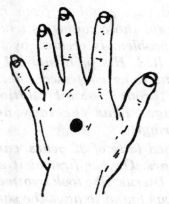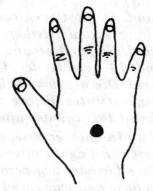

Back of Left Palm   **Fig. 25**   **Back of Right Palm**

Now if there is no pain on point no. 16, but only on the back of the palms, the problem is not serious as there is no malignant growth and can be cured within 15 to 30 days.

Degeneration in Uterus :

Now, when there is painful hurting on point nos. 11 to 15 and also on point no. 16, it clearly indicates degeneration, i.e. the deterioration and loss of specialized function of the cells of a tissue or organ (otherwise known as Cancer). This degeneration is detected even at a very early stage even if it is less than 10 %. In case the degree of pain on point nos. 11 to 15 & 16 is acute, it indicates advanced stage—even malignant growth. This can be confirmed easily by Biopsy.

Do not upset the patient in any manner. Assure the patient that all types of degeneration are curable within 45 to 60 days by proper treatment as mentioned later in this book – Part 2.

Infertility :

Now, in the cases of complaints about infertility, there could be acute pain on point nos. 11 to 15. But in all such cases, call the patient's husband. I have observed that in more than 80 % cases, the problem lies with the husband.

Case Studies :

(1) A young lady of about 27 years of age, looking healthy, was complaining about frequent itching in the vagina. On examination, point nos. 11 to 15 and 16, were found to be tender without any signs of degeneration. She was suspected to have inherited this problem from her husband. In most such cases, except those countries which may have sexual freedom, such problem is created by the husband. So her husband was called. His point nos. 11 to 15 and 16 were tender. On inquiry, he confessed having Venereal Disease which he got through sexual relations with prostitutes before marriage. Thus the lady had developed this disease after marriage.

(2) In another case, a married lady of 32 years, came to our Centre again after two years. On her first visit she was found to have degeneration in Uterus. She took treatment for 45 days and was cured. She was found to have the same complaint and an additional problem of degeneration in blood. On enquiry, she informed that her husband was away in Dubai and would come home for a month after every six months. That indicated the husband was involved in an

extramarital affair and suffering from V.D. which was the root cause of the lady's agony.

During the past three years, I have started calling the husbands along with their wives (the patients) and insisted on examining them in case of such doubts. And in more than 1000 cases of the degeneration of the Uterus, the root cause was found with the husbands who were either suffering from veneral diseases or had HIV infection.

In few of the cases, where the husbands were frank, they confessed about their ignorance about the sexual facts of life.

(3) A boy of 8 years, was brought to me by his mother. She told that her son was indulging in masturbation. When the foreskin (prepuce) was drawn back, there was a scar of about $\frac{1}{4}$ inch on the glans of the penis. On examination, the points of Pineal gland and Sex glands, the Thyroid, Parathyroid were found to be tender. The mother was examined. Even though she looked healthy, she had degeneration of Uterus. Her husband was called and on examination, his points of Sex glands and even lymph glands were found to be tender. In the beginning he refused, but on prodding he admitted having done excessive masturbation before marriage and having sexual relations with prostitutes whenever he had to go out of town. The result was he had acquired V.D. The three were put under treatment. Within 15 days, the boy stopped masturbating and the scar on the glans of the penis was healed within one month. The couple was asked to have restraint on sexual relations and to use contraceptives if control was not possible. Within 2 months, they became a happy, healthy couple.

(4) A lady of about 26 years, came to our Centre and complained about having 3 miscarriages. On examination, her point nos. 11 to 15 were found to be very tender. She was given proper treatment and advised not to have child for at least two years. She and her husband co-operated. They took proper treatment and also drank charged water. They planned for a child, as per my book. And after about four years, this happy couple came to our Centre with a healthy young baby boy.

(5) *"A lady of about 22 years came to me with her mother-in-law. She complained about having no issue even after 4 years of marriage. Her palm was cool and the nails lacked half-moons. There was hurting on point nos. 11 to 15 and even slight pain on point no. 16. On inquiry, she confessed about having irregular menses from the beginning and discharge of white fluid, since the last 5 years. She was given proper treatment and advised not to have children for at least 2 years. Later on, the young lady reported being free of her complaints."*

(6) *"In the case of another married lady of 26 years, she looked pale and her, nails showed half-moons only on thumb and first finger. There was acute pain on point nos. 11 to 15. She confessed about Leucorrhoea and that she had a miscarriage six months back. If she had given birth to a baby, under such condition, the baby would have been very weak and may have had some hereditary problem. She was advised proper treatment and asked to desist from having children for at least 2 years."*

It must be informed to the patients that there are no shortcuts in Nature. Mother nature is very kind and so with proper treatment taken over six to twelve months, any woman will become capable of conceiving. When such advice has to be given to a lady patient, it is always in her interest to call the husband. Get him checked and advise him to co-operate and take proper treatment even though no problem is found with him. Such a treatment will correct his hormonal balance. It will make him more virile and after 12/15 months, such couple will have a better chance of becoming parents.

Serious effects of Leucorrhoea :

"A child of about 3 years was brought to me. On examination, it was diagnosed that the young boy was suffering from Thalassemia minor. The boy's mother, was then examined. She had an advanced stage of degeneration. She was asked to come again with her other two children and husband. On their examination, both the pale children were found to have Thalassemia minor and also worms in

the intestines. The husband was suffering from sexual weakness and admitted having masturbated before marriage. The wife (the mother of the children) admitted of having irregular menses and leucorrhoea. The whole family was put on proper treatment and cured successfully."

Thus it will be observed that negligence and ignorance about irregular menses and Leucorrhoea can lead to serious consequences. I am very sorry to say that even educated ladies neglect this problem of irregular menses which is very widespread. On discussion with many such patients, including educated ones, it was revealed shockingly that all these women accepted such complaints of irregular menses as being natural. Such problems were accepted as a regular consequence of being a woman. It is high time that, proper awareness is created in girls and women about such irregularity. It is a very important problem not only in India but also in all the developing countries. For better and healthy progress of girls/women, it is most vital that they take hygienic care of their periods and have regular menses. Proper menses denotes hormonal balance. And if there is no proper hormonal balance in the couple, the baby to be born will be weak and will have health problems. Hence, there is higher infant mortality in India and other developing countries. It may be noted, that with early treatment, such problems can be prevented and cured with minimum cost.

Menopause :

For women in the mid-forties, this problem starts because of the hormonal changes. Around this age the cycle of menstruation comes to stop. There is a change in the balance of sex hormones in the body. Even such problem is observed for women who have undergone operation to remove ovary and stop menstruation. After menstruation ceases, the women are no longer able to give birth to children. Some women may experience emotional disturbances. In all such problems, just press on point nos. 11 to 15, these points will be found to be rendering pain. Suggest cure and women who are dull, timid and of worrying type will become normal just within 30 to 40 days. During such treatment it is advisable for the women to drink 2 glasses of charged water reduced from 4 glasses. Such treatment can also prevent Osteoporosis, even cure it.

Excess Weight :

In the case of females, damage to endocrine glands of Thyroid/Parathyroid is very common. Moreover, their Sex glands are damaged during pregnancy or delivery because of worry. And so when these two endocrine glands do not function properly, these women start putting on weight more around the waist. Because of damage to these two endocrine glands, sometimes even Pineal gland is damaged and so there is more retention of water in the body, which is also one of the reasons for excess weight.

When such patients come, their obese figure obviously shows their problem which can be confirmed by pressing on point nos. 8, 11 to 15 and no. 3. At this time of checking, it is advisable to check other endocrine glands too, so you can locate any further damage, if any. For cure, first it is necessary to treat these two endocrine glands for 15/20 days and only then start dieting and treatment on not only these two endocrine glands but also on the other endocrine glands. I have treated many cases, where the weight loss was from 2/3 kgs to 10 kgs per month. Once the weight has reached normal then ask the patients to continue Acupressure treatment and they will be able to maintain their weight and pleasing figure.

Tenderness :

Women are gentle and tender by nature, and so their endocrine glands easily get damaged. And if these endocrine glands are not rectified, it leads not only to physical problems but also to many psychological problems. And so it is advisable, to check up one by one all endocrine glands of all the patients irrespective of their age.

It has been observed that because of the damage to one or more endocrine glands, a psychological problem is created, and which has not been understood properly. Therefore, a separate chapter has been devoted to these psychological problems.

CHAPTER 10

PSYCHOLOGICAL PROBLEMS

Our mind has a great effect on the body. However, all the endocrine glands act as buffer and try to absorb shock of such bad effects. During my long years of practice, I have observed that in all these psychological problems one or more endocrine glands are damaged and when you press on their points you will find them to be tender. And so when you give treatment on these endocrine glands, surprisingly the psychological problem is corrected. It may be true that everyday problems of life may still persist, but the patient gets enough strength to face them and fight them.

So when any patient comes to you with such psychological problems, check-up their endocrine glands. The details about effects of malfunctioning or overworking of the endocrine glands are given in Chapter 2 of this book. As these endocrine glands play a very important part not only in our body but also on our mind for developing of our character, it is advisable to read and refer this Chapter as often as possible till all the details are properly settled in your mind. If these details are followed strictly then any practitioner of Acupressure can become a Psychologist or a Psychiatrist.

It may be noted that the treatment of Acupressure on the relative points of the endocrine glands have been found very effective to get rid of bad habits like drug dependence and masturbation both in males and females.

Case Studies :

(1) *"A young man of about 23 years was brought to me. He had become a drug addict and was also a chain-smoker. His family had spent lots of money on his treatment. But the problem was becoming worse day by day. The young man had started stealing from the house for satisfying his drug habit and he also threatened his mother. On examination, point nos. 8, 11 to 15, 28 and 3 and also point on head which controls all drug addiction were found to be tender.*

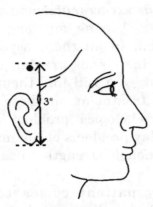

Fig. 26

The young man also confided that he regularly indulged in masturbation. His brother was a good, successful actor. And so he suffered from an inferiority complex. In the first instance, this was a psychological case. The patient was advised treatment. His mother co-operated by giving the boy charged water + green juice mixed with health drink and honey + fruit juices. She was not to be strict with her son, but show love and affection. Within 40/45 days of the beginning of the treatment, not only did the drug addiction stopped but the patient also got rid of smoking and masturbation, and became confident of himself."

(2) A 16-year-old boy wrote to me that he was a chain-smoker and wanted to quit the habit. I replied about the treatment to be taken. Accordingly, he started the treatment as mentioned in my book and within 40 days he stopped smoking.

(3) One of the Airport Managers of the Indian Airlines was posted at Karachi. From his personal satisfying experience, he had become an ardent follower of Acupressure. Now, he found surprisingly that even in Karachi (Pakistan),

there were lots of cocktail parties being held. And in these parties, many people would get heavily drunk and they would not be able to stand steadily. At that time, this officer gave the treatment of rubbing the tip of the nose of these drunk persons who vomited within 3 minutes, became sober and went home on their scooters / two wheelers.

Fig. 27

(4) A girl of 17 years complained that she was not able to co-ordinate the activities of both sides, i.e. right and left hands and feet, of the body. As a result, she had great difficulty in walking. She had this problem since childhood and though she tried every treatment, none was found effective. On examination, point nos. 3-4-8 and 5 at the base of thumbs, were found to be tender. She was advised to take treatment for the problems of the brain as mentioned later in this book. And within 10 days, she reported 80% improvement and within month, she became normal.

(5) A woman of about 35 years complained that she would feel that her fingers and hands have become dirty and she would wash them about 50 times in a day. On examination, point no. 28 of the Adrenal gland was found to be tender. While inquiring the past history of her case, she informed that 10 years before, she was shocked to get the news of the sudden death of her beloved mother. As she was very much dependent on her mother, she could not cope with the situation arising after her mother's death. Since then her queer habit had started. She was advised treatment and in 15 days, she was happy to report that she had become normal.

(6) A mother came with her eight-year-old son. The boy had become naughty, disobedient and had started stealing from the house. This, she said, happened since last fortnight. On examination point nos. 3-4 and other endocrine glands were found to be tender. The mother was asked to give treatment and not to scold the boy. Within a week, the mother was happy to see her son completely normal.

(7) A married woman of 32 years was having several fits of hysteria and her distressed husband thought of giving her divorce. But before this extreme step was taken she approached me. On examination, point nos. 11 to 15 were found to be tender. Most of the time her husband had to go out of town. He could give little time to his wife. Because of this she had become frigid and lost interest in marital life. The husband was also called for and I observed that his point nos. 11 to 15 were tender and had very little half white moons. The husband later confessed that he suffered from premature ejaculation which left his wife sexually dissatisfied. Both the husband and the wife were asked to take treatment for six months. Now, they are considered to be an ideal 'Made for each other' couple.

Thus, you will observe that in all these and hundreds of other similar cases, the patients come to me as a last resort. In all these cases, the root cause found was the malfunctioning of one or more endocrine glands and when treatment was taken, the results were amazing.

In the case of retarded children, when their Pituitary and Pineal glands are overworking, their body develops fully, sometimes becoming bulky and there is an early awakening of sexual desires. The parents are confused and greatly worried and become disheartened seeing new problems being created everyday by their child. In all these cases, the treatment of brain problem plus giving blue light produced wonderful results.

(8) Once a mother brought her 12-year-old son, who looked like 18. When I asked him his name, I got the reply

on my cheek-a resounding slap. As the boy was not taking blue light when awake the whole day, it was decided to give blue light when he slept. The mother and son visited me after a month. There was a complete transformation in the boy. The boy shook hands with me. There was a smile on his face of understanding. The parents were happy because their son had now started taking interest in playing games and painting.

So, whenever you come across psychological problems, check the endocrine glands and you will find out the root cause. While treating such patients, blue light + biochemic medicines blended with Acupressure treatment will give amazing and desired results.

Females :

The females are immediately disturbed, because of tenderness of heart, and develop many problems considered to be psychological. However, any of these problems of timidness, fear, loss of interest in sex or hysteria are due to the damage to their endocrine glands and as they are not rectified, these problems worsen as days pass by. Therefore, as mentioned earlier, treatment on these endocrine glands + charged water give wondrous and marvellous results.

Prevention of Psychological Problems :

If any girl is taught to take Acupressure treatment from the age of at least 8/10 years, not only she will have proper development of her body but also of mind. She will be able to cope with all the problems of life. She will not have psychological problems and will become capable of being an understanding wife and a good mother, besides being a dutiful citizen.

In the same way, the boys should also be taught the method of Acupressure from an early age of 8/10 years. This will not only build their bodies but also make them of sound and noble character. Then the aim of education "A sound mind in a healthy body" will be achieved.

Moreover, these children can be saved from any type of delinquencies like smoking, drug addiction or even sex. Today, the problem of paedophilia, i.e. sexual attraction to children (of either sex) by older men, which affects the development of sexuality in the children, is worsening and has become a mega issue seriously damaging the very foundation of our society. On the other hand, in order to control HIV/AIDS, condoms are freely available to the youngsters. But this is not the solution of the problem. This will only lead to premature sex indulgence. The right solution is to control the sexual desires which is possible only by Acupressure.

In the same way, if we want to stop and prevent crimes, wars, atrocities, etc. we will have to go back to Nature and accept its Health Science of Acupressure. If proper survey is made, it will be surprising to observe that most of the political and social leaders of the World suffer from malfunctioning of the endocrine glands and the liver; So they mislead their nation and disturb the world. Therefore, if the Pituitary, Pineal and Adrenal glands are properly controlled, and the liver is made to function properly, we shall be able to control our nature and our habits. We will be more tolerant and face the battle of life bravely and calmly.

CHAPTER 11

SCIATIC NERVE

This problem is not understood properly by most of the practitioners. When a patient complains about pain in the lower part of the back, i.e. lower lumbar or pain from the waist to toes or pain in the knees, generally the patient is told that it is Arthritis. Sometimes in a female patient of advanced age of 50 years, it is diagnosed as Osteoarthritis and the patient is given painkillers and Oestrogen, which have severe side-effects. But when not cured, the patient is advised to get an X-ray done of the spinal cord. And in cases of a little advanced stage where there is a swelling around the damaged vertebra it is labelled as slipped disc and the patient is asked to undergo an operation.

In X-rays, the damage to the sciatic nerve is not found, because it is not a bone but it is a nerve extending from the pelvis down the back of the thigh to the toes. Only when a M.R.I. (Magnetic Resonance Imaging) test is done, such damage to the sciatic nerve is located. It is a costly examination and even in the advanced and rich countries, people do not go for M.R.I. tests – because such expenses are not covered under the Insurance scheme. Moreover, the costly machines doing M.R.I. are available only in a few hospitals of big cities. Consequently, the patient has to remain dependent on the painkillers. But long term use of such painkillers leads to acidity and ulcer and life becomes miserable. **And so under misery and pain, the patient goes for unnecessary operation.** And in turn he/she becomes a lifelong patient as some vital nerves are operated.

So in all such cases, or when the patient has trouble in walking or climbing up the stairs or in squatting or getting up from the ground, just check-up the line of point no. 9 leading to point no. 16 on the back of the palm, the right palm in the case of the problem on the right side or the left palm if the problem is on the left side.

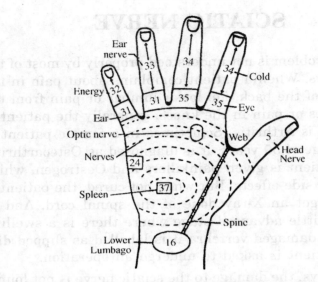

Fig. 28 (a) : Back Side of the Left Hand

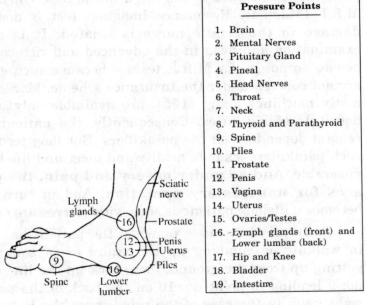

Fig. 29 (a) : Inside of Foot

Pressure Points
1. Brain
2. Mental Nerves
3. Pituitary Gland
4. Pineal
5. Head Nerves
6. Throat
7. Neck
8. Thyroid and Parathyroid
9. Spine
10. Piles
11. Prostate
12. Penis
13. Vagina
14. Uterus
15. Ovaries/Testes
16. Lymph glands (front) and Lower lumbar (back)
17. Hip and Knee
18. Bladder
19. Intestine

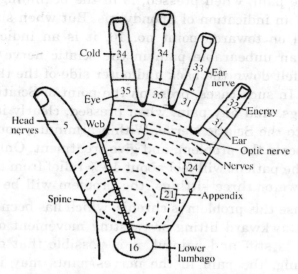

Fig. 28 (b) : Back Side of the Right Hand

Pressure Points
20. Colon
21. Appendix (front)/Allergy (Back)
22. Gall Bladder
23. Liver
24. Shoulder
25. Pancreas
26. Kidney
27. Stomach
28. Adrenal
29. Solar Plexus
30. Lungs
31. Ear
32. Energy
33. Nerves and Ear
34. Cold and Nerves
35. Eyes
36. Heart
37. Spleen
38. Thymus

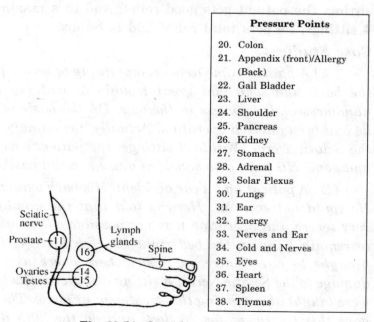

Fig. 29 (b) : Outside of Foot

If the pain, when pressed, is in the beginning of that line, it is an indication of Spondylitis. But when such pain is located on towards point no. 16, it is an indication of sciatica, an unbearable pain in the sciatic nerve or pain which is felt down the back and outer side of the thigh, leg and foot. In such cases, press on the point of Sciatic Nerve on the legs. And any pain, when pressed, clearly indicates damage to the Sciatic Nerve. Within a minute, you will be able to locate the problem, and give treatment. Only in one sitting, the patient will feel about 40 % relief from the pain. And in two or three sittings, the problem will be cured.

In case this problem is chronic, which has been brought on by an awkward lifting or twisting movement or where the back is stiff and painful, it is possible that after the first sitting, the pain in the nerves/joints may increase. But when the treatment is continued, then after the second sitting, the patient gets good relief. And in a maximum of 4 sittings, he gets total relief and is happy.

Case Studies :

(1) A patient came to me complaining of severe pain in the back and who had great trouble in walking due to numbness and weakness in the legs. On the basis of X-ray, he had been advised operation. Actually, the damage was to the Sciatic Nerve. Within 3 sittings, the patient's weakness had gone. His pain also subsided and he could easily walk.

(2) A patient had a car accident. His back was crushed. He could not even sit. He was told that the damage was very severe and operation was not possible. He would have to remain lying in the bed right through his life. He was brought to our Centre on a stretcher. There was severe damage to the Sciatic Nerve. A sitting was given. His brothers were taught about giving this treatment at home. They daily gave this treatment for 25 days and on the 30th day, the patient walked to the bank, where he was working as a manager.

(3) A very peculiar case came to me. The patient had a twist from the waist on the right side. He was neither able to sleep on a single bed nor sit on a chair. He was rich and so went round the world for cure. At last he came to our free Centre. The damage was located in the Sciatic Nerve. Treatment was given and in one sitting, he felt relief. In another 6 sittings, his waist straightened and he became straight – normal.

Arthritis-Rheumatism :

In the case of Arthritis or Rheumatism, there is a pain when pressed on point nos. 8 and 11 to 15. At that time, just check-up point no. 36 of the heart. If that point is paining or hurting, it is a case of Rheumatoid Arthritis. Therefore, the patient should be given treatment for both Heart and Arthritis.

Paralysis :

In such cases, where there is total or partial loss of the power of muscular contraction or of sensation in right or left side of the body, you will observe pain on point nos. 1 to 5, 8, 11 to 15 and 28. Also press on the base of the middle toe. There may be severe pain. See fig. 29.

With proper treatment as mentioned in my book "Health in Your Hands : Volume 1", such paralytic patients, whose muscle weakness varies in its extent, severity and degree, recover totally in 30/40 days.

CHAPTER 12

DETECTION OF SERIOUS DISEASES

Today, such detection – Diagnosis has become complicated and costly. When the family physician has doubts about some serious problem, he refers the patient to an expert. However, before coming to any diagnosis, he asks for various tests of urine, stool, blood, blood sugar, X-ray, Sonography, Cardiogram, CT Scanning, even M.R.I., etc. And many times, in spite of all these tests, the opinions of different experts differ and so proper treatment cannot be given to the patient.

In the case of a serious problem, the Diagnosis must be as quick as possible, so proper treatment can be started immediately. Here, Acupressure has an edge over all the therapies. *The Diagnosis is instant and proper and that too without going into details about the past history or any tests.*

In the case of any serious problem, one or more endocrine glands are damaged. It is, therefore, utmost necessary, to study again and again about endocrine glands and the effects of malfunctioning of these vital endocrine glands.

(1) In all such cases point no. 8 of Thyroid/Parathyroid gland will be tender. Refer to page no. 43 and find out the degree of the problem.

Now in the case of pain on point no. 16 also, it indicates Hypothyroidism, treatment of which is just the same as that of Cancer.

(2) As all the endocrine glands are interconnected, check up other endocrine glands. And this will give a vital clue to the problem. Afterwards, check the corresponding points of the organs which indicate a problem. In Acupressure, one need not worry about the names of the diseases. Most important is to find out the endocrine glands which are disturbed and also the organs from which this problem has started and so are badly damaged.

Now, let us study separately about the main serious problems.

(a) **Heart Problem :** In the case of any pain in the chest, the patient will come running to you. After having a handshake, and giving a look at his face, hold the left palm in your hands and give pressure on point no. 36 of the Heart. If there is a pain even on pressing slightly, it indicates Heart Problem/Heart Attack. Then ask the patient to go home immediately by the first available transport. But see that the patient does not drive the car himself. Ask the patient to have complete bedrest for 72 to 96 hours and do the treatment. Assure him not to worry. In all such cases, the heart requires complete rest. Within 3 to 5 days, the pain on point no. 36 will subside, so ask the patient to see you after 4 to 5 days. Ask the patient to have 2 glasses of liquid diet-charged water reduced from 4 glasses, fruit juices (preferably pomegranate juice) and pressing of both the palms and point no. 36 of heart twice a day. In the second sitting, try to find out the root cause of such Heart problem. Check point no. 8, if it is paining then the problem is malfunctioning of Thyroid/Parathyroid.

(b) Then check point nos. 11 to 15 and if these points are paining it denotes weakened Sex glands. At that time, observe the nails and your findings will be confirmed.

(c) In the case of advanced stage of Cancer, V.D. and HIV/AIDS you will observe pain on point no. 36 of the Heart. So, check these points and advise treatment accordingly.

(d) It will be surprising to note that in about 80 % of such cases of pain in the chest or/in the case of enlarged heart, when pressed even harder, there is no pain on point no. 36 of the heart. That means that it is NOT Heart Attack. In that case, check up the Solar Plexus and correct it.

(e) It could be a muscular pain starting from vertebrae 6 to 8 of the Spinal Cord. In that case suggest treatment on the point on the back of hand as per fig. 28 (a), (b) & 30.

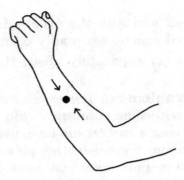

Fig. 30

Later on, ask the patient to rub Eucalyptus oil or pain balm on the chest as well as around vertebrae no. 4 to 8 of the Spinal Cord.

Even a feeling of slight pain on point no. 36 of the Heart is a premonition of coming heart trouble. So the best cure in such cases is to start pressing point no. 36 and point nos. 1 to 5 for 1 to 2 minutes 3 times a day and take bedrest for 24/48 hours.

Case Studies :

(1) Once during a marriage function, I observed profuse sweat on the face of my relative with whom I was talking. He was also finding difficulty in speaking which is indicative of breathlessness. Immediately, I pressed his point no. 36, and pain was observed. I virtually ordered him to go home and take bedrest and treatment. After 72 hours, he showed himself, to a Cardiologist, who after thorough examination of the cardiogram, declared that he had passed through a Heart Attack. After that, he is following my book and has no problem even after 10 years.

(2) Once I had to go to a hospital to see a 68 year-old relative who was admitted in the Intensive Care Unit for heart trouble. I examined his point no. 36 and observed that it was not paining even when pressed hard. I then corrected his Solar Plexus, which had shifted upwards causing trouble to the heart. I advised my relative to ask for a discharge and go home. He did so and even after 14 years now, he enjoys good health.

(3) "Once we had gone on a pilgrimage with our 35 year-old nephew. The temple was on a hill about 3000 ft. above the sea level. We had to climb and walk for $2\frac{1}{2}$ miles to reach there. As such pilgrimage was being done after 2 years, we hired a 'Doli' (a sitting square hanging on a 3" thick wooden stick-arrangement which is carried by 2 people on their shoulders.) Our nephew preferred to climb. After just a quarter mile of climbing, we were resting in a place. After ten minutes our nephew came panting and sat opposite me. I saw him going blank and falling down from his seat. I immediately grabbed him and with help of our dolimen, laid him on the ground. He had become unconscious. I immediately started giving him treatment on point no. 36 and then on point no. 8 and on the earlobes. Within 3 minutes, he opened his eyes and drank water. Then we called for another 'Doli' and forced him to sit into it and then completed our pilgrimage. In the evening, at our native place Bhavnagar, (30 miles from the place of pilgrimage) he was examined by a Cardiologist, who was surprised to observe that my nephew had survived a massive heart attack. He started taking treatment and during the last 12 years, he has no problem whatsoever about the heart and enjoys robust health".

(4) "A 3 year-old, girl, was finding difficulty in breathing, so she was examined by a Cardiologist. On further examination, a hole was found in her heart. It was decided that when she would reach the age of 12 years, an operation would be performed to correct the hole in the heart. She was brought to me. I advised her mother proper treatment on point no. 36 of the heart and also on all the endocrine glands + drinking of charged water. Within three months, she started responding properly and continued treatment. When she was of 12 years, she was again examined by the same Cardiologist. He was surprised to observe that the hole in the heart had healed and there was no necessity of any operation".

You may kindly assure the patients that they should not worry about a heart problem. With rest and proper treatment not only of the heart but also of the root cause, the heart will function properly and stop only at the time of death.

Nervous Tension / Depression :

This is the curse of modern development of life – which requires every one to be on the roller-coaster ride. The simple, ordinary people have to face many sudden dramatic changes in life. This results in a little tension in the beginning which goes on accumulating and results in severe nervous tension, leading to depression. Only Acupressure has an unfailing system of measuring such tension.

First ask the patient to remove shoes and socks, and to lie down on a flat bench or table. See fig. 31, then go towards the legs and press the base of the middle toe of the right leg and then the left leg. The patient may even cry out in agony – this indicates the tension – refer to page 43 and find out the degree of the problem. If such degree is more than 70, then there is lot of mounted tension and the patient may collapse – have nervous breakdown.

Treatment :

Secondly, take the five toes of one leg in one hand and the five toes of the other leg in the other hand. Try to bend them backward, you will find them stiff as per the degree of tension. Then in order to give instant relief, force these

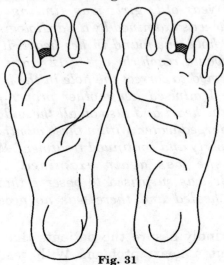

Fig. 31

10 toes backward as much as possible, hold them in that position for fifteen seconds, release them – repeat again. The patient will feel relieved of his/her tension in two minutes. Ask the patient to get it done accordingly twice at home by other person and all tension will be reduced within a week. Then ask the patient to do so every evening or at least two to three times a week. He will enjoy a tension free life like a bird. And so if this depression is due to excess tension, it will be cured. For long-term cure refer to my book, "Health in Your Hands : Volume 1" and suggest treatment accordingly.

Diabetes :

Generally, the patient is aware of this problem of Diabetes. When such patient comes to you and asks cure for Diabetes, tell him/her not to speak anything more. Then press on point no. 16 of the Lymph gland and carefully observe the degree of pain.

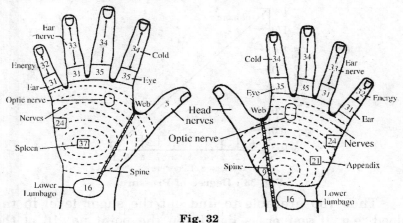

Fig. 32

Then press on point no. 25 of the Pancreas. If it is not hurting on point no. 25, then this Diabetes is less than 200-2 % and will not be found in the urine. If it is paining on point no. 25, then such blood sugar is definitely more than 200. Depending upon the degree of pain on point no. 16, you will be able to tell the exact percentages of such blood sugar. The patient will then have full confidence in you. You may note that such reading of glucose/sugar in blood may only vary by 2 %. Thus you can find out the degree of Diabetes the patient has. Assure the patient, that such Diabetes will be brought under control, within 30 to 40 days with the treatment mentioned in this book.

How to carry out a Sugar Test :

In case of any doubt about this problem of Diabetes, you need not ask the patient to get such Glucose / Sugar Test of Urine and Blood. Refer to fig. 16 (a) and (b).

(1) Press on point no. 16. If it is not hurting, even when pressed hard, then the sugar level in the blood is normal.

(2) When you press a little hard on point no. 16 and there is slight hurting, it denotes that the sugar/glucose level in the blood is more than normal.

Study the following charts :   **Chart no. 1**

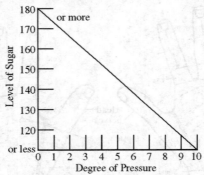

Fig. 33 : Degree of Pressure

Thus you are able to find out the sugar level in the blood, e.g. if you press lightly on the point no. 16 of the Lymph gland and if there is hurting, it denotes that the sugar level is higher than 200. In that case, when you press on point no. 25 of the Pancreas on any palm, there will be hurting. This denotes that the sugar is not only in the blood but also in the urine.

In that case refer to chart no. 2 given on next page.

Please note that chart no. 2 is to be referred only when there is hurting on point nos. 16 and 25.

Chart no. 2

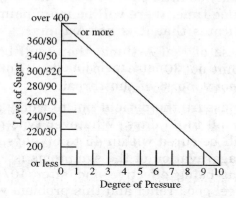

Fig. 34 : Degree of Pressure

With experience, you will be able to find out exactly the level of sugar in the blood. I have found that this reading hardly varies + or − 2 % than the test made in a laboratory.

In order to get confidence about this reading, in the case of a Diabetic patient, ask him not to tell you the sugar level, check the patient, find out the sugar level and then compare it with the patient's report.

Any person / patient can use this method.

Case Studies :

"A small girl of 6 years was brought to me. She had more than 3.50 % blood / sugar. She inherited it from her mother. Her father had V.D. and mother had infection in uterus. All three of them were put under treatment. Within 45 days, all were cured of their sufferings.

Assure the patient that with Acupressure treatment, the Pancreas can be reactivated and so once the Diabetes comes under control, then with proper care about chewing and diet, the patient will not get Diabetes again".

Asthma :

I have discussed this problem at length under common cold. When patient comes to you and if on pressing point no. 30 of the lungs there is no pain, then it is not Asthma but 'cold due to excess heat'. Only in the case of such complaint of more than 10 years, the lungs get damaged and so there may be little pain on point no. 30 when pressed. But at the same time, there will be more pain on point no. 28 which indicates that it is not Asthma.

In the case of real Asthma, there will be pain, when pressed on point no. 30, also on point no. 27 of the stomach and also on point no. 6 of the throat.

You may assure the patient not to worry and continue treatment for 30 to 60 days. Whatever type of Asthma, it may be, it will be cured within 45 to 60 days. Also tell the patient that aggravation of the symptoms is a good sign of this treatment being effective and after 10/12 days, the patient will feel good relief and this problem will get cured shortly and permanently.

Breathlessness :

If with the treatment for Asthma, such breathlessness does not come under control, it could be due to blockade in the arteries of the heart. And with proper treatment of the heart such blocked arteries open up and any bypass surgery could be avoided.

Serious Problem of Eyes :

Any normal complaint about the eyes will be traced to pain on point no. 35 of the eyes. However, if there is any problem like the damage to the optic nerve which in turn

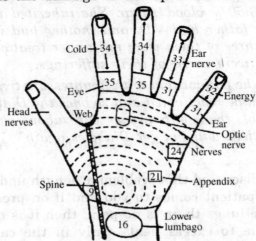

Fig. 35 : Back of the right palm showing points of optic nerve

damages the retina, or if there is any developing problem of cataract or glaucoma, check up point for the optic nerve. This point is shown on the back of the palms. (See fig. 35)

Now in the case you find pain on point of the optic nerve, check up point no. 3 of the Pituitary gland. It will also be found to be paining. So proper treatment, as suggested in my book, should be started immediately. Also check up point no. 37 and if it is hurting it could be HIV.

High Blood Pressure :

In such cases, there will be pain on point no. 4, and which in turn damages other endocrine glands. So treatment on all endocrine glands + charged water reduced from 4 glasses to 2 glasses are necessary.

Now, when you find such symptoms of High B.P., try to find out the root cause, because High B.P. is a symptom and not a disease. It could be high tension, even V.D. or Cancer of prostate/uterus, HIV infection, etc. And so correct the same as a long-term treatment.

Low Blood Pressure :

This denotes that vital energy of body is being wasted. First check up point no. 25 of the Pancreas. Its overworking is a major factor for Low B.P.

Then check up point nos. 11 to 15. Indulgence in excessive sex, masturbation in the case of males or Leucorrhoea in the case of females could be the root cause.

Also check up the Solar Plexus, and if necessary, correct it.

Lastly, check up point no. 28 of the Adrenal glands. If it is functioning less, it leads to less oxygenation and consequently to Low B.P.

Arthritis – Rheumatism – Rheumatoid Arthritis – Paralysis i.e. Stroke :

Generally, this is a disease of old age indicating deficiency of calcium and phosphorus and so when pressed, there will be pain on point nos. 8 and 11 to 15. However, in most cases, such pain is due to the damage to the Sciatic Nerve, so check it first.

Now in patients below the 50-55 age group, the root cause is found in the malfunctioning of the Heart and so when pressed, there will be pain on point no. 36 and so along with the treatment of Arthritis, treatment for the Heart should also be prescribed.

In all such cases of Arthritis and Rheumatism, check up about the tension as mentioned earlier. Because High tension plus Arthritis leads to Paralysis/Stroke. Timely check-up and immediate treatment can thus prevent Stroke/Paralysis. Further it is found that in the case of pain in different parts of body and in all joints, it could be due to HIV and so check up point no. 37 also. Because as this disease is not traceable in most cases it is treated for Arthritis and the painkillers/steroids aggravate HIV into AIDS.

Cancer :

First understand this dreaded disease and for which read Chapter 2 of this book. It will be surprising to note that detection of Cancer is possible in its initial stage in the body. At that time when pressed, there will be pain on point no. 16 of the Lymph gland. However, before coming to any conclusion of Cancer, find out whether –

(a) The patient has any infection. Many times the female patient may have pus in the urine and the male patient may have Venereal Disease.

(b) The patient may have boils, infection in cuts and injury.

(c) The patient could be Diabetic.

When these possibilities are checked up, only then such a pain on point no. 16 denotes the degeneration popularly called as Cancer.

To detect Cancer in the different parts / organs of the body :

Another pointer for detection is the organ where Cancer is developing is damaged and there is pain in the corresponding point on the palms and soles. For example, in the case of Cancer of the breast, there is pain in the middle point on the back of the palm as shown in fig. 24 or in the case of Cancer in colon, there is pain in the corresponding point no. 20.

In the same way, for Cancer in

There is pain on

Throat, teeth	: Point no. 6.
Windpipe, gullet	: between Point nos. 6 and 27
Stomach	: Point no. 27
Small Intestine	: Point no. 19
Large Intestine	: Point nos. 20 and 10
Liver	: Point nos. 23 and 22
Lungs	: Point no. 30
Brain	: Point nos. 1 to 5
(It is also called tumour)	
Blood	: Point no. 37
Bones	: Point nos. 9 and 37

Now, if these signals are ignored, the declining process starts disturbing other glands also and reaches a dangerous point where these endocrine glands become tired and stop secreting hormones. During that time, more and more wastes/toxins accumulate forming a duct and start multiplying and thus a fast malignant growth starts in that part of the body damaging the very metabolism of the body.

Thus you will observe that Cancer can be detected at a very early stage, and it can be controlled very easily. Moreover, you will observe that if regular Acupressure treatment is taken daily or at least 3 times a week, the lethargic spleen or the lymph gland can be reactivated, and factors leading to Cancer can be checked. Thus **Acupressure can prevent Cancer.**

To detect Cancer of the Uterus :

It is more common in the females who do not take proper care of internal hygiene. It is due to continuous irregularity of menstruation, continuous Leucorrhoea, etc.

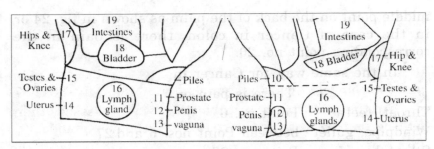

Fig. 36

This type of Cancer can be easily detected. In the case of any doubt, press on point nos. 11 to 15 on both the sides of the wrists of both the hands. If there is pain on pressing these points and also on point no. 16 of the lymph gland, it denotes degeneration.

To detect Cancer of the Breasts :

Just press on the circle in the back of the right palm for the right breast and the left palm for the left breast. If there is NO PAIN when pressed, it means there is NO CANCER in the breasts. Even if there is pain on these points, but no pain on the point no. 16 of the Lymph gland at that time, it denotes that there is NO CANCER. And just by giving treatment on these points on the back of palms, the minor problem like accumulation of milk in the breast, etc. will be cured. Only pain on the circle on the

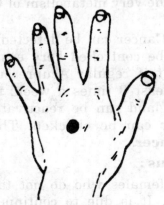

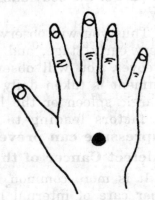

Back of Left Palm   **Back of Right Palm**

Fig. 37

back of the right palm and also on the point no. 16 of the Lymph gland denotes Cancer degeneration in the right breast. In the same way, Cancer in the left breast can be detected by pressing the circle on the back of the left palm and the point no. 16 of the Lymph gland. (Refer fig. 36 & 37)

At that time, it is possible that when pressed, there will be pain on point nos. 11 to 15 of the Sex glands.

Severe pain on those points on the back side of the palms and on point no. 16 when pressed, denotes that Cancer has spread more.

Hundreds of cases can be quoted. In all such cases, Diagnosis is impeccable and so with the treatment mentioned in this book, fantastic results are obtained. At our Centre, we can give assurance of cure to all those patients suffering from Cancer. **Please inform the patients that all types of Cancer are curable and it is the easiest disease to be cured.**

I am of the firm opinion, based on my experience of thousands of successful cures of these Cancer patients, that Cancer can even be eradicated. If all the people of the World practise Acupressure regularly, such serious problems will not develop.

Thalassemia :

It is a dreaded disease found in children. In acute cases, total blood has to be changed every 15 to 30 days. Patients suffering from Thalassaemia major, are given repeated blood transfusions. In spite of the best treatment and blood transfusions, chances of recovery are considered to be very limited. On examination of such children, it has been found, that their endocrine glands are severely damaged and even all the organs of the digestive system are found to be sluggish.

So in the case of any doubt about any child patient, who will be looking pale, check up point no. 37 of the spleen. If it is hurting, check up point nos. 22-23 of the gall bladder and liver, which also will be tender. Then check point no. 27 of the stomach. When you find tenderness on all these points of the organs of the digestive system it indicates

Thalassemia. In that case, point no. 8 will be very tender, denoting deficiency of calcium. The next point to be found tender will be point nos. 11 to 15, denoting deficiency of phosphorus. And because of damage to these organs and the endocrine glands, you will find point no. 28 of Adrenal glands to be tender. In the advanced stages, you will find even point no. 25 of the Pancreas and point no. 16 of the Lymph gland to be tender. Many times such children get Diabetes.

Also press the middle of the nail in the small finger and there will be pain which denotes worms in the intestines making these children more anaemic. (See fig. 23)

Once you find that the child has Thalassemia or if you have doubt about it, call the parents and check them. Except in a few cases, the blood group of the mother and the father is not matching which is the root cause of these children inheriting Thalassemia from their parents. After the check-up, you will find the root cause in the mother and the father and so your diagnosis of Thalassemia gets confirmed. Also call for the patient's brothers and sisters and check them. Because, if this Thalassemia is due to HIV, V.D. or Gynaecological problem other members of the family may suffer from similar problem.

In all such cases, assure the parents that this dreaded disease is also CURABLE. See Chapter 9 in Part 2 of this book.

Case Study :

One child had Thalassaemia major and every 20/25 days blood was given to him. Treatment of Acupressure was started. Within two months, the progress was so remarkable that further blood transfusions were not required. Similarly hundreds of successful cases can be quoted.

Kidney Problem – Pyelitis – Stone :

In the case of any swelling in the body or legs, check-up point no. 26. And in most of these cases, you will find that point to be tender. Then refer fig. 16 (a), (b) of Chapter 5 and you will be able to find out the damage to the kidneys, i.e. Pyelitis or inflammation of the part of the kidney. Tenderness on this point no. 26 on the right hand denotes that the right kidney is damaged. While such tenderness on such point no. 26 on the left hand indicates damage to the left kidney. At that time, when you press on point no. 8, and if there is a little severe pain, it indicates that there is stone or a condition which causes obstruction to the free flow of urine.

Now, in case there is no pain on point no. 26 of the Kidneys and in spite of it there is retention of water in the body, then check up point no. 4 of the Pineal gland. You will get the root cause.

During the last 18 years, many patients who were on Dialysis and even those who were later on advised tranplantation of kidney have approached me. In all such cases, I have observed that the damage to the kidneys was not more than 60 %. But on examination, it was found that in the case of the male patients, the root cause was venereal disease or Cancer of Prostate and in the case of the female patients, it was Cancer of the Uterus. And in all these cases, with proper treatment, not only the transplantation of kidney was prevented but also Dialysis was stopped. Within 30 to 45 days of treatment the same doctors who had prescribed Dialysis and advised transplantation of kidney agreed that the kidneys of the patient were functioning satisfactorily.

Even in the cases of skin problems, check up point no. 26 of the kidneys and if necessary, advise cure of it. It may be noted that with such a cure, not only do the kidneys start functioning normally, but even a stone formed (due to calcification, i.e. malfunctioning of the Thyroid / Parathyroid glands) is removed in 80 % of the cases. You can assure the patient not to worry about the failure of the kidneys.

Case Studies :

(1) A gentleman approached me for prolonged trouble of stones. He had five operations to remove stones. On examination, I found that his Thyroid / Parathyroid gland

was malfunctioning and so instead of Calcium being digested it was forming stones. Then that gentleman told me that my Diagnosis was perfect because after several costly tests, the expert had given the same opinion. He took proper treatment and since then, even after eight years, he has no complaint about stones. Every winter he drinks 'Black Tea' for twelve days, as per the advice given by me.

(2) "A lady was asked to go for transplantation of kidney by a reputed hospital of Mumbai. As her mother's kidney was found to be suitable, the date of the operation was fixed. Just ten days before the kidney transplantation operation, she came to me. On examination, the damage to the kidney was found to be not more than 55%. The root cause was Cancer in the Uterus. She was advised to postpone the operation for one month. She took proper treatment at home. After a month, when she went to the hospital, the expert was surprised to observe that both her kidneys were functioning properly and there was no necessity of transplantation of kidney or even Dialysis".

More than 400 successful cases can be quoted, where such dialysis is stopped and in more than 200 cases, such operation for kidney transplantation has been prevented. I have therefore to appeal to all the patients suspecting—suffering from kidney problems and all the medical practitioners advising dialysis or transplantation of kidney; to read the Chapter 7 from Part 2 and try treatment for Pyelitis (an advanced stage of damage to kidney) just for fifteen days and see the fantastic results.

Sometimes, it is found that even in HIV, the kidneys are damaged. So press on point no. 37 and verify the root cause.

Problems of the Brain :

Case Studies :

(1) A young lady of 24 years came to me for continued severe headache. On examining her, I found that it was the beginning of tumour in the brain. It was not easy for her to accept such a diagnosis. So next day, she went for CT Scan

and on getting the report after 2 days, she came immediately to me and thanked me for exact diagnosis made without any test. She had developed faith and so she started treatment as suggested. After 2 months treatment and on getting green signal from me, she went to the same hospital for another CT Scan and she was given a report that she was totally cured of the tumour in the brain.

(2) "Similarly, a lady was having pain in legs and not able to control her steps (a lack of balance) while walking. As the sciatic nerve was found to be damaged, four sittings were given. Her pain subsided, but she could not control her steps. So on further examination it was found that the root cause was in the brain. I pressed her thumbs on point nos. 3 and 4 of the Pituitary and the Pineal gland and point of controller as per fig. 27. They were found to be tender. Thus there was the beginning of tumour in the brain. With proper treatment of 72 days, she is now able to walk briskly and run".

Thus it is observed that in the case of any problem in the brain, instant Diagnosis is possible with Acupressure.

Now thumb represents the head and so in the case of pain on point nos. 1 to 5 when pressed, it denotes trouble in the head. It could be headache. In most cases, it could be congested cold due to heat.

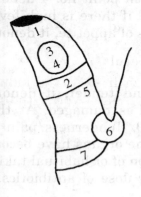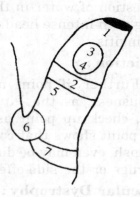

Fig. 38

But when the patient has long-standing complaint or symptoms denoting damage in the brain, after pressing point nos. 1-2-5, also press point nos. 3 and 4. After that, press point as shown here (fig. 38) in the base of the thumb. If the flow of electricity or cerebro-spinal fluid is being hampered, you will find pain on point in the base of the thumb and with the same treatment for 3 to 6 days, and drinking of charged water which has been reduced to 2 glasses from 4 glasses this complaint will disappear.

In case of any doubt, press point no. 16 of the Lymph gland. If there is pain, it denotes problem in the brain (popularly known as brain tumour).

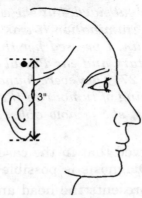

Fig. 39

Meningitis :

At the same time, severe pain on point no. 4 denotes congestion of water in the brain and if there is high fever, along with intense headache and loss of appetite, it denotes Meningitis.

Addiction :

Further, if point no. 3 is found tender, it denotes seriousness, as the Pituitary gland is damaged. At that time, check up point as per fig. 39. Tenderness/pain on that point shows that control over the organs have become sluggish, even may be due to addiction of or habitual taking of drugs or the side-effects of heavy dose of antibiotics.

Muscular Dystrophy :

Now, when you observe such pain on all points of nos. 1 to 5 as per fig. 38 & 39 and there is pain in the calves of legs, it could be Muscular Dystrophy. Then go into details.

Even in the case of retarded children, you will find pain, when pressed on these points plus point nos. 8, 11 to 15 and 28.

It may be noted that Polio, Parkinson's disease are due to damage in the brain, so check these points.

Do not scare the patient. Assure the patient that these diseases are curable but the curing process will be slow. With proper treatment and brain wash given to the patient as mentioned in this book, unbelievable results are obtained.

Case Studies :

(1) *"A mother brought a good-looking son of 4 $\frac{1}{2}$ years. Since fifteen months, he had a severe pain in both the calves of legs, sometime even in the head. And since the last 4 months, he had trouble in climbing even one step. Thorough examination revealed that it was a case of Muscular Dystrophy and proper treatment was started. After three months the mother came to me complaining that it is very difficult to control her son. They were staying on the sixth floor. The boy would go down by the lift and climb up the steps again several times a day".*

(2) *"A gentleman of 52 years old, approached me for his complaint about Muscular Dystrophy (Muscle Weakness), which he got around the age of seventeen. He had been in touch with all the leading hospitals and health institutions for treating this dreaded disease. He was asked to undertake Acupressure treatment. After about 4 months, he was able to get up from his chair without support, could limp and afterwards was able to drive the car. As this was an old problem 95 to 100% cure could not be achieved. But he was happy to have 80% improvement and to be free from dependence on others".*

Parkinson's Disease :

When dealing with patients of Parkinson's Disease, check up also about Nervous Tension and advise treatment accordingly.

Case Study :

"A leading paediatrician and surgeon, had problem of Parkinson's disease. I advised him proper treatment for the problem of the brain and showed method to remove tension. As a result, his shivering stopped and he became fit to perform operations."

HIV/AIDS :

It is advisable to read chapter 12 and study about HIV. Once one gets HIV infection, just because it is not understood properly, it develops silently and the first victim is the life partner – wife or husband – and then all the children born afterwards. The treatment of the popular therapy of Allopathy only worsens the matter. It will be surprising to observe that Diagnosis of HIV is very simple and easy.

In the case of any doubt while examining a child patient or a female patient, without hesitation call the family, i.e. father–mother and other children.

First, verify that they have had not any Malarial fever in the near past (30 days). Of course in that case, there will be obvious symptoms. Then press point no. 37 of the spleen. Now if there is pain, it is a clear indication of HIV infection. Such pain on point no. 37 is also observed in the case of Cancer of the blood / Thalassemia, but in that case the symptoms are very obvious. *Moreover, in that case, the family is not affected.* Now, when you find such pain on point no. 37, just check up point no. 37 of other members of the family. In case of such HIV infection, you will observe that all the members of that family have pain on point no. 37. Thus you become confident to declare the problem as HIV infection which I call as 'impurity in blood.'

Now, if the patient has acquired such HIV infection casually, he will be looking healthy and there will not be pain on any other points except point no. 8. But if it is due to sexual relations, there will also be pain on point nos. 11 to 15. Now, if this HIV infection has developed into AIDS, you will observe pain, when pressed, on point nos. 8, 11 to 15 may be on point 16 also, point no. 28 and then point no. 25 and in quite advanced stage on point nos. 22-23-30 and even on point no. 3 and point no. 4.

In the case of females, if this problem has developed, you will find pain on point nos. 11 to 15, also on point no. 16 (the Lymph gland) and there would be degeneration in the Uterus.

In the case of children over and above pain on point no. 37 of the Spleen, you will find pain on all organs of the digestive system, i.e. point nos. 22-23-25-27 and 28 and in advanced stage on point no. 3 and also 4, i.e. in short the symptoms are that of Thalassemia.

This is a delicate problem and therefore do not go into the cause of how the patient got the HIV infection. Let them think for themselves. It is not always due to having sexual relations with HIV-affected person. Assure the family that this is only a paper Dragon, and with proper Acupressure treatment for about 50 to 60 days, the problem will be cured.

Only in the case of advanced case of AIDS that it may take 75 to 90 days, but it will be cured. However, it must be specifically noted that if the stage of AIDS has reached over 80 %, then the chance of survival may be less. But with the treatment, agony, severe pain, burning sensation will definitely come under control.

Thus you will observe that Diagnosis is possible of all the serious and dreaded diseases.

Lastly, remember and always keep in mind the Motto – *Any feeling of pain, when pressed on the points of any functioning organ or endocrine glands, denotes PROBLEM.* One need not worry about the names of such diseases. Just find out the location of such pain and its degree and intensity and advise treatment for the same as per my books "Health in Yours Hands : Volume 1" and as per Part 2 of this book.

CHAPTER 13

FIND YOUR FRIENDS

Last but not the least, we have to change our thinking. We have got to believe that these diseases are not our enemies. You will observe that our body creates Common cold to remove excess heat from the body. And if such excess heat is not removed but suppressed inside, we become lifelong patients of cold – Sinus, then Allergy and then Asthma. Thus, Common cold is our friend.

In the same way no serious diseases appear overnight in the body. As we ignore mild, friendly complaint/advise of minor problems, it develops into a major problem, e.g. Cancer, which is the last friendly notice from our body-Nature.

Moreover, if such diseases, which are our friends, do not warn us to take immediate and necessary steps to remove such toxins or correct malfunctioning of any endocrine glands, then such toxins go on accumulating and bad effects of malfunctioning of endocrine glands increases and which results in irreparable damage to the Heart. And this may cause premature death.

For example, swelling on liver and gall bladder denotes that there is excess heat in the body. When it is neglected the body sends another powerful friend Jaundice. Many times this is not understood, and on the basis of Sonography, crystals of dried bile – look like stone called gallstones are formed in gall bladder and the gall bladder is removed. Consequently, the patient has a lifelong problem of acidity and indigestion. Very recently, a case came to me. *On the basis of Sonography, the gall bladder was removed. But as the flow of bile would not stop, Endoscopy was done. However, that created infection to the Pancreas. The condition of the patient became critical and he had to be admitted to the Intensive Care Unit of a hospital. As the Doctors were not confident of the survival of the patient, they agreed to allow Acupressure treatment as suggested by me. Within 10 days of the treatment the patient got cured.*

Thus it is observed that these diseases are our Friends and this book shows you an easy way to 'Find out and know your Friends'.

Once you know your friends, i.e. the diseases and their root cause, then the cure is very simple and easy and has to be done by you / your relatives. **Further reading of my books "Health in Your Hands : Volume 1 & 2" will make you your own Doctor and you will be able get back your birthrights, your Health and Happiness.**

P.S. : Readers, before phoning or E-mailing for consultation, please press two palms on front and back side as per fig. 16 (a) & (b) and 18 (a) & (b). Find out which points are hurting when pressed. And inform these points to the author or any Acupressurist.

****

SC

HEALTH IN YOUR HANDS

Part 2

(formerly "Defeat the Dragon")

Analysis
and
Cure of Dreaded Diseases

DEVENDRA VORA M. D.

FOREWORD

I have had the privilege of reading the manuscript of "DEFEAT THE DRAGON" authored by Dr. Devendra Vora. He is also the author of India's Best-Seller titled "HEALTH IN YOUR HANDS" based on Acupressure and other natural therapies. It is surprising to observe that even though Dr. Vora is a Commerce Graduate and a retired Exporter, he has carefully analysed all the dreaded diseases like Common cold, Asthma, Cataract, Diabetes, Kidney problems, Heart, Brain's problems, Cancer, Thalassaemia and HIV/AIDS and made Researches about the CURES of them. This is a great achievement, because even the W.H.O. has admitted its helplessness about these dreaded diseases and even about Common cold.

Today, the whole World is terrified about Heart Diseases, Cancer and HIV/AIDS. Dr. Vora has made useful research about them, tried the same on thousands of patients over the years. When found successful, he has revealed them for the benefit of mankind in this book in a simple and fluent language. This book will greatly enhance the importance of Alternative therapies – especially Acupressure. It has also given credit to the Open International University for Complementary Medicines, which has conferred upon him the honorary Degrees of D.Sc., M.D. and F.R.C.P. and has also awarded him Gold medal for his Research about Cancer. For the past ten years Dr. Vora has been associated with us in his researches.

No doubt mankind will greatly be benefited by his useful books. It is gratifying to note that now this dragon of dreaded diseases can be easily defeated in our homes and that too without cost. I am confident that very soon all the Medical Faculties of the World will include Acupressure and alternate therapies in their curriculum and accept these two valuable textbooks in their course programmes. I sincerely hope that these two books of his will be available in all the main languages of the world.

My best wishes and congratulations to Dr. Vora.

15th March, 1996   **Lord Pandit Prof. Dr. Sir Anton Jayasuria**

PREFACE

I was in search of health from the age of fifteen. I was suffering from cold and tonsilitis. My father had arranged to have my tonsils removed by operation. However, being an ardent follower of the apostle of peace and *ahimsa*, Mahatma Gandhiji, I believed in nature cure and somehow managed to avoid such an operation. Afterwards, my father never insisted on such an operation. However, this problem of cold and tonsilitis persisted. In spite of my regular habits of healthy diet and exercise, my tonsils would flare up, become enlarged and I would get fever every 40–45 days. When I had fever, I used to fast and drink hot water with black pepper added to it, apply Glycerine Tannic acid on the tonsils and gargle with salt water. Sometimes I took Homoeopathic medicines. This problem in minor or major form persisted for 35 long years.

Then, on one of my business trips to U.S.A. and Canada, I came across a book on acupressure "Reflexology" (in hand) written by Mrs Mildred Carter. I was taught by my *Guru,* that, if we press very hard in the middle of two thumbs with small fingers, sneezing can be stopped. And so, when I read this book, I was convinced that this health therapy is based on the same principle. I tried this method on myself. The result was instant and astonishing.

When away from home for more than 10/15 days, I would feel homesick and would not get proper sleep. But by following this method, I started getting good sleep. Again, this therapy was put to test, when I was travelling by bus from Montreal to New York. Late at night, I could not resist scratching my teeth. As a result the silver filling of one tooth came out and I had severe cramps and pain. I was scared. However, I remembered how to create anaesthetic effect with Reflexology. As my last tooth on the right side was hurting, I pressed hard the tip of my small finger of my right hand. To my great surprise, my pain subsided within a minute and I had no toothache for the 30 days of my tour in the U.S.A. and the Continent. After reaching Mumbai, I got the filling redone by my dentist.

During this tour, I visited my niece in the States. Her ten-year-old daughter was suffering from severe bronchitis for about 15 days. I was by then confident about the therapy of Acupressure, so I assured my niece that I would cure her daughter of bronchitis just by pressing certain points on her palms. My niece asked me to discuss this matter with her husband, who was an M.D. In the evening, I put forward my suggestion before him. He agreed that just pressing on palms could do no harm and allowed me to go ahead with the treatment. The next morning, I started giving treatment to my first patient. Two sittings were given on the first day. Within half an hour of the third sitting, the little girl vomited and all the congestion, thick mucus came out. After another half an hour, her constant fever came to normal and she felt well. In the evening, when her doctor-father examined her, he was surprised to observe that her severe bronchitis was cured. He gave me encouragement.

When I came back to Mumbai, I made cyclostyled pamphlets and started propagating Acupressure among my relatives and friends. My business friends just laughed and made fun of me and my therapy. But when the mother of the then Chairman of our Export Promotion Council, got cured of her paralysis within 15 days, it was a tremendous boost to my confidence.

Later on, I was introduced to Shri Morarjibhai Desai, who was then the Prime Minister of India and also held the portfolio for Health and Family Welfare. He accepted this therapy but asked me to propagate this therapy through benevolent organisations. But I could not find even a single organisation which would adopt and spread such a useful therapy for the service of the people. I requested the Prime Minister to arrange to propagate this therapy at the government level. But before anything could be finalised, the Janata Government was toppled. Later on, after a period of two years, when I met him in Madurai, he virtually ordered me, like a father, to write a book on Acupressure. But before writing such a medical book, I studied in short about all the therapies of the world. Later on my book "Health In Your Hands", was published in 1984. It became a best-seller in India and is available also in languages such as Hindi, Marathi, Gujarati and Bengali. At that time, I had not written about Cancer. Somehow, all these dreaded diseases posed a challenge to me. I devoted my time for the study of Cancer and within six months, I got considerable success.

Then, I continued to work on Muscular Dystrophy and problems of the Brain for another 5 years. Even the study of books about the brain prescribed for the course of M.D., could not enlighten me about the working of the brain. In these books, the expert doctors have admitted that they know very little about the Endocrine glands and the working of different organs of the brain. Therefore, I diverted my study towards India. And to my great surprise, I found, that the working of different organs of the brain is very well explained in *Rigveda,* supposed to have been composed about 3000 to 4000 years ago. And so I could tackle the dreaded diseases of Muscular Dystrophy and Brain problems.

Later on, watching an episode of *Ramayana* on TV gave me a new insight into the disease of Diabetes. The same way just observing a bench, gave me an insight into the treatment of Sciatic Nerve. Similarly, observing the repairing of the lights of my car, gave me an insight into the working of the eyes and thus the prevention for cataract was found out. Since 1977, I have been giving free guidance to all types of patients and I am getting very good results for Common cold, Tonsilitis and Asthma. Later on, when I retired from my export business of rayon fabrics in 1985, I devoted more time at our free consultation centre at Arya Samaj, Linking Road, Santacruz (West), Mumbai – 400 054 near my residence. At our centre, till now more than 2600 medical practitioners have come to me with their own problems. Among them, there were many M.Ds. My dentist friend sent me his friend who was an M.D., M.R.C.P., F.R.C.S. This has given me great confidence in the impeccable and instant diagnosis made by just pressing the palms and the efficacy about the cure by practising this therapy in homes by the patients. According to acupressure, Cancer is one of the easiest diseases to be cured.

Now, the most dreaded disease which remained to be tackled was AIDS, which I was confident of curing. But the hospitals in Mumbai did not permit me to see patients of AIDS. In 1994, during my visit to the U.S.A., one of my relatives, an M.D. took me to his hospital in Harlem, New York – where there were several patients with AIDS. I examined them and during my two months' stay with my daughter in Minneapolis, I studied about AIDS and was very happy to find its cure. I have tried this method of diagnosis on more than 30,000 patients. In case of doubt about HIV infection in any patient, even if it's a child, I send for its parents, brothers and sisters. And I am shocked to observe such HIV infection in all of them. I have observed such HIV infection in college-going boys and girls. I have observed that this dreaded disease has silently spread its vicious tentacles in a big way in our society. The cure for the same was prescribed and the results are simply fantastic. Within 60 to 90 days, the cases of this dreaded disease have been cured. Even the most expert medical practitioners have sought my help and consulted me for their HIV patients.

The diagnosis about HIV infection is made within a minute without any tests and costs. The diagnosis made by this Nature's Health Science of Acupressure/ Reflexology is so accurate and exact that it is equal to any diagnosis made by Magnetic Resonance Imaging (M.R.I.) test. I have personally examined over 2,00,000 patients and my confidence about this God-given therapy increases day-by-day. My experience and insight has led me to write another book about 'Diagnosis'.

I am most happy to announce that all the dreaded diseases such as Common cold, Cataract, Cancer, Heart, Kidney problems, Diabetes, Thalassaemia, Muscular Dystrophy, problems of the Brain and now HIV/AIDS are curable. We can not only defeat these Dragons of dreaded diseases, but can also eradicate Asthma, Cataract and even Cancer.

I fervently appeal to all the people engaged in medical services, to forget their prejudices and vested interests, and try this Nature's own Health Science of Acupressure and provide health and happiness to the mankind.

I am thankful to all the patients who have tried my Researches and informed me about the results.

I am also thankful to my dentist friend Dr. Narendra Bandrekar and his wife Pratimaben with whom I could always discuss about my researches and who have always given me proper guidance. I am also thankful to our family physician Dr. Harshad Pandya for giving me inspiration and guidance. I am also thankful to Dr. Pradeep Shah, M.D. (U.S.A.).

I am very much thankful to Sri Lord Pandit Prof. Dr. Sir Anton Jayasuria, Chairman of The Open International University for Complementary Medicines, Colombo, Sri Lanka who has conferred upon me the Honorary Degrees of D.Sc., M.D. and a Gold Medal and has kindly written the Foreword for this book.

Before I end this note, I humbly bow before the Supreme Power, which controls the cosmos, to give me insight and energy to be useful to the mankind with these revolutionary Researches.

In the end, I only have to say that this Supreme Power has put health and happiness in our own hands. Now, man need not fear the dreaded diseases. He can stop depending on others and become his own doctor.

Last but not least, I would be failing in my duty, if I do not thank my publishers, for bringing out this book and my other books on health in a commendable style and also at a minimum possible cost.

In the end I pray that :

"**W**elfare be to all the **W**orld;
May all be interested in helping others;
Diseases and misery may perish;
And may all the people be
Healthy and **H**appy."

P. S. I am grateful to my publisher who is combining my two books, "Defeat The Dragon" and "Instant Diagnosis" in one as "Health In Your Hands : Volume 2" and which will be avilable at a very reasonable price.

30th December, 2001   **–Devendra Vora**

CONTENTS

CHAPTER 1

DREADED DISEASES

The diseases, which develop and reach such a stage that the patient cannot be saved, are considered to be dreaded, for example – Cancer. The first thing about such diseases, is that when such a disease is in the preliminary stage, its diagnosis is not made, sometimes it is not even possible. It is admitted by popular medical therapy that Cancer is detected only when it has developed up to 30% or more. Later on, chemotherapy is given to the patient. Consequently, heat increases very much in the body. The liver and gall bladder get damaged to the extent that the patient gets jaundice and cannot be saved. Medical experts take solace that they have cured Cancer (Dr. Dagli in his booklet "Cancer"), but the patient has died of jaundice. The patient and his relatives are interested in the complete cure. It makes no difference to them what disease the patient has died of.

Many times the disease is suppressed with antibiotics or powerful drugs but after a few days, may be a few months or years, there is a relapse and the patient cannot be saved. The main object of any medical treatment should be to save life. The object of any medical practitioner is as per Materia Medica – "utmost interest of the patient". A patient is not a guinea pig – on whom experiments could be made.

Moreover, all medical practitioners are health scientists. Therefore they should be ready to accept any truth coming from any other direction, may be from the other medical therapies dealing with different methods of treatment and healing. However, habits and prejudices die hard.

In his conquest of nature, man has forgotten the kind mother nature. The great inventors, discoverers scientists, astronomers and astronauts admit that the knowledge so far acquired by human beings is just a drop in the ocean.

Experts of popular health science have admitted in their books, viz. "Diseases of Nervous System" by Dr. Lord Brain & Dr. John Walton and "Clinical Neuro-Anatomy" by Dr. Richard Snail, (prescribed in medical colleges for the degree of M.D.) that they are not aware of the working of some of the organs of the brain and they have little knowledge about endocrine glands and do not know how to control them. They maintain that if the pancreas functions less, a person gets diabetes. But what if the pancreas works more? The overfunctioning of the pancreas leads to deficiency of glucose in the brain, cerebrospinal fluid and often leads to migraine, a recurrent throbbing headache that affects one side of the head. To subdue the same, painkillers are administered which in the long run lead to acidity and ulcers in the intestines and mouth.

The experts have admitted the great importance of proper functioning of all these endocrine glands and also that these important glands sometimes work less and sometimes more. They are also aware that unless all the endocrine glands function properly, an imbalance is created in hormones which consequently leads to many problems; which later on can become fatal. e.g., AIDS.

More importance is given to the germs which cause diseases, and less to the power of the body which, if empowered, can create antibodies and get itself cured. Milk is considered difficult to digest. But when bacteria turns it into curds it becomes more digestible. And when this curd is churned and turned into buttermilk, it is accepted as very useful for digestion and removal of excess heat from the body.

Surprisingly, the function of very important organs of body like the Liver and the Gall bladder is not understood by them. These twins work like a radiator in a car. They neutralise the acidity from the food which goes into the small intestines. However, when excess heat is created in the body, they are damaged. The liquid stored in the Gall bladder dries up and becomes crystal which leads to jaundice considered to be surgical and in spite of curing liver and Gall bladder, unnecessarily an operation of Gall bladder is done and it is removed from the body. Consequently, the patient suffers, for the remaining life, with acidity and burning sensation.

The body is not treated but the symptoms of different organs are treated. Without going deeper into the root causes, these symptoms are suppressed and so the drugs create side effects which sometimes prove fatal.

Somehow, the very basis of the body syndrome is not understood. It is an accepted fact that during masturbation or sexual intercourse semen is ejected by the male and this important semen is not stored in any gland in the body. This semen contains spermatozoa which, when it enters the female's egg (ova) in the uterus, fertilises the egg and a child is conceived. A virile person is capable of becoming a father even at the age of 80 or more. It is important to know how the semen is produced in the body. It may be noted that out of about 40 kilos of food we digest, only one litre of blood is formed and out of one litre of blood, a few

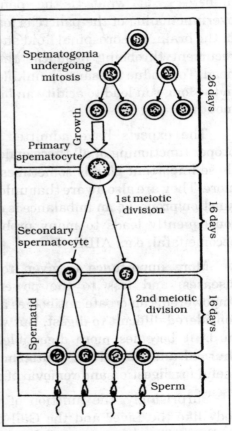

Fig. 40 : Reproduction of sperms

drops of semen are formed in 49 days in a sequence of seven steps of (1) Liquid (2) Blood (3) Fat (4) Muscles (5) Bones (6) Bone marrow (7) Semen.

After sperms are created, it takes another 74 days to get them multiplied significantly as shown in fig. 40.

Now, this semen starts being produced in the body from the birth. It is stored throughout the body and its level is reflected in the nails as per fig 41.

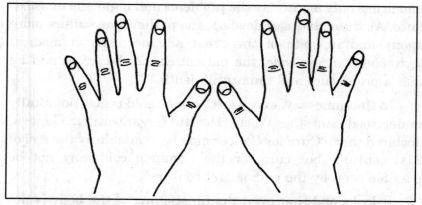

Fig. 41 : Picture showing half white moons in the nails

This semen is converted from blood through a combined process of proper functioning of all the endocrine glands plus electric process plus the heat process in the body. This semen is not produced in any laboratory.

This semen or ova, creates a syndrome of the body. And at the age of about twelve when the sex glands become more active, and due to the heat process in the body, this semen gets matured and half-moons in the nails become more and more milky white and spread in all the nails of the hands and toes.

This semen forms the syndrome of the body and so, the more powerful the semen, the more powerful is this syndrome. And in turn this syndrome protects the body against the diseases.

It is very surprising to observe that the popular medical therapy has not understood these facts about the syndrome. And so the modern medical practitioners are not able to understand AIDS. It is an accepted fact that if the disease itself is not properly understood and diagnosed, it cannot be cured. And so, these diseases are considered to be dreadful.

Heavy bombardment of antibiotics and powerful drugs like steroids – main weapons of this popular medical therapy – failed to cure these diseases. The doctors get into a panic mode and resort to frighten the world branding these as 'fatal, dreadful diseases'. In fact, such heavy dosages of antibiotics and drugs only aggravate the problems and make the diseases fatal. As these diseases develop, the patient has suffers more agony and in spite of the great advancement in medical technology and science, the patient cannot be saved and he dies a premature and unnatural death.

In the same way, even the Common cold is also not totally understood and the World Health Organisation, Geneva, declared that, "Cure for Cancer may be available by the end of 21st century; but cure for the Common cold may not be possible even by the end of 21st century".

It looks odd that even the functioning of the body is not properly understood. Only a few years ago, they have accepted Acupuncture but not its basis, the electricity of the body. And so the therapy of Acupressure/reflexology which is based on this Bioelectricity is not given recognition.

Further, the concept that "our body creates antibodies to fight out – throw out the foreign matters, toxins, germs of disease from its system" is accepted by all the medical therapies. However, under the popular medical therapy, very little chance is given to the body to do so. Right from the early stage, bombardment of antibiotics and heavy dosages of drugs are administered, thereby producing so many side-effects. Even the internal immune system becomes lethargic and does not extend proper cooperation in the process of healing. On the contrary, it creates resistance against these anti-biotic drugs and so in case of relapse of the disease, it is necessary to give more powerful antibiotics or heavier doses of drugs.

It is an irony, that life-saving costly injections are prepared in Japan from urine, but this Urine Therapy is not advised to the people.

It is our common experience that sometimes we breathe through the right nostril and sometimes through the left nostril. There is an automatic change in our breathing. Why? It has not been understood by even the experts of popular medical therapy.

Even the concept of the solar plexus is not accepted or understood by them. And so, unnecessary operations of hiatus hernia and piles are performed. They are not able to prevent loose motions due to downward shifting of the solar plexus. By just correcting the solar plexus, all these problems can be cured.

It will be a great surprise for the world to note that *Yogis* and *Rishis* in India were fully aware of the human body, its endocrine glands, the syndrome of the body, the solar plexus and about Bioelectricity even 5,000 years ago. They were even able to control the organs and endocrine glands through internal Acupressure and breathing exercises. They were disciples of nature and found out that the Creator of the universe, has put this wonderful therapy not only in the human body but in the bodies of all living animals with five senses of touch, taste, vision, hearing and smell. Even the cats and dogs are aware of this health science of nature and so if they have any problem, they lick and rub their paws.

If mankind wants to survive these dreaded diseases, eradicate Cancer and Cataract, be healthy and enjoy the great happiness provided to us by nature, then we have no other alternative but to surrender our prejudices to nature and abide by its abundant TEACHINGS.

In this book, I will explain the Common cold, Asthma, Allergy, Cataract, Cancer, Diabetes, Kidney problems, Heart's problems, Brain's problems, Thalassaemia and HIV/AIDS which are easily detectable, even preventable and curable. **We can defeat these dragons of dreaded diseases – We can CURE all types of serious diseases.**

CHAPTER 2

USEFUL IMPORTANT HINTS

How to empower the battery?

In order to get faster relief and break the vicious cycle of diseases it is advisable to do the following to recharge the battery – to empower the immune defence system :

(1) Perform Pranayam : The easy four-step way :

1st Step : Inhale the air counting 1-2-3-4.

2nd Step : Then keep the air in the lungs counting 1-2-3-4.

3rd Step : Then exhale the air counting 1-2-3-4.

4th Step : Pause – do not inhale counting 1-2-3-4.

Then repeat 10 to 15 times, three to four times a day and with practice go on increasing the count to 10. During the pause, the lungs get rest and are revitalised. This type of controlled breathing called Pranayam was tried on patients suffering from tuberculosis in a hospital in Chicago and the results were beneficial.

Once you reach a count of 10, you may do Pranayam, as follows :

Inhale counting	10
Retain counting	20
Exhale counting	10
Refrain-pause counting	10

i.e. in the ratio of 1 : 2 : 1 : 1.

(2) Control of the five basic elements through Pranayam-Mudras : While doing pranayam, even the five basic elements of the body can be controlled because they are represented by the different fingers as follows :

Thumb	— fire or sun
Index finger	— wind or air
Middle finger	— sky or space
Ring finger (4th finger)	— earth
Small finger	— water

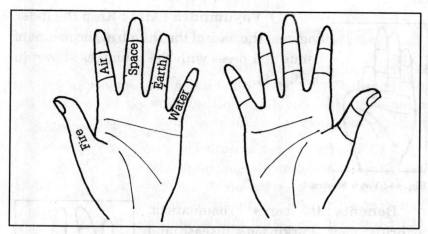

Fig. 42 : Five fingers represent five elements

Now, through different combinations of these fingers-mudras – we can not only control these elements but also cure many diseases. This can be done in any position but 'Padmasan' (sitting in a lotus position) or 'Sukhasan' (sitting in a normal position) is advisable for better results. These mudras can be started for 10 minutes and can be done for at least 30 to 45 minutes. Some of such mudras are shown below and **are to be performed by both hands simultaneously.**

(1) Meditation Mudra : Simply touch the thumb with the index finger. Pressing is not necessary.

Benefits : This helps in increasing the brain power, mental concentration, memory, etc. and cures the problems of sleeplessness, tension and lack of concentration.

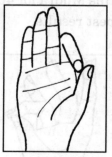

Fig. 43 : Meditation Mudra

Fig. 44 : Vayu Mudra

(2) Vayumudra (Air) : Keep the index finger on the base of the thumb at the mount of Venus and press with the thumb as shown in the fig. 44.

Benefits : It cures rheumatism, arthritis, gout, Parkinson's disease and blood circulation defects. For better results, also do Pran Mudra.

(3) Shunya Mudra (space) : Keep the middle finger at the mount of Venus and press it with the thumb as shown in fig. 45.

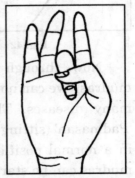

Fig. 45 : Shunya Mudra

Benefits : It helps in curing earache, deafness, vertigo, etc. It is necessary to do this Mudra for 40 to 60 minutes to get the best results.

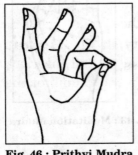

Fig. 46 : Prithvi Mudra

(4) Prithvi Mudra (earth) : Put the ring finger together with the thumb as shown in fig. 46.

Benefits : It cures weakness of the body and the mind. It increases life force *(chetna)* and gives new vigour to an ailing person. It also gives peace of mind.

(5) Varun Mudra (water) : Put the tips of the thumb and the little finger together as shown in fig. 47.

Benefits : It cures impurities in blood, skin problems and makes the skin smooth. Useful in gastroenteritis and any other diseases that cause dehydration.

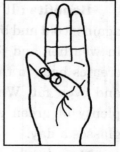

Fig. 47 : Varun Mudra

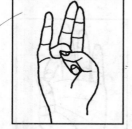

Fig. 48 : Sun Mudra

(6) Sun Mudra : Bend the ring finger and on its outer side on the second fold, press with the thumb as per fig. 48.

Benefits : It creates heat in the body, helps digestion and also helps in reducing fat in the body.

(7) Pran Mudra (life energy) : Bend the little and the ring fingers so that their tips touch the tip (front edge) of the thumb as shown in fig. 49.

Benefits : It increases the life force and cures nervousness and fatigue. It also helps increasing the power of the eyes and in reducing the number of eyeglasses.

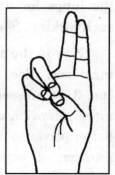

Fig. 49 : Pran Mudra

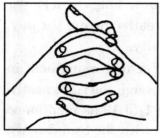

Fig. 50 : Ling Mudra

(8) Ling (Shiv) Mudra : Join both the palms and interlock the fingers, keep the thumb of the left hand vertically straight and encircle it with the index finger and the thumb of the right hand as shown in fig. 50.

Benefits : It increases the resistance power of the body against cold and bronchial infections and also against changes in weather and fever due to cold. It gives power to lungs, creates heat in the body and burns up accumulated phlegm and even fat. While practising this mudra one must drink plenty of green and fruit juices and water, at least eight glasses a day.

Now, while performing these mudras if pranayam is done, you will get better results.

Retention of air : While doing pranayam, after inhaling air, press the upper part of thumb no. 1 with the index finger. You will be able to retain air easily in the lungs for a longer time than without such locking. See fig. 51.

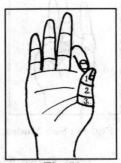

Fig. 51

Now if, the middle of thumb no. 2 is pressed, the retention increases. See fig. 5. Now if the base of the thumb (no. 3) is pressed, the retention is the maximum. If there is more retention of air in the lungs, it is fully utilised, gives better power to blood and body. This will also mean that fewer number of breaths are taken. According to the Indian philosophy, our life span is measured not in minutes, days, months and years but is fixed in the total number of breaths. Now by doing pranayam and retaining air in lungs for a longer time, we reduce the total number of breaths during the day. This will help us to increase our longevity.

1st Method (Sun Pranayam) : For increasing heat in the body, close the left nostril, inhale through the right nostril and exhale through it whilst counting 1 to 10 as mentioned above. As the right nostril is connected with the Sun (known as *Pingala nadi* in Yoga) inhaling and exhaling through it will produce heat in the body. Therefore, this pranayam is very useful in winter and monsoon and for the cure of diseases like cold, asthma, polio, paralysis, bronchitis, arthritis, TB, etc. where heat is required.

2nd Method (Moon Pranayam): For increasing coolness in the body, close the right nostril, inhale and exhale through the left nostril whilst counting as above. The left nostril is connected with the Moon (known as 'Ida' in Yoga). So, it produces coolness in the body. Therefore, this pranayam is useful in diseases like fever, sunstroke in summer, etc. where coolness is necessary.

3rd Method (For balancing of heat and cold): Inhale through the right nostril and exhale from the left nostril and then inhale through the left nostril and exhale from the right nostril. This will control the heat of the body.

During the period the breath is held inside, pull the stomach inside for more effective results as well as for reducing the fat around the stomach.

Please see to it that while inhaling, your chest expands by five to seven cm. Better results can be obtained by breathing as above. Pranayam should be done in a comfortable posture, by sitting upright on the ground or a chair/sofa, or can be done in a standing position or even while walking.

Breathing from the desired nostril – right or left – can be effected by closing the other nostril. Otherwise, if you lie down on the left side of the body, the breath will flow from the right nostril. In India, people are advised to lie down for 10 to 15 minutes on the left side after lunch or dinner so that the breath is linked with the sun, producing heat in the body and helping digestion. Similarly, if you lie down on the right side, the breath will flow from the left nostril which is useful during too much heat or fever.

4th Method (Kapalbhati) : Sit upright in a quiet place. Inhale and exhale very fast through the nostrils. Start with 10 times and go up to 50 times in a minute through the nostrils. Do this pranayam for two minutes twice a day.

5th Method (Bhastrika) : Open the mouth, inhale slowly through it and then immediately blow out hard. Do it 1 to 15 times. Do this pranayam every time after you do 'kapalbhati'. These will clear any congestion in the head.

Sheetli, i.e. How to create cooling effect in the body :

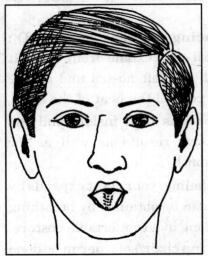

Open the mouth, put out the tongue and inhale (draw in) air through the mouth. Close the mouth and retain the air as much as possible. Then exhale through the nose. Repeat 15/25 times. You will immediately feel cool. This method is called *Sheetli* (शीतली) in Yoga and found to be useful in summer, sunstroke, fever or whenever cooling effect is necessary, e.g. in Kaposis's sarcoma.

Fig. 52 : Picture showing how to create cooling effect in the body

Regular practice of pranayam and breathing exercises will ensure proper oxygenation of all the parts of the body and cure many diseases. Proper oxygenation helps in purifying the blood and removal of toxins and carbon dioxide from the body. This, in turn, will reduce the unnecessary burden on kidney, reducing the possibility of skin diseases and failure of kidney. Moreover, pure blood enables proper functioning of all the organs and thereby increases vigour and vitality.

These breathing exercises are beneficial to all and should be practised daily. However, these exercises are a must for the treatment of cold, cough and asthma, TB and mental disorders like polio, meningitis, nervous breakdown, muscular dstrophy, etc.

Blue Light & Red Light :

(1) (a) 90 minutes from sunrise and 60 minutes before sunset; keep a glass of the desired colour (blue or red) in the sunlight in such a way that the rays will fall on the affected parts of the body. While taking this sunlight, care should be taken to see that the patient is not exposed to strong, direct wind.

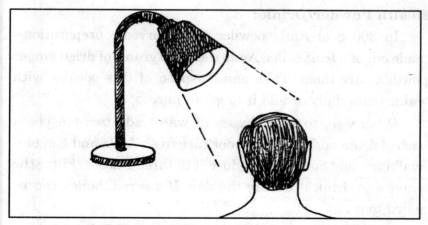

Fig. 53 : Picture showing how to take blue or red light

(b) If it is not possible, take a coloured bulb of 60 to 100 watts. If such a coloured bulb is not available, take a plain bulb, a gelatin paper of the desired colour, fold it four times and wrap it around the bulb. Light the lamp, keep the affected part 18 to 20 inches away and take the red light for 1 to 2 minutes or 5 to 10 minutes of Blue light twice a day as recommended. (See chapter 7 in Volume 1)

(2) Drink lukewarm water, preferably iron/copper/silver/gold charged water at least two glasses reduced from four glasses.

(3) Drink 2 to 3 cups of green juice

adding to each cup   1 teaspoon health drink

also adding to each cup   1 tablespoon honey.

Sleep :

(4) The battery of our body is recharged during sleep. So it is most important to sleep for 6 – 8 hours.

The above four things help to recharge our unchangeable battery. **This battery is capable of curing almost all the diseases.** And that is why it is most important to recharge this inner battery.

Health Powder/Drink :

In 300 g of Amla powder (an ayurvedic preparation – made out of a fruit called Amla) add 100 grams of dried ginger powder. Mix them. Take one teaspoon of this powder with water twice daily or add it to green juice.

Otherwise, to four glasses of water add two teaspoons each of Amla and ginger powder (use fresh Amla and ginger if available) and boil it and reduce it to three glasses. Filter the water and drink it during the day. If desired, honey can be added to it.

Amla is a concentrated form of Vitamin 'C'. It has 16 times more vitamin than lemon. Such a drink will give protection to the body against cold and other diseases and increase digestive powers.

People in the West take apple cider which is also beneficial. The health drink is beneficial to all, especially to the convalescent people, old people, expectant mothers and growing children.

Green vegetable juice :

25 gm mixture of the fresh juice of the following green leaves and vegetables is also beneficial.

Leaves of tandaljo or spinach, leaves of methi (fenu-greek), cucumber, leaves of phudina (mint), tulsi (holy basil), lettuce, coriander and cabbage leaves. **All types of non-poisonous leaves can be used.** Even carrots and radish can be added.

How to prepare the green juice :

First, wash all these leaves, vegetables, etc. first with salted water, then with clean water. Then crush them or blend them. Collect the paste (चटनी) in a piece of clean cloth and squeeze and filter it. And green juice is ready.

Face mask :

The remaining paste (चटनी), can be mixed with little cream, turmeric powder and applied on face as a face mask. Keep it for 10/15 minutes. If possible, take blue light on the face for 5 to 7 minutes. Wash it with fresh water. In 10/15 days, the face will glow. Even white spots and pimples will vanish.

Copper/Silver/Gold and Iron charged water :

It has been found that the following minerals are useful for treating diseases connected with the organs as follows :

(1) **Copper :** Useful for all diseases and problems connected with the nervous system, e.g. high B.P., arthritis, polio, tension and leprosy.

(2) **Silver :** Useful for the diseases of the organs connected with the digestive system and the urinary system.

(3) **Gold :** Useful for the disorders of the breathing system, lungs, heart, brain and as a general tonic. It acts as an antibiotic.

The charged water can be prepared as follows :

(a) **Copper charged water :** Put 60 gm of pure copper plate/ingots/wire or six to eight copper coins in a vessel containing four glasses of water and boil it.

(b) **Silver charged water :** Put 30 to 60 gm of silver-pure bullion or pure coins (.999 purity) in a vessel containing four glasses of water and boil it. (Never use silver ornaments.)

(c) **Gold charged water :** Put 15 to 30 gm of gold-pure bullion gold coin or ornaments (chain or bangles) of 20 – 22 carat gold in a vessel containing four glasses of water and boil it.

(d) **Iron charged water : (In case of deficiency of iron in blood, anaemia or during pregnancy)** Put 60 gm of unrusted, not galvanised, piece of iron (nails, etc.) in a vessel containing four glasses of water and boil it.

All these metals can be put together in water, in the proportion of gold 15 to 20 gm/silver 30 gm/copper 60 gm/Iron 60 gm. It should be borne in mind that all the metals put in the water are thoroughly cleaned and are not rusty. Use stainless steel, copper or pyrex glass vessels.

Boil and reduce 25 % of the water, i.e. retain three out of four glasses of water after boiling. Filter this water, keep it in a thermos if possible and drink it lukewarm/hot during the day. Drinking one glass of this water the first thing in the morning is very beneficial. This water is a good tonic. When

4 glasses of water is reduced to 2 glasses, it gets medicinal value and is useful for all the types of serious and chronic diseases. In acute cases, this water may be boiled down to one glass or even half a glass. When you drink such concentrated water, avoid sour things like lemon, sour buttermilk, etc.

This charged water is found useful for good health. And it is a must for the treatment of any problems connected with the improper flow of the current of Bioelectricity, i.e. high B.P., polio, rheumatism, arthritis, paralysis, chronic diseases including cancer, etc. The use of concentrated gold charged water has given wonderful results in the cases of mental retardation, muscular dystrophy, TB, heart attack, HIV/AIDS etc. and is a good brain tonic too.

Endocrine glands :

Before you proceed to learn about Diagnosis, please read chapter 2 : part 1 about endocrine glands again.

CHAPTER 3

COMMON COLD

Common cold – coughing – fever – tonsils – sinus allergy and asthma :

Even though these are not dreaded diseases, they are not properly understood and treated so they have become the biggest enemies of mankind. They are responsible for the highest loss of working hours. Though they are not deadly unless they develop into pnuemonia, they make you most miserable. We have to properly understand our body in order to ascertain the root cause of common cold.

We are all aware that our body consists of about 72% of water. Heat and cold have the same effect on the water inside our body as on the water outside. Our body has an airconditioner as well as a heater. In summer, even when the outside temperature is 110°F or in winter it is 20° or 30°F below zero; our body maintains the same temperature of 98.4°F (about 37°C). The water in our body gets heated during the day due to activity and due to outside temperature, while during the night, it cools down, creating moisture in the lungs or head. In nature, it is thrown out in the form of dew. In case of our body, it is thrown out by sneezing or running of the nose. Therefore, according to Ayurveda, sneezing in the morning is considered to be a good sign of health.

In our head, brain cells create H+ which in turn is transformed into electricity. The excess of such H+ is thrown out of our system through exhaling of the air and some through perspiration. But due to any reason, if there is an excess of such H+, it damages the brain cells. In order to throw it out, through electric process in our body, one atom of oxygen is taken from the air we breathe in and mixed with two atoms of H. This combination becomes H_2O, i.e. water. And in turn, this water is thrown out of our system. This water, gathered in our head, drips down resulting in running nose and watering of the eyes, etc. When this water drips down further, it affects the throat and develops into tonsilitis. At this time, if lungs are examined, they would be clear. Now, in a healthy person, the body tries to throw out such excess heat twice a year through sneezing and running nose, which is known as common cold. This phenomenon lasts for three to four days each time. We need not worry about such cold or try to stop it. It is jokingly remarked that in common colds if you take medicines you will get cured within six days but if you do not take medicines, you will be alright within four days.

When an attempt is made to subdue this cold, this toxic water dries down temporarily. And when our body becomes normal, again it tries to throw out this water from the system. We again subdue it by taking heavier doses. But the process continues and so later on it is declared as an allergy. During these attacks of cold, the first endocrine gland to be disturbed is thyroid/parathyroid. During long term cold, as the working of this important gland is impaired, it digests less calcium and so a deficiency of calcium is created in the body and so in cases of allergy, when biochemic salt of calcium – known as calcaria phos is administered to the patient, this allergy is cured.

When the common cold is subdued, semi-liquid mucus is formed and it is gathered into pockets around the nose and head known as sinuses. Sometimes, puncturing is done and such mucus is removed from the sinus-pockets. But as the root cause is not removed, the mucus occurs again and the patient gets sinusitis.

When this problem continues, along with thyroid/parathyroid, even the sex glands are damaged. This important gland controls heat of the body. As it is disturbed, control in the production of phosphorus in the body weakens and in turn because of less supply of phosphorus, less heat is produced. And this leads to less evaporation of water from the body. Consequently, there is an increase in the content of water in the body putting more pressure on the lungs and it turns into symptoms of asthma. In more than 80 per cent of patients of asthma, their problem is due to the "excess heat in the body" and administering of more antibiotics and powerful drugs only create more and more heat in the body and subjects these patients to a life of misery because then acidity and ulcers develop.

Another root cause of such "cold due to heat" is sluggish liver. This vital organ is often damaged by unwise use of drugs to remove "worms" from intestines. These drugs do remove worms, but damage the liver and even gall bladder in the process. Unless proper steps to cure, revitalise the liver are taken the patient complains of indigestion, and acidity. Due to sluggish liver, less bile is produced; consequently the acidic food of stomach is not neutralised in intestines. This leads to more acidity called "pitta" (आम्लपित्त) in intestines, further leading to warming of air in the stomach. This heated air occupies the empty spaces in the head and the face. Now during the day, whenever this heated air is cooled due to cold wind, overhead fan or sitting in an air-conditioned room, it turns into moisture and becomes water. This cooled water contracts the nerves, leading to headaches and sinus troubles. When accumulated, the cold starts coming down. It irritates the throat and the nose. This in turn also leads to tonsilitis and causes sneezing and running of water through the nose and the eyes. In such a cold, the chest is clear. Now in case of such colds-tonsils-sinus-Asthma, any pain reliever or antibiotics upsets the stomach, increases the excess heat in the body and in the long run leads to ulcers and hyper acidity. It is also observed that this type of cold aggravates in summer and autumn.

Another cause of cold is the effect of the moon on the body :

The moon is the satellite of our earth, and it being very near has great effect on the water on the earth. The obvious proof of this is that the time of the ebb and flow of the tide changes daily along with the moon-days and when there is a change in the shape of the moon.

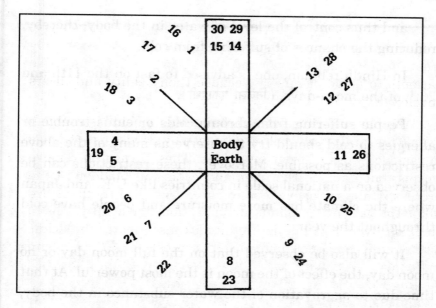

Fig. 54 : Rotation of the Moon round the Earth

From the above fig. 54 about the rotation of the moon around the earth, you will observe that on the 4th, 5th, 8th, 11th, 14th and 15th, 19th, 23rd, 26th, 29th and 30th of moon-days, the earth and our body come directly against the moon. At that time, the level of water in the sea and our body rises.

Now in order to curb the bad effect of such a rise in the level of water in our body, in the Indian religions, particularly, in Jainism, people are advised on these moon-days :

(a) to observe complete fast (not to drink even boiled water, if possible) or drink only boiled water before sunset.

(b) to eat only once a day and drink only boiled water before sunset.

(c) to eat only twice a day and drink only boiled water before sunset.

(d) at least to avoid eating green vegetables (as they contain about 90 % water) and thus control the level of water in the body, thereby, reducing the chances of suffering from cold.

In Hindu religion, one is advised to fast on the 11th and 26th of the moon-days. (निर्जला एकादशी).

People suffering from chronic colds or sinus trouble or allergies to cold should try to observe as many of the above restrictions as possible. Moreover, these restrictions can be observed on a national scale in countries like U.K. and Japan where the climate has more moisture and people have cold throughout the year.

It will also be observed that on the full moon day or no moon day, the effect of the moon is the most powerful. At that time due to aggravation of the water substance in the body, the heat in the body decreases and thereby the air content increases, which travels to the head and causes mental disturbances. Recently a scientist in Chicago (U.S.A.) has confirmed the existence of such an effect of the moon on mental diseases. Consequently, more suicides are committed during these days.

Real Common Cold :

The water in the blood and the body is controlled by the heat of the body which in turn depends upon the digestive power. So, whenever the digestive system weakens, the internal temperature goes down. This reduces the evaporation of water and consequently the gathering of excess water in the body. In turn this excess water reduces the heat, and the process of turning liquid food into blood slows down, there is more phlegm (कफ) and it goes up and there is a congestion in the chest, lungs and throat. This if not controlled, develops into bronchitis, which the body tries to remove by coughing. But when such a congestion is not removed, there is fever and tonsilitis. This cold due to excess of water is further aggravated by the consuming of cold drinks, heavy foods, sweets, sour things like curds, buttermilk, lemon juice, etc. and exposing the body to cold winds or coldness through air-conditioning. All these add to the prolonging and the aggravating of the real cold.

The best way to remove this real cold is to –

(a) Fast and drink boiled water.

(b) Keep the bowels clean and avoid constipation.

(c) Take only light food and more of green salads, green juices, etc.

(d) In case of congestion in the throat and chest, drink at least one glass of hot water with little salt and $\frac{1}{2}$ teaspoon of turmeric powder added to it.

(e) Gargle with luke-warm water with salt and turmeric powder added to it.

(f) Rub the chest as per fig. 55 shown here.

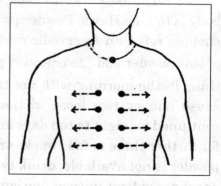

Fig. 55

(g) Put hot dry pack on the chest.

One need not worry about fever. It is a good sign that the body is trying to dry up congestion and remove it. Only thing is that one must be careful to control the temperature and not allow it to rise more than 103°F. Such temperature can be controlled by putting a cold pack on the stomach and head and as per treatment given below :

(h) The body should be empowered. The method is narrated in Chapter 2 of this book.

(i) And with Acupressure treatment. (Health In Your Hands : Volume 1)

Diagnosis :

(1) In case of **real cold,** when you press point no. 27 of the stomach and no. 30 of the lungs, they will be found to be tender. And if congestion has affected the throat, there will be pain on point no. 6 of the throat also.

(2) In case of **"cold due to heat",** you will feel pain, when pressed, on point no. 28 and in case of excess of heat point. nos. 22 & 23 also. Moreover, owing to the congestion of water in the head, and throat you will observe pain on point nos. 1 to 5 and that of point no. 6 of the throat.

Cure for "cold due to excess heat" :

(1) The best way to remove this excess heat from the body is to take Harde Powder (हरितकी चुर्ण) (powder of terminalia chebula refz), an Ayurvedic medicine. In about one teaspoon of this powder add $\frac{1}{2}$ teaspoon of ground sugar and take it first thing in the morning with hot to lukewarm water. This may cause one or two loose motions. This treatment is to be continued for eight to ten days and then twice or thrice a week for further three to four weeks or till completely cured. If such powder is not available, drink two to three glasses of water or one glass of fruit juice or one cup of green juice (details about the same are given in Chapter 2) first thing in the morning after cleaning the mouth.

(2) All points connected with the cold are to be pressed, i.e. point nos. 1 to 7, 30 and 34 and in case of sinusitis, tips of all the fingers.

(3) The points of the adrenal gland, liver, gall bladder, stomach and solar plexus, i.e. point. nos. 28, 23, 22, 27 and 29 are to be pressed.

(4) In case of chronic complaints, it is necessary to empower the digestive system and so it is useful to take the following medicine for six weeks.

Nux Vomica 200×6 to 8 pills once a week.

Nux Vomica 12 or 30×3 to 4 pills twice a day

(This is a homoeopathic preparation.)

(5) Check up about the worms in the intestines and remove them in the following method :

When pressed on the point on the outer side in the middle of the smallest toe or last finger of any of the legs or palms, if pain is observed, it is an indication of the presence of worms.

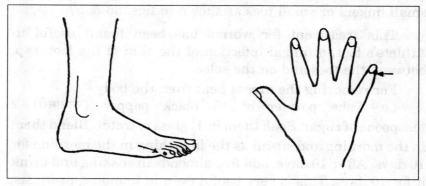

| Fig. 56 | Fig. 57 |

Picture showing how to detect worms

This is a common problem with the children. Whenever, children complain :

(1) of pain around stomach, (2) their hunger is reduced (3) growth has stopped (4) look pale (their eyes will look whitish) then first of all try and find out about worms. **In case of worms, the children even get ear infection** and in that case, point no. 16 of Lymph gland will be found to be tender and paining.

Cure :

Cina 200 (a) Homoeopathic medicine

Children under 6	Under 10	Over 10 & Adults
4 pills	6 pills	8 pills

Once a day for four days preferably before going to bed. Then stop the medicine for four days.

After four days, repeat the medicine for four days. On the 13th day, give some powerful laxative so that it causes 3 to 4 loose motions. From 14th day give Cina 12 or 30, three pills once a day for 30 days. If allopathic medicine is taken for worms, supplement it with medicine for liver, because such medicines for worms damage the liver. Also empower the liver, gall bladder by giving treatment on point nos. 23 and 22.

Also give treatment for a minute each on points of both the small fingers or small toes as shown in figs. 56 & 57.

This treatment for worms has been found useful in Athlete's foot, a fungal infection of the skin of the foot, esp. between the toes and on the soles.

For removing the excess heat from the body –

(a) Take powder of 15 black pepper (कालामरी) + 2 teaspoons of sugar. Soak them in $1\frac{1}{2}$ glass of water. Blend them in the morning and sip all as the first thing in the morning for 10 days. After 10 days, add five almonds in soaking and drink it for 10 days. This is very useful even in jaundice, psoriasis, sunstroke, Kaposi's sarcoma.

(b) Take five black peppers + 10 to 12 black dried raisins + 1 teaspoon of saunf (सौंप); soak them in one glass of water in the evening. Next day, blend them and drink it in the afternoon. It is a useful tasty drink in summer.

(c) Take equal quantity (about 50 grams each) of (1) cumin seed (जिरा) (2) black pepper (3) saunf (4) amla (आमला) (5) ginger (6) crystal sugar (मीसरी). Grind them into powder and keep it in a bottle. Take one teaspoon of this powder with the water any time in the morning and evening.

Tonsils :

Mix 3 to 4 drops of Glycerine Tannic Acid (available with the chemist) with $\frac{1}{2}$ teaspoon of turmeric powder. Apply it on the inner-both sides of the throat and then gargle with lukewarm salted water. Do this two or three times a day. Just within two to three days, these and even septic tonsils will get cured.

Asthma/Breathlessness/Suffocation :

In most of the cases the root cause is "cold due to heat" and so by taking the treatment mentioned above, this disease can be controlled and cured. In such cases, the lungs would be clear and when pressed there would not be any pain on point no. 30 of the lungs.

In case the real cold continues over a long period, the power of lungs becomes weak and the patient gets asthma. It may be noted that this is a curable disease. The following treatment, over and above the treatment suggested previously for real cold, will be found to be useful.

(a) Treatment on point nos. 1 to 7, 30, 34 and tips of fingers and toes.

(b) Add $\frac{1}{2}$ teaspoon of turmeric powder (हलदी) and $\frac{1}{2}$ teaspoon of powder of cumin seed (जिरा) in one teaspoon of Health powder and take it twice a day with lukewarm water. If possible, also add $\frac{1}{2}$ teaspoon of "Mahasudarshan" powder (An Ayurvedic bitter powder) to the above.

(c) Drink two glasses of Gold/Silver/Copper/Iron charged water reduced from eight glasses of water. This is a very effective tonic for lungs.

(d) Take red light on the chest and back for two to three minutes, once a day (10 days only). This melts the mucus inside. Then take blue light for five to seven minutes twice a day – till the disease is totally cured. This blue light gives power to the lungs to throw out the congestion. (see fig. 53)

(e) Ask the patient to lie down on back and to open full mouth. Pour one tablespoon of pure honey directly in throat so that it does not touch the tongue. This helps to clear all the congestion in the throat – wind pipe and gullet.

(f) Perform sun pranayam as much as possible and ling (Shiv) mudra (details are given in Chapter 2).

(g) Do the following twice a day and also when under an attack.

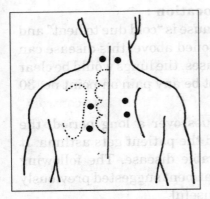

Fig. 58

Press hard on the back of neck and on back on the points shown in fig. 58 for 10 seconds and pause.

Repeat for 2 to 5 minutes.

At the same time ask the patient to rub from the middle of the chest to the sides for a few minutes. Also give treatment for a minute on the point shown below the neck. (see fig. 59)

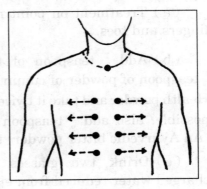

Fig. 59

Eosinophilia :

In cases of continued cold, Asthma, TB, etc. the percentage of eosinophilia in the blood is more. In addition to taking the treatment, it is advisable to take the following for 15–20 days.

After sunrise, take a half tablespoon of half ground Bishops seeds (अजवाइन), soak them in lemon drops and keep them for at least 2 hours before eating it, latest before sunset.

It should be noted that when you start the treatment, the body will be empowered and will start throwing out all the subdued cold-toxins from the body and **it will look as if the cold has aggravated. This is a sign of recovery.** And so, one need not worry. But during these two to three days, avoid food, milk and its products. Eat fruits and drink only lukewarm charged water and heated green juices. One need not worry, if one's temperature rises. Just keep the fever under control and do not allow it to go over 103°F. (method to control fever is narrated in Health In Your Hands : Volume II page 67 of this book.)

Once this real cold or cold due to heat and asthma are controlled and cured, with the regular treatment of Acupressure and control of diet, these diseases will remain under control.

As explained before, it is possible that one would get common cold for 3/4 days twice a year. This is a useful process whereby excess heat is thrown out from one's system, and as such one need not worry about this common cold.

CHAPTER 4

ALLERGY

When cold continues even after taking regular treatment over a period of 2 to 5 years, it is termed as 'cold' due to Allergy and when there is congestion, it is termed as Bronchial Allergy. In spite of Researches, this Allergy is not understood and so it is not cured. And as a result, the patient has to suffer for entire life and be in a perpetual fear of catching Allergy any time.

It is true that painful tests are taken to find out the cause which creates Allergy. Then Anti-allergic injections are prepared and given to the patients. The Allergy seems to be cured for a short while, but appears again and makes the life of the patient more miserable. Although Allergy is not fatal, it is considered to be dreaded.

The basic fact is that common cold is not understood and neither is Allergy. Most of the common cold, as you will observe under Chapter 4 titled 'Common Cold' is due to excess heat in the body. Now when such common cold continues, the endocrine gland of Thyroid and Parathyroid is the first to be disturbed. As no treatment is taken to correct the function of this gland, it starts functioning less efficiently. This endocrine gland controls the digestion of calcium and so when this endocrine gland does not work efficiently slowly, but steadily a deficiency of calcium is created in the body. Disturbance in the Thyroid/Parathyroid gland leads to disturbance of Adrenal gland, which controls 'fire' element of the body, i.e. spleen, liver and gall bladder and it also controls proper oxygenation. Thus, less functioning of these vital endocrine glands reduces the of resistance power of the body.

This vicious cycle continues. The drugs consumed to cure common cold only increase heat in the body which in turn damages the liver – the radiator of the body. Moreover, due to the continuation of cold for a period of two to three years, even the lungs lose their capacity to throw out toxins gathered from the blood. The net result is that the body develops Allergy for something. The overburdened nerves develop irritation against certain things like perfumes, pollen, dust, etc. And so when the patients come in contact with that particular thing; the nerves get excited.

The Allergy point no. 21 on the front and back of the right palm sends signals, one to the liver to slow down its functioning so the excess heat can be produced and the other an SOS to the brain to defend against this enemy. The body knows only one language of defence – it creates Heat. The Brain produces more H + i.e. Histamin. After a while, the brain comes to know that Allergy point had sent a wrong signal and realises that nothing has gone into the system of the body. And so, in order to remove the excess heat from the body it creates cold by taking one atom of oxygen from the air we breathe and mixes it with two atoms of Hydrogen, i.e. H_2O = water. This results in sneezing, watering of the nose and eyes, coughing, vomiting, etc. This fight in the body between the excess heat and cold results in breathlessness, depression, etc. This is not understood and so instead of helping to remove the excess heat and increasing the power of resistance of the body by reducing the deficiency of calcium, drugs like anti-histamin are given to curb the Allergy. For the time being, this process of removing the excess heat from the body is arrested. But very soon, the body starts this process of throwing out the excess heat – which is considered to be another attack of Allergy. The vicious cycle continues. And so, even Adrenal gland is more damaged – which damages oxygenation in the body – creates more breathlessness and creates more and more weakness in the body – leading to more depression and the power of resistance of the body becomes so low that the patient develops Allergy even against microscopic dust.

Now, once we have understood about Allergy, 'cure' is very easy. For immediate cure; give treatment on point no. 21

on the front and back of palm on the right hand – as shown here in the figure of right palm.

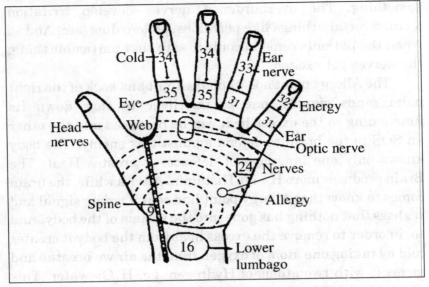

Fig. 60

(2) Start taking Cal. phos 6 or 12 i.e. 3 pills in the morning and 3 pills in the evening – This will reduce the deficiency of calcium.

(3) Take Kali Phos 200 – 8 pills on the first day and then once a week. Then take Kali Phos 12 – 3 pills in the morning and 3 pills in the evening. This Biochemic medicine will soothe the excited nerves, and the Allergy will be under control. During this treatment, drinking of charged water of 2 glasses reduced from 4 glasses is also advisable.

To remove Allergy permanently the patient must do the following :

(a) Treatment to remove the excess heat from the body as mentioned on pages 151 – 165 – 166 of this book.

(b) Drink 2 to 3 cups of green juice adding in it 1 tea spoon of Health Drink + 1 tablespoon of honey. This will supplement Vitamin "C" and digestive power and increase the power of resistance of the body.

(c) Drink 2 glasses of charged water reduced from 4 glasses. This will empower the brain and the resistance power.

(d) and also take the following Bio-chemic salts :

Cal. Phos. 6 or 12 − 3 pills in the morning & evening for 45 days.

Kali Phos 200 − 8 pills once a week.

Kali Phos 12 or 30 − 3 pills in the morning & evening.

(e) Treatment of Acupressure is a MUST.

(f) It is very likely that during this treatment, cold-sneezing may increase − that brings out the suppressed cold and so you need not worry. At that time, take the treatment for Tonsils as mentioned on page 151.

(g) Also take the treatment as mentioned on page 166.

(h) And take Blue Light on the chest and back for 5 to 7 minutes twice a day. That will empower the weakened lungs. It is also advised to do breathing exercise mentioned on page 153.

(i) In case of breathlessness, do the following :

Ask the patient to lie down on the back between 11 A.M. to 4 P.M. and open his/her mouth wide open. And pour 1 tablespoon of honey directly into the throat in such a way that honey does not touch the tongue. And thus, just in 45 days, the body would have built up enough resistance power − removed the deficiency of calcium and also empowered all the endocrine glands. So the patient will become free from Allergy and its fear.

————

CHAPTER 5

CATARACT

To get cataract is a common thing in anybody's life. And due to ageing process, anybody of 55 years or more can get cataract. Previously, the life expectancy in underdeveloped countries like India was less than 50 years. But now this has gone up and so the chances of more people getting cataract is on the rise. Once cataract sets in, the eyes become opaque and unless this cataract is removed, one becomes blind. From the facts given below, one would realise how such a small matter has become a dreaded problem.

"Dr. Allen Jones, Director of Royal Commonwealth Society for the Blind (U.K.) has informed in his address in Mumbai on 24-4-84 that at present there are about 4.9 million blind people in India and every year there is a further addition of 1.3 million blind people. Out of these 1.3 million blind, hardly 2,00,000 are blind by birth or due to infection at the time of birth. About 1 million people become blind due to cataract only. And the others, about 1,00,000 people become blind due to the diseases of the eyes and/or by accidents. This way within 4 to 5 years, there will be over 10 million blind people in India". This is alarming. Now the population has increased and so in India alone, it is feared that about 2.5 million people get cataract. And even when 50% people are operated for removing the cataract, about 1.25 million people become blind due to cataract. It is not true that this problem of cataract exists only in India or similar underdeveloped countries. Even in rich countries like the U.S.A., there are about 20% to 25% people, who get cataract and because they are not insured and so cannot afford such operation to remove cataract, they become blind. Thus, it is quite possible that every year, about 9 to 10 million people get cataract out of whom about 2.5 million people become blind.

However, this dreaded problem of cataract can be tackled. If one eye specialist does five such operations daily to remove cataract, he can do about 1,500 operations in a year (300 days). And to operate on 9 to 10 million cataract patients, it would require about 6,500 eye specialists. The total number of eye specialists in the world is over 15,000. Unfortunately, most of them live in big cities and so the villagers have few chances of being cured of their cataract. If we can harness the services of all the eye specialists and if they do only 20 operations of cataract per day in a year, over 10 million operations for cataract can be performed and just within 4 to 5 years, all the cataract patients can be cured and not a single person will become blind due to cataract. Additionally, if the drive for eye donations is given priority, eye specialists can even perform more and more eye transplantations and thus blindness can be reduced.

Donation of eyes :

Social workers and religious preachers all over the world should make concerted efforts to persuade the people to donate their eyes after their death. When anyone dies, the body is either cremated or buried. Whatever the custom, the valuable eyes are destroyed. These eyes do not help the dead person. Then, why not donate the valuable eyes and earn the satisfaction of giving eyesight to two blind people? Such a donation is more precious than even a donation of a million rupees. It is true that prejudices die hard. But the educated people should reconsider. I appeal to all the progressive people of the world to donate their eyes after death, and persuade others to follow their noble example.

Eradication of cataract :

Such a major problem can be tackled if only we can prevent cataract.

The American Association of Eye Specialists have admitted that "approximately two-thirds of blindness from cataract is of the over 55 years type, for which no cause has been proved. This has been labelled the senile type – a term that unfortunately implies helplessness. More and more people are living long enough to have "senile" cataract. In spite of a great deal of experimental work, the basic causes of senile cataracts in humans are still not clearly understood". According to the Eye Association of the most advanced nation prevention of cataract is not possible.

However, nature's own health science of Acupressure is capable of tackling the problem of cataract and also blindness.

Eyes :

Now in order to understand about cataract, we must know about our eyes. The great role played by Arjun in *Mahabharat* is played by our eyes in our life. Arjun, a great Archer, had a bow called "Gandiv". Nature has provided all of us with this type of bow.

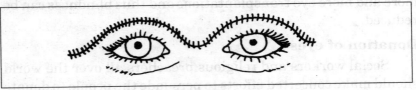

Fig. 61

If perspiration goes in the eyes, it can cause irritation to the eyes. So in order to prevent such perspiration from the forehead from entering the eyes, nature has grown brows over the eyes. Please study carefully the following figure of the eye.

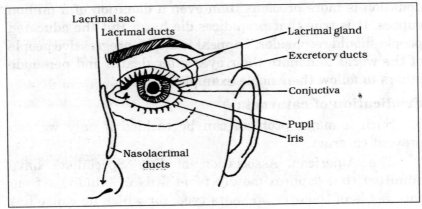

Fig. 62

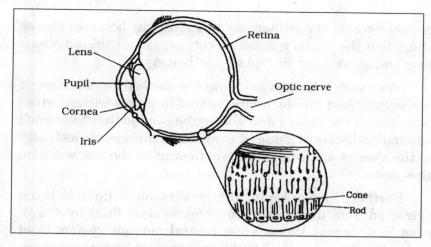

Fig. 63

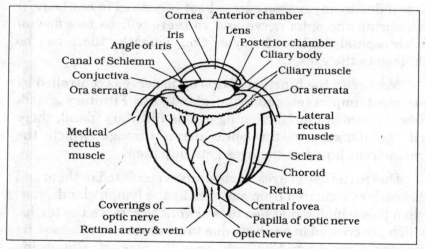

Fig. 64

The working of our eyes is not like an ordinary camera but more like the most sophisticated electronic automatic camera. To adjust the focus, the pupils of the eyes open up. Accordingly, the muscles of the eyes expand or contract to allow proper light inside. Colours are identified and the proper picture develops in our mind. All these processes are automatic.

Now, in all electronic cameras there is a battery so that all the working of camera becomes automatic. If this battery becomes weak, the recharging of flash light becomes slower and when the battery becomes very weak, all the functions stop and so we have to replace the battery.

Now, such a battery is created in our body at the time of conception. And the electricity created from this battery, gives power to all the organs and also to the eyes so that they work automatically. Now, if due to any reason, the flow of electricity to the eyes is disturbed, the functioning in the eye will also slow down.

Further, in our brain, the cerebrospinal fluid is being extracted from the blood. This cerebrospinal fluid rotates in most vital organs through the central nervous system. And such nutrition is supplied to the eyes through the optic nerves. Now if due to any reason excess heat is created in our body, it can shrink the optic nerve and so there will be less flow of cerebrospinal fluid to the eyes. Consequently, there can be damage to the eyes.

Moreover, the function of this optic nerve is controlled by our most important endocrine gland – the Pituitary gland. Now, in case of malfunctioning of this Pituitary gland, there will be damage to the optic nerve through which the transparent liquid in the eyes gets nutrition.

Due to the use of eyes, carbon-toxin is created in them and this carbon is cleared from our eyes by the lymph gland. Now, when this lymph gland has to overwork to remove the toxins, which are created in our body due to other serious diseases, its function slows down. Similarly, even the process of removing the carbon from the eyes also slows down.

Root Causes of cataract :

Thus, the root causes of cataract are :

(1) Lesser supply of electricity to the eyes.

(2) Damage in the optic nerve, or to Pituitary gland, when the eyes do not get enough nutrition and

(3) Slower function of the lymph gland, the removal of the toxins-carbons from the eyes becoming lesser and lesser.

(4.) When Diabetes continues for a long time, there is deficiency of glucose in the cerebrospinal fluid and so the eyes do not get enough glucose to work efficiently and throw out the carbon.

So, when there is an increase of carbon in the transparent liquid of the eyes, the vision is reduced, i. e. becomes hazy. This is the beginning of cataract. Now, because of the internal pressure, the carbon starts gathering around the lens of the eyes – diminishing its transparency. Later on, when more carbon is pressed – gathers behind the lenses, the

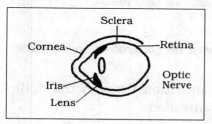

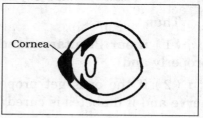

Fig. 65   **Fig. 66**

Picture showing how cataract is formed

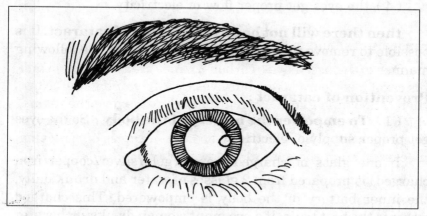

Fig. 67

Picture showing cataract in the eye

transparency is blocked – the lenses become opaque. And operation of cataract is performed and brownish jelly-like substance – carbon is removed.

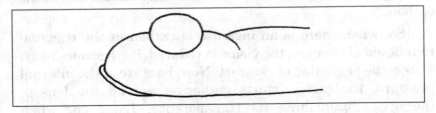

Fig. 68
Picture showing jelly like cataract after removal

Thus,

(1) if our Pituitary gland can be controlled to function properly and

(2) if the eyes get proper nutrition through the optic nerve and if diabetes is cured / controlled.

(3) if the lymph gland is made to function normally, so all the carbon from the eyes is properly removed and

(4) the eyes get proper flow of electricity.

then there will not be any formation of cataract. It is possible to remove the root causes of cataract in the following manner :

Prevention of cataract :

(1) **To empower the battery of the body :** So the eyes get proper supply of electricity :

If one glass of charged water (gold/silver/copper/iron charged) is prepared from 2 glasses of water and drunk daily, the inner battery of the body is empowered. This charged water is the best tonic. If a pregnant woman drinks such water throughout pregnancy, the possibility of the child becoming blind becomes very remote. Moreover, if the foetus develops properly – physically and mentally; the possibility of the child becoming retarded, getting polio, deafness, muscular dystrophy and even hereditary diseases is greatly reduced.

And so after the age of 50, drinking of such water is advised. That will keep the battery powerful and eyes will get enough supply of electricity. Moreover, all the organs of the body will also be reactivated and with the daily treatment of Acupressure, even the ageing process can be slowed to a great extent.

(2) Refer to figs. 16 & 69 and you will observe that it shows the points of all the working organs and endocrine glands on the front palms and on the back are shown of nerves, spinal cord and optic nerve.

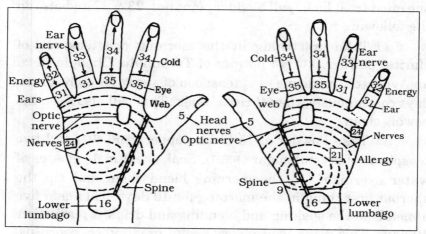

Fig. 69

Now, if the palms are pressed on both the sides for five to six minutes once daily, all the organs are reactivated, all the endocrine glands are controlled and when the point of optic nerve is also pressed, it is activated and so it supplies nutrition from the brain to the eyes properly.

(3) Moreover, when excess heat H+ is created in the body, this important optic nerve shrinks and its working is impaired. In order to remove such H+, the body mixes two atoms of hydrogen with one atom of oxygen and so H_2O (water) is formed and this water is thrown out of the body in the form of Common cold. As we are not aware that this Common cold is beneficial to our body, we suppress it with powerful drugs—

pain killers and antibiotics. Consequently, instead of excess heat being removed from the body, more heat is created in the body damaging the optic nerve.

Moreover, the function of the liver/gall bladder is not properly understood. They work in our body like a radiator in a car. If they do not function properly, acidity increases in the body – thereby excess heat is generated and consequently eyes are damaged. **Thus, you will observe that there is a direct relation between the liver and eyes.**

And so, in order to remove this excess heat from the body, one must treat liver/gall bladder point nos. 23 & 27 and also do the following :

(a) Take first thing in the morning one teaspoon of Haritki powder (हरडे चुर्ण Powder of Terminalia Chebula Retz, an Ayurvedic medicine) + $\frac{1}{2}$ teaspoon of sugar for eight to ten days continuously, then thrice a week. This will also keep the bowels clean.

(b) Take Powder of 15 black pepper (काला मरी) and two teaspoons of crystal sugar (मीसरी). Soak them in $1\frac{1}{2}$ glasses of water overnight. In the morning blend them and sip the sherbat first thing in the morning for 10 days. Then add five almonds to the soaking and blending and drink it for further 10 days. This drink is also very useful in jaundice, psoriasis, sunstroke and for removing excess heat due to chemotherapy, etc.

(c) Take 5 black pepper (काला मरी) 10/12 black raisins (काली द्राक्ष – मनुका) + 1 teaspoon of saunf (सौंप). Soak them in a glass of water overnight. Next day, blend them and drink it in the afternoon. It is a useful drink in summer.

(d) Take equal quantity of cumin seeds (जीरा), black pepper (काला मरी), saunf (सौंप), Amla powder (आमला), crystal sugar (मीसरी), ginger powder (सुंठ). Grind them into powder and keep in a bottle. Take one teaspoon of this powder with water in the morning and evening.

(e) Moreover, in the analysis of the transparent liquid of the eyes, it has been found that it contains a large quantity of vitamin C and glucose, also a small quantity of vitamin B complex and very little quantity of phosphorus. In order that this important liquid of eyes gets proper nutrition, one is advised to do as under :

Take sprouted Chinese green peas (मुंग) + green leafy vegetables like spinach, tandaljo (तांदळजो), fenugreek (मेथी) + cabbage + carrot + green coriander leaves + any leafy vegetables/non-poisonous leaves – crush them/blend them and in one cup of such juice add one teaspoon of health powder (i.e. mixture of 300 grams of amla powder + 100 grams of ginger powder) + one tablespoon of honey and drink it twice a day.

(4) To activate the lymph gland, give Acupressure treatment on its point no. 16 for a minute in the morning and evening. Take proper treatment for any serious diseases, like cancer, venereal diseases and HIV/AIDS infection. And if this lymph gland starts working properly, it will be able to clear the carbon from the eyes. Consequently, the possibility of getting cataract will become remote.

(5) Moreover, if diabetes continues for a long time, the percentage of glucose required in the cerebrospinal fluid becomes less and so there is a considerable reduction in the amount of glucose supplied to the eyes and that causes damage to the eyes and the retina.

This Diabetes can be cured as under :

(1) Drink two glasses of gold/silver/copper/iron charged water reduced from four glasses.

(2) Drink $\frac{1}{2}$ cup of fresh juice of green coriander leaves as the first thing in the morning for 35/40 days. After 10 days, check the glucose content in the blood. When it is found to be reduced, stop the medicine for the diabetes slowly in five to ten days. Within 35 to 40 days, this diabetes will be brought under control.

(3) Chew the food thoroughly.

(4) Take Acupressure treatment and activate the endocrine glands – including the Pancreas.

If such proper care is taken, not only cataract, but even the possibility of one's getting glaucoma will be greatly reduced.

Glaucoma :

Now in case one has already got glaucoma, or damage to retina, when pressed you will find pain on the points of optic nerve and those of eyes point no. 35. At that time, the above-mentioned treatment will be able to cure this disease.

Cure for the beginning of cataract :

(1) When cataract starts forming in the eyes, first the vision becomes hazy. At that time, it is advised to do as mentioned earlier and that will cure this beginning of cataract.

(2) Moreover, healthy urine (which does not contain either sugar or pus) – should be collected in the morning and allowed to cool down. Then fill it in an eye-glass and wash the eyes by opening and closing – by blinking the eyes in the urine.

This experiment of self urine was tried by India's former Prime Minister Shri Morarjibhai Desai at the age of 67, when cataract had just begun forming in his eyes. So for further 25 years, he could avert the operation to remove his cataract.

(3) Rub one black pepper with water on clean stone and apply it in the eyes. There will be burning sensation – water will come out of the eyes. And along with it the carbon in the eyes will get diluted and removed in 40/45 days.

(4) Put the lemon drops in the eyes twice a day and observe the improvement.

Thus, one can prevent and even cure the beginning of the cataract – at a very low cost and one can do it himself. Consequently, the eyesight can be preserved throughout life. The above mentioned care can also prevent colour blindness and night blindness.

Now, when we have understood about how to prevent and even cure cataract even if it is set in about 25 to 30 %, then let us understand about eyecare and how to do away with spectacles and eradicate blindness.

Eradication of blindness :

The problem of blindness has grown to a mega size and with each passing day, it is becoming bigger. However, Acupressure can play a great role in defeating this dreaded dragon and that too without any cost. Let us examine how it can be done.

Causes of Blindness :

(1) A child can become blind in mother's womb.

(2) At the time of delivery, the baby's eyes catch the germs from the vagina – if mother has infection there and if not treated immediately, the baby loses eyesight.

(3) Due to diseases of the eye, the eyesight is lost.

(4) Due to cataract, one can become blind.

(5) Due to accidents.

(1) **Blindness in mother's womb** : The foetus develops eyes in the third month. And if at that time, there is neglect and lack of proper nutrition, child's eyes do not develop properly and so the child becomes blind from birth.

Now, as mentioned earlier, if the expectant mother, in the second month, starts pressing her two palms – both the palms 5 minutes each daily, she will be able to prevent any disease, her health will remain good and there would be proper development of the child in the womb.

Moreover, she should drink copper/silver/gold/iron charged water at least one glass reduced from two glasses every day; or at least two cups of green juice.

Just by doing these two things, there will be proper development of the child and so the possibility of blindness or even mental retardation, polio, muscular dystrophy and hereditary diseases will be greatly reduced. And thus, the birth rate of blind children can be reduced to a great extent. Later on, there will be possibility of giving eyesight to this small number of blind children with eye transplantations.

Shri G. S. Sharma, an Ayurvedacharya reports, "A lady in Kolkata, twice gave birth to sightless children. Third time, when she was pregnant, she started taking charged water from the second month till delivery. She gave birth to a healthy child with perfect vision."

(2) **Due to infection** : The expectant mother should have a medical examination before delivery and should take treatment for vaginal infection or venereal diseases. And immediately after the birth of the child, treatment should be given to the child's eyes, so that it does not lose the eyesight due to the mother's infection. The nurses and midwives in the rural areas should be trained for this treatment.

It is unpardonable that a child with fully developed eyes should lose the eyesight only because of such infection. The total responsibility for this is of the father and mother. With proper care before and after the delivery, we can prevent blindness due to this factor.

(3) **Eye Diseases** : If proper care is not taken of the eye diseases which appears mild or wrong treatment is given, there is a possibility of losing the eyesight. Moreover, if regular treatment is taken on point no. 35, the possibility of getting disease of the eyes like watering and reddishness, etc. will be very less.

(4) **Due to cataract** : About 80% of blindness is due to cataract. In this chapter, this matter is discussed at length by which we can prevent cataract and which will enhance the chances of operations of cataract of those unfortunate blind people.

At this stage, it is the bounden duty of the Governments of all the nations to prohibit all eatables and drinks which damage the eyes, e.g., vegetable hydrogenated oil, margarine, etc. While manufacturing these items, the manufacturers add hydrogen in a faulty way and it has been found from the experiments on rats, that they become blind in 3rd to 5th generation. In the same way, humans also can suffer from blindness within five generations.

Thus, in all other cases except blindness caused by accidents, **blindness can be prevented.** Very few people will remain blind. If more people donate eyes, these few blind persons can also be given sight with eye transplantation.

Now, that cataract can be cured and blindness can be eradicated, let us see how to take proper care of our precious eyes. Just do the following :

1. Splash cold water on closed eyes three to four times a day. If possible, keep the eyes in eyeglass filled with cold water and blink the eyes for two minutes three to four times a day. (See fig. 70)

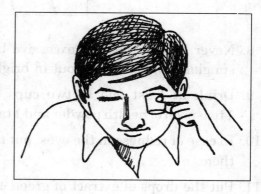

Fig. 70

2. Apply a little saliva in both the eyes when you get up in the morning.

3. Before retiring in the night, apply ghee made of milk of a black cow, if available.

4. Add a grain of alum to 8 oz. of rose-water, shake it well and put these drops in the eyes.

5. Give Acupressure treatment on point no. 35 of the eyes and that of the optic nerves – along with the treatment of all the endocrine glands. This will activate the eyes and prevent and cure any disease of the eyes.

6. Make a regular practice of blinking the eyes. And never watch the cinema or TV at a stretch, without blinking the eyes.

7. Do palming for a few minutes of the eyes two to four times a day. (See fig. 71)

Fig. 71

8. Never read in poor or excessive bright light. And wear sunglasses when going out in bright sunlight.

9. Drink at least one to two cups of green juice adding 1 teaspoon of health powder and 1 tablespoon of honey in it.

10. In case of redness in the eyes, put the pack of cold milk on them.

11. Put the drops of extract of green coriander leaves.

12. Drops of cooled self urine can be put in the eyes. Or the morning self urine, when cooled can be filled in the eyeglass and eyes should be blinked in it for two minutes. This also cures the cataract if it is in the beginning stage.

13. Cure problems of liver and acidity and also that of excess heat in the body.

14. **Take proper care of teeth :** In case one gets pyorrhoea, the toxin from the mouth goes into stomach with the saliva and upsets the stomach. Not only that, but it damages the transparent fluid in the eyes. In case of Pyorrhoea (getting bad smell from the mouth) you may immediately do the following :

Cure :

Fill up the mouth with morning's first urine and wobble for 5 minutes. Then gargle with lukewarm water. To a good toothpowder add 10% alum+10% fine salt+10% Mahasudarshan powder and use it as a toothpowder, thrice a day (after each meal and in the morning). Then massage castor oil (otherwise coconut oil or any edible oil) on the gums. After every meal, take a little salt and chew it, then gargle. It is more beneficial to add $\frac{1}{4}$ lemon in water for gargling. That gives freshness to the mouth. Within 30/45 days, this problem can be overcome.

15. Give pressure treatment around the eyes as shown in fig. 72 shown here two to three minutes on each eye thrice a day. Pressure is to be given on the bones around the eyes and not on the eye ball.

    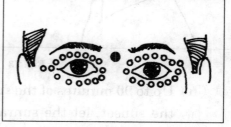

    Fig. 72

    Also give pressure treatment on the points of optic nerves and points no. 3 & 4 of pituitary and pineal glands and on point no. 35. This will help reduce the optical number of spectacles.

16. Make a mixture of 300 grams of amla powder + 100 grams of ginger powder + 200 grams of pure honey. And eat one tablespoon of it every morning followed by one cup of hot milk and repeat the same in the evening.

17. Do some exercises for the eyes as follows :

(a) Up to 30 minutes of sunrise or 15/20 minutes before sunset, let the sunrays fall directly on the eyes. At that time roll your eyes in a clockwise and anticlockwise direction.

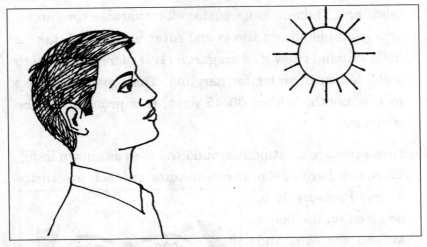

Fig. 73

(b) Up to 90 minutes of the sunrise or 60 minutes before the sunset, let the sunrays fall on the closed eyes. Then do palming of the eyes for a few minutes.

(c) During the moon nights of 8th to 23rd moondays, lie down on your back and while blinking, see the moon for 10 to 15 minutes. The eyes will get great relief.

(d) As per fig. 74 given below, close the eyelids in such a way that there is pressure on the eyes. Keep in this position for 15/20 seconds, then remove this pressure and keep the eyes closed for 15/20 seconds. Repeat thrice.

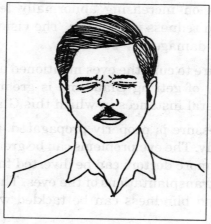

Fig. 74

(e) Do the lion's pose as per fig. 75 given here for 30/40 seconds.

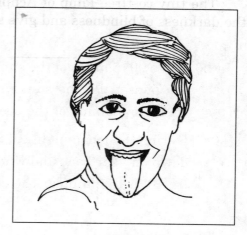

Fig. 75

If these instructions are followed properly, one would not get spectacles and even if anybody has got spectacles up to −4 (minus four number); they will be able to get rid of the spectacles in a few months.

Glaucoma :

When the eyes do not get proper supply of electricity, the muscles in the upper corner of the eyes or the end of the passage for letting out the transparent liquid of the eyes, get contracted and so the pressure in the liquid inside the eyes goes on increasing abnormally leading to severe headaches and redness in the eyes. The vision is blurred and then retina is damaged.

Now, if care to cure the eyes mentioned as above is taken, the possibility of getting Glaucoma is greatly reduced. And there are several instances in which this Glaucoma is cured.

If Acupressure is properly propagated, more people will become healthy. The eye problems can be greatly reduced, and so services of more doctors can be diverted to do operations of cataract and transplantations of the eyes. These eye problems of cataract and blindness can be tackled within five to ten years.

The tiny costfree lamp of Acupressure can thus remove the darkness of blindness and give sight and happiness.

———

CHAPTER 6

DIABETES

According to the medical world, Diabetes is more dangerous than even cancer, in the case of which comparatively fewer people suffer from it and further it remains local. Only in the case of blood cancer it affects different organs. While in the case of Diabetes, it affects the organs of the body one by one and quite a number of people suffer from this dreaded disease. Once Diabetes sets in the body, the patient's life becomes miserable, as he has to avoid the pleasant taste of sweets and has to take care of his diet throughout life. Moreover, this disease is considered to be hereditary.

When Diabetes crosses the level of 2 %, it starts damaging many organs like kidneys, brain, heart, retina and does not allow the injuries to heal up fast. Moreover, if one of the parents is a diabetic, when the child is conceived the child to be born surely has some trouble from the birth-retardation, blindness, deafness and so dumbness, juvenile diabetes, etc. It is, therefore, absolutely necessary to know about this dreaded disease, Diabetes.

Glucose/Sugar :

Our body requires glucose for energy. Nature has put such glucose in fruits, cereals, milk, honey, etc. and so if these foods are consumed in their natural way, their fructose is easily digested when mixed with saliva. Therefore, in order to PREVENT Diabetes, it is most necessary to chew every bite at least 15 times. This habit of chewing should be formed and taught to the children from their early age. If such habit of chewing is formed, one can enjoy sweet items of food throughout life without worrying about Diabetes.

How Diabetes sets in :

In our body Pancreas, one of the endocrine glands, produces insulin and that digests the glucose/sugar from the food/drink we take. Such digested glucose gets mixed in the blood. Now, when blood goes to the brain, there is a special process of manufacturing cerebrospinal fluid – an extract from the blood. During such extraction, glucose is also extracted and mixed with cerebrospinal fluid. It has been found out that –

100 ml of Cerebrospinal fluid contains :

Protein   15 to 45 mg.
Glucose   40 to 50 mg.
Chloride   7.20 to 7.5 mg.
Cells   0.5 to 1 lymphocytic, etc.

In about every $5\frac{1}{2}$ hours, 125 ml of cerebrospinal fluid is produced, i. e. about 545 ml of cerebrospinal fluid and 200 to 250 ml of glucose is produced in 24 hours. Now this cerebrospinal fluid circulates in the body through the central nervous system and gives necessary energy – created from glucose to the main functioning organs.

Now due to tension or high blood pressure (which is a symptom of something seriously wrong in the body), this process of extracting glucose from the blood is weakened or damaged, and so instead of extracting all the glucose from the blood leaving only 75 to 1.2 % glucose in the blood (which is considered to be normal level in the blood – in fasting test), less glucose is extracted and so the blood which goes back in circulation contains more glucose/sugar and increases the level of glucose and when blood is tested this unextracted glucose is found in such testing, e. g. 1.5 to 5.00 % and even up to 6 % in some cases. Thus when the level of glucose at the time of fasting test goes over 1.2 % and remains so continuously for a long period, it is said that Diabetes has set in and the patient is called a Diabetic.

In further research, it has been found that when the percentage of glucose increases more than 2 %, it damages the kidneys and glucose is then found in the urine of the patient.

Second root cause of Diabetes :

When more sugar is consumed regularly and Pancreas

has to overwork for a longer period, this endocrine gland gets tired and works less, so less insulin is produced. Thus, sugar/glucose is not properly digested and its level in the blood increases. This extra glucose in blood is not being extracted in the brain and thus the level of sugar increases in the blood. As under the popular therapies, Pancreas cannot be reactivated, the patient is told to take proper care of diabetes throughout life and to forgo the pleasure of sweet taste. The patient is kept on drugs-pills at first and for careless patients or in the case of gynaecological problem or some other serious problems in the body, when the level of sugar remains high in spite of pills for Diabetes, the patient has to take injections of insulin.

Third Root cause of Diabetes :

When unnecessary heat increases in the body (called तजागरमी in Ayurveda), it affects the Pancreas resulting in less production of insulin leading to Diabetes. At that time, one gets excessively thirsty.

These facts are not understood. In India, such diabetic patients are given bitter powder that increases more desire for sweets and if control is kept on the intake of sweets, Diabetes comes under control, but not cured.

How to find about Diabetes :

When any person gets :
(a) More and more tired.
(b) Gets excessive thirst.
(c) Calf muscles are constantly paining.

one needs to check up his Diabetes. The doctors advise to get sugar test for blood and urine regularly.

According to Acupressure, such test can be done at home without any cost.

(1) Press on point no. 16 of the Lymph gland (see figs. 16 (a), (b) & 76). If it is not hurting, when pressed, it means that the sugar level in blood is normal. So, try to find out the other root cause for the above symptoms.

(2) When you press little hard on point no. 16 and there is slight hurting, it denotes that sugar/glucose level in blood is more than normal.

With practice, one can easily find out the sugar level in the blood with the help of this chart.

Chart No. 1

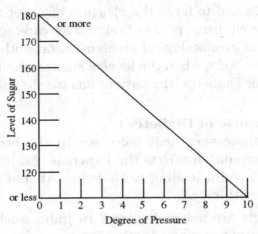

Fig 76 : Unit of Pressure

When on slight pressure say on unit 1 this chart if there is pain on point no. 16, it denotes that the sugar level is around 200 and when pressed, there will be pain on point no. 25 (of Pancreas). At that time, if urine test is done, sugar will be found.

When there is pain on point no. 16 and also on point no. 25, the sugar level is more than 200 and with the help of the following chart, one can find out approximately the sugar level in blood.

Chart No. 2

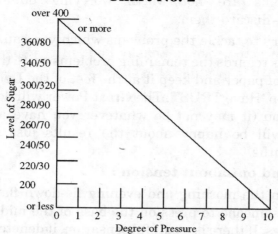

Fig. 77 : Unit of pressure on point nos. 16 & 25

At our Free Centre at Arya Samaj, Linking Road, Santacruz (West), Mumbai – 400 054, whenever any patient informs me about Diabetes, I tell the patient not to tell me how much the sugar level is. I press their point nos. 16 and 25 and tell them the present level of glucose in their blood.

Accordingly, such reading has been within a range of plus or minus 2 %. The patients are just surprised. After trying the method on thousands of patients of Diabetes, the above charts are prepared. And with experience, one will be able to find out almost accurately the level of glucose in the blood without any test.

Cure :

Do not panic, when you get Diabetes, one by one all the main three factors / root causes of the diabetic can be removed and **Diabetes can be CURED within 35 to 40 days.**

How to remove tension :

To stop worrying and to be free from tension do as mentioned below :

(A) Write down on a paper all your problems which worry you very much. Then you will realise that most of the problems are not worth worrying but are just imaginary – discard them.

(B) Try to tackle the problems which you can.

(C) As regards the remaining problems write them down on a piece of paper and keep it at the feet of the Deity, whom you worship. Have TRUST. The Great Power will do which is good for you (it may not be whatever you have asked for) and you will be happy about the results just in a few weeks/months.

How to find out about tension :

(D) In the morning and evening lie-down flat on your back. Ask someone to press on the base of the middle toe in both the legs. If there is a painful sensation, it denotes nervous tension. If the pain is unbearable, it means that the person is on the verge of collapse and needs immediate attention.

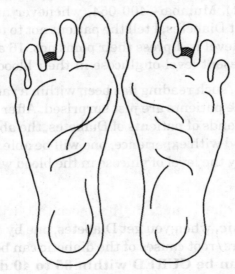

Fig. 78 : How to find out about tension

Cure :

(1) While the patient is lying on the back, bend all the toes of both the legs backwards. This may hurt, but give little more pressure and bend these toes as much as possible. Repeat this three times till tension is cured.

(2) Clasp your hands tightly, interlocking the fingers. Then with the left hand fingers press on the back of the right palm and then with the right hand fingers press on the back of the left palm. Repeat for about 1 to 2 minutes , – 3 to 4 times a day.

(3) Whenever possible, lie down flat on the back relaxing all the muscles of the body – keep the eyes and mind closed for 15 minutes each time (शवासन) like a corpse. You will get much relief.

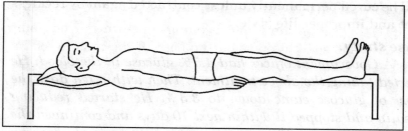

Fig. 79

How to activate Pancreas :

(A) Give acupressure treatment – pressing intermittently not only on point no. 25 of the Pancreas but also on the points of all the endocrine glands.

(B) Drink 2 glasses of gold / silver / copper / iron charged water reduced from 4 glasses of water everyday.

How to reduce excess heat and reactivate proper production of insulin :

(A) As the first thing in the morning, drink $\frac{1}{2}$ cup (2 ounces) of fresh juice of green coriander leaves. Avoid any food / drink for the next 15 / 20 minutes.

(B) OR in case green coriander leaves are not available take 2 lady's fingers (भींडी) cut them in half – soak then in half a cup of water. Keep it overnight, squeeze them in the morning – strain this water. The sticky water covers the inside wall of the stomach and prevents sugar being sucked from the stomach. And thus helps in curing Diabetes.

(C) During the day, drink 2 to 3 cups of green juice adding in each cup 1 teaspoon of mixture of 300 grams of Amla powder (a fruit grown in India having 16 times more vitamin 'C' than 16 lemons)+100 grams of dry ginger powder.

The net effect of all these treatments will be that just within 10/12 days, Diabetes will be arrested. Now go on reducing the intake of tablets, pills of insulin injections in such a way as to stop all the other medication within 10 days.

Continue the treatment for 35 to 40 days and Diabetes will be cured permanently unless contracted again by reckless diet and improper life style.

Case study:

A Government officer had 4.5% glucose in the blood. He started taking the above treatment. Then within ten days the level of glucose came down to 3.5%. He started reducing insulin and stopped it within next 10 days and continued the treatment. On the 36th day, he got a full medical check-up done to find that the sugar level was normal in fasting as well as post lunch tests. Before the treatment, he was not able to walk. Now he walks 6 to 8 kilometres at a stretch.

Diet :

After Diabetes is cured, eat any type of food you can digest—you can take some sweets/icecream; but chew properly and avoid over-eating.

Continue Acupressure and drink 2 cups of green juice.

Do some exercise daily. Swimming and walking are good exercises.

Lead a normal life and forget worrying about Diabetes.

Juvenile Diabetes :

When the mother/father has serious problem of Diabetes/Venereal disease/Cancer/Gynaecological problem/Thalassemia/HIV/AIDS, etc. the child in the womb is affected. And so, they may be born with Diabetes. As such, parents having any of the above problems should get their children checked up as early as possible, for Diabetes. And if

Diabetes is detected the above mentioned treatment has to be started. Along with this treatment, it is most necessary to keep the child away from any tension and proper treatment be given for any other serious problem, if any. Please note that Juvenile Diabetes can easily be cured.

Case study:

One gentleman phoned me from Kolkata about the cure of Diabetes for his 8-year-old daughter, who was found to have 5.5% sugar in blood. I suggested the cure – to read my book and follow it. After four weeks the happy father informed me that the level of glucose has come down to 1.5%. The girl was then sent to school. She was absent for 30 days and so had to work hard to cope with the lost studies – that created tension and the glucose level went up to 2.1%. I asked the father to stop sending her to school and allow the girl to relax. And within just 3 weeks, this juvenile Diabetic was cured. Then, I asked the parents to inform me if they had observed pain on point nos. 37 – 16 – 11 to 15 and they admitted that they had. In fact this was an indication of HIV / AIDS. So they were also asked to take treatment and desist from having another child for at least two years. The result, they are extremely happy today.

This incident clearly shows the effect of tension on the sugar level.

Glucose :

It is a vital source of energy in the body. It is also the only source of energy for the brain. It is observed that many people observe strict diet restrictions and create a starvation of glucose. That leads to low blood pressure, dullness, loss of interest in all activities of life, including sex.

In fact, sugar / glucose should be consumed in its natural form, chewed properly and digested.

Honey :

In many cases honey is given to Diabetic patients without any bad effects or increase in the sugar level.

Mankind need not worry about Diabetes, which can be easily defeated in a month. Let man enjoy sweet taste and enjoy life to the utmost.

CHAPTER 7

KIDNEY PROBLEMS

Modern age has brought with it an increase in the number of cases related to the kidney problems. Day by day, this problem is growing bigger and bigger and in spite of new equipment for dialysis and operations for transplantation of kidney, it has become a mega problem. The demand for kidneys is so great that it has even lured the doctors to remove kidneys from the innocent, gullible patients and do illegal trading in the same.

Surprisingly, the popular medical therapy has not understood the function of the kidneys and so do not know how to repair the same. They are making a big hue and cry about the same making the poor, illiterate people scared. They have introduced dialysis and operations for transplantation of kidneys and have made it a big business but at the cost of mankind.

It should be noted that kidneys are like metal filters (e.g.-sieve, which we use to filter flour – filter tea, etc.). And these kidneys are supposed to work for a lifetime. Now in case the flour is wet and gets stuck in the holes of the metal filter, further filtering is stopped. At that time do we throw away this metal filter? No. We clean it and use it for a long time. Then why not clean the tiny holes in the kidneys and allow it to function normally for life?

Mother nature is very kind. It has grown tea, and we use it daily without knowing its therapeutic value. Before we learn about the use of tea, let us examine why there is failure of kidneys – or to say correctly how and why the tiny filters of our kidneys are filled up and prevent the function of filtering toxins from the blood.

Today, more importance is given to the heart and less to the most vital organs – lungs. Whatever toxins are gathered in the blood during the circulation, is cleared in the lungs. And only whatever toxins remain uncleared are cleared by the kidneys. More and more attention of mankind is directed towards the taste—more and more restaurants—more fast foods, etc. However, the health department does not care to see the quality of the food—oil, vegetables, spices, etc. used in these hotels and restaurants. Eating of more oily, fried and spicy junk food brings only more toxins in our blood on the one hand and on the other hand, breathing exercises are not followed. Pollution in cities has greatly increased. In the same way, the habit of smoking is increasing in spite of warning. All these have resulted in reducing the capacity of our vital organs, lungs. And so, day by day, the burden on kidneys increases. Moreover, the use of white oil, hydrogenated oil and consumption of certain drugs also directly damage the kidneys.

All these toxins get stuck in the minute holes in the kidneys and slowly and steadily they are not able to clear all the toxins from the blood.

Another root cause of damage to the kidneys is the increase in venereal diseases, gynaecological problem, which develops into cancer of the uterus, cancer of the prostate and HIV/AIDS, etc. In all these serious diseases, toxins in large quantities are produced in the body and bring heavy pressure on the kidneys.

Now when the level of toxins increases in the body above a certain level, it starts breaking the proteins, which produces more of Nitrogen. This vicious cycle goes on and thereby increasing the level of creatinine in the blood. When such a level goes over 8.00 % in the blood, the doctors declare it as failure of kidneys. The patient is asked to go for dialysis.

In the same way, when the water content in the body increases due to its retention and the weight goes on increasing, the doctors consider it to be a failure of kidneys and advise dialysis.

Before dialysis can be started, it is necessary to do operation for the Artery vein, Fistula—called A.V. Fistula, so that through one tube, blood can be sucked into the machine, where it is filtered and through the other tube, the blood can go back into the body. At that time sodium free liquid is mixed/injected into the blood. Now, it is surprising that the patient and his/her relatives are not informed that this operated hand will become totally useless for the rest of life. And if proper care is not taken, about not wearing band/bangle or watch on that hand, not to take any weight, not to keep this arm under the head during sleep, etc. then this operation of A. V. Fistula will have to be done again. Thus after this operation is done, the patient leads a miserable life.

The most regrettable aspect is that the family physician or the expert does not care to find out the root cause for the damage to the kidneys. And so the poor patient remains a patient throughout the life and has to undergo dialysis two times a week in the beginning and then three times a week. And after few months, if creatinine does not come under control, the patient is advised to go for transplantation of the kidney.

Patients who cannot afford to buy a suitable kidney request his/her relatives to donate one of their kidneys, while the rich people buy such a kidney and are involved in the illicit trading of the kidneys. Even after such a transplantation of one kidney, the patient has to take utmost care for three months so that he/she may not get infection.

However, dialysis, and even transplantation of a kidney is not a guaranteed cure. As the root cause is not found out and treated, the toxins go on gathering–increasing in the body and damage the kidney.

During this treatment of kidneys, nobody except the patient and his/her relatives bother about the high cost of such dialysis, which costs about Rs. 1000/- per dialysis in India and even if two dialysis are done in a week the cost of such dialysis comes to Rs. 1,00,000/- per year and the cost of transplantation of a kidney is so much more costly an affair, that very few people can afford it.

Easy cure :

In all such problems about the kidney, one need not worry or panic. This problem is created because of the breach of the laws of nature and inviting diseases and so one must go back to nature and its therapy of Acupressure. Acupressure goes to the root cause to find out why kidneys are damaged, and suggests treatment which can be easily taken at home at no cost. It may be noted that even in the case of blood cancer and HIV/AIDS it takes maximum of 75 to 90 days to set complete cure (Read my books – Health In Your Hands : Volume 1 & 2). And as regards kidneys, the damage can be repaired within just 15 days and that too without cost. The patient can do this treatment at home.

Treatment for curing kidney ailments :

(1) Before starting the treatment, gather the first urine of the patient in the morning in a glass and one will observe that this urine is not clear but hazy and has bad smell. It denotes that the kidneys are not functioning properly.

(2) Put one cup of water to boil. Put one teaspoon of **any tea** in it. Do not add sugar or milk. Boil 1 cup of water till it is reduced to half a cup. Filter it, then add half a cup of regular water. Sip it hot. Regular breakfast can be taken after 15/20 minutes. It is possible that one may get nausea. In that case put some crystal sugar or 1 or 2 cloves in the mouth. Do not worry even if there is vomiting. Continue drinking this black tea for 10/12 days. And again examine the first urine. If it has become clear and there is no bad smell in it, it denotes that the kidneys have started functioning normally, continue the treatment for 15 days.

(3) During the day, drink 2 glasses of silver charged water reduced from 8 glasses of water.

Method for preparing silver charged water :

Put 8 glasses (225 ml about each glass) in a stainless steel or earthen vessel. Put 30 to 40 grams of pure silver coins or a bar of ·999 touch purity in the water. Clean this metal properly before putting it in to the water. (Please do not use silver jewellery or utensil – these generally contain white metal which is very harmful to the kidneys.) Boil the water till it is reduced to 2 glasses. Filter it and keep it lukewarm in a thermos. And drink it three / four times during the day. This silver charged water will reactivate the kidneys, bladder and also help to reduce the excess heat from the body.

(4) Drink 2 to 3 cups of green juice without adding salt or any spice to it.

(5) Perform Acupressure treatment –

Within just 15 days, you will observe amazing results. There will be a proper flow of urine and even if there is stone in the kidneys, that will break and be thrown out through the urine. When the kidneys start functioning properly, it will help the body to clear other toxins.

(6) Remove the root cause. Before starting the treatment for repairing kidneys, find out the root cause and start the treatment for the same at the same time. Within just 50 / 75 days, the root cause will also be cured. Thus, patient will get a new, healthy life.

Retention of water – Water content in the body is controlled by Pineal gland. When there is serious problems like V. D., Cancer, HIV / AIDS, etc. one by one the endocrine glands stop functioning properly and later on Pineal. This malfunctioning of the Pineal gland leads to the retention of water. This is misunderstood as the failure of the kidneys. And doctors restrict intake of water and other liquids. In such cases, when the patient takes proper treatment plus drinking black tea, the Pineal gland starts functioning normally and there is enough flow of urine and the problem of water retention gets cured.

In fact, for the cure of the problem of the kidneys and removing of toxins (which are acidic), it is most necessary to repair the kidneys by drinking black tea, etc. and also increase the intake of green juices (which is alkaline) and which neutralises the acidity of toxins.

Charged water activates all the endocrine glands and organs of the body and thus assists the body to throw out toxins and get itself cured. In his book, 'Spontaneous Healing' Dr. Andrew Weil, eminent M. D. of U. S. A. has proved that body has the capacity to heal itself. So, nature should be allowed to do its work.

More intake of liquids (8 to 10 glasses) and free flow of urine is like a natural way of dialysis.

At this point, it may be noted that when such patients of kidney problems are advised to take 3 to 4 cups of green juice and 2 to 4 glasses of charged water, they ask the opinion of their family physician or the expert under whose treatment they are. And as these doctors are not aware of the great benefits of such green juices and charged water (they have a fear that such metal-charged water will damage the kidneys) hence they advise the patients not to take these green juices or charged water. It may be noted that green juices are alkaline and have great energy and help the body to clear toxins and give energy while in charged water those metals gold/silver/copper and iron are in such a microscopic form that they are not harmful to kidneys but activate all the endocrine glands and organs and thus assist the body to heal itself.

Preventions :

In order to avoid any problem of kidneys, it is advisable to drink the above mentioned black tea for 12 to 15 days in a year. Preferably in cold season, drink plenty of water – 8 to 10 glasses in a day – plus consume 2 cups of green juices. Perform Acupressure and forget any worries about the kidneys.

Case study :

Thousands of patients on dialysis have been benefited and after starting the above mentioned treatment have been able to stop further dialysis and live normal lives. In most of the cases, damage to the kidneys is not even 50% but they have other serious problems.

In the same way in more than 200 cases we have been able to prevent transplantation of kidney and their dialysis. Once a lady of about 35 years of age, came to our centre. She informed that her mother's kidney was found to be suitable, she was going to have operation of the transplantation of kidney only after 10 days. On examination, the kidneys were not found to have been damaged much, but she had cancer of the uterus. She was asked to postpone the operation just for a month and advised treatment. She religiously followed it. After 35 days she went to the same hospital and the experts declared that she was alright and the operation for transplantation of kidneys or even dialysis was not necessary. Thus, very pleased, this lady came to our centre with a purse of Rs. 25,000 /-. It was not accepted and she was advised to donate the amount for whatever purpose she thought proper.

In short, I have to advise mankind not to worry about the problems of kidneys. Go back to nature, get the root cause properly diagnosed and follow Acupressure treatment and be free from this problem about the kidneys in 60 / 70 days and enjoy life.

CHAPTER 8

HEART'S PROBLEMS

Killer No. 1 in the U.S.A. and the World.

Heart is a specially designed muscle – a non-stop pump, so it can work non-stop from birth till death. In fact, it starts functioning from the mother's womb. So, proper care should be taken by the mother to be during pregnancy about her health and diet.

Secondly, the parents to be should correct their hormones – especially sex hormones before a child is conceived. We take great care in selecting the seed to be planted so that the plant becomes strong and gives maximum yield. In the same way, the father to be should take care of purifying and strengthening his semen. In the same way, the mother to be should take care of her ova. If her sex glands are functioning properly, she will have regular menses. This can be done very easily :

(1) Remove excess heat from your body.

(2) drink two glasses of charged water reduced from four glasses of water.

(3) Drink at least 2 to 3 cups of green juice.

(4) Start Acupressure treatment at least 4 months before. That will correct the working of all the organs and also all the endocrine glands.

If this is done religiously, the child to be born will be healthy – no problems about retardation, deafness or dumbness and not even blindness and the possibility of hereditary disease will be reduced to a minimum.

The case of Alexander the Great is well-known. He was born as a weakling. He became an Emperor. But at the age of only 32, he died of Heart Attack.

To know about : (a) How to – prepare charged water; (b) How to remove excess heat; (c) How to prepare green juice.

Please read my book "Health in Your Hands : Volume 1 & 2."

We must know the language of our body. Whenever there is any problem in any organ of the body due to less supply of bioelectricity or gathering of excess toxins around it, that organ informs us through pain. We must immediately give attention to such a notice. In case of Heart, such pain in the chest, Heart inform that its require full rest. And if neglected there is a possibility of Heart Attack. And so instead of getting panicky and rushing to a cardiologist and then as advised by him going into Intensive Care Unit of a Hospital, one can go home and take complete bed rest for 72 to 96 hours. During the rest, one should forget worries, watch comedy shows on TV, read comics, laugh heartily, take light diet (if possible only fruits and green juices-green salads) and listen to soft music, pray to God and take the treatment for the Heart. And to one's astonishment, the Heart will start functioning normally. It may be noted that the pills given in the Hospital contain 50% pain killer and 50% sleeping medicine. They also give medicine to thin the blood—which can be easily done by drinking at least 8 to 10 glasses of water + fruit juices daily. The best medicine for the Heart is complete rest— "SHAVASAN"—lying down like a corpse.

Once, when I was attending a marriage, I saw my relative perspiring profusely—he had also trouble in chatting with me. I immediately checked his heart point no. 36. That point was very tender and painful when pressed. I virtually ordered my relative to go home and take complete bed rest and treatment for the heart which included Acupressure and drinking of charged water. After four days, he went to a cardiologist. After a thorough examination, he told my relative that he had passed through a massive heart attack and heart thereafter was functioning normally. Even after 15 years my relative is hale and hearty at the age of 75 years.

Cholesterol and the blockade in the arteries of the Heart :

Suprisingly, more importance is given to the heart – than to the lungs and liver. Lungs work to purify the blood and the liver neutralizes the toxins. **Moreover, in order to produce bile, the liver uses cholesterol.** So, in case of any problem about high cholesterol, along with change in the diet (light diet), one must pay attention to activate the liver and to do the following :

(1) Press point nos. 22 and 23 those of Gall Bladder and Liver.

(2) Eat 2 pieces of black pepper or clove after each meal.

(3) Eat 1 teaspoon mixture of 50 % powder of dried coriander seeds and 50 % powder of dried cumin seeds (known in India as Dhania – Jira (धनीया-जीरा). This is an anti-oxidant and can be taken throughout life.

(4) Eat a mixture of 50 % powder of Cinnamon + 50 % pure honey – twice a day for 45 to 60 days.

(5) Take Blue light on Liver – stomach area for 4 to 6 minutes twice a day for 12/15 days.

And see the wonderful result just in 15 to 30 days. This treatment is so useful that even if angioplasty or even bypass surgery is advised on the basis of angiography; it will not be required. But along with the above-mentioned treatment, one must take treatment for the heart also. It may be noted that this treatment is tried in the hospitals of Canada and England and wonderful results are obtained. Even in case bypass surgery is again advised, such operations can be averted.

After the birth of a child, proper check-up (which is possible through Acupressure without cost) of its body should be made within three months and if necessary, correct the working of all the endocrine glands and other organs including the heart.

In case any problem is found, even a hole in the heart, it can be corrected e.g. Once a baby was not developing and so was checked by a cardiologist. He found a hole in its heart. As an operation to correct the hole could not be done before the age of twelve, she was asked to see the doctor later on. The mother brought the baby to me. She was advised to take the treatment mentioned for the heart and just within six months, the baby started growing satisfactorily. At the age of twelve, she was again examined by the same cardiologist and he was surprised to observe that there was no more hole in her the heart. And so, the operation was not necessary.

Thus, all types of Heart problems can be corrected – better if detected at an early age. The cure will be faster.

Varicose Veins :

One must understand that the heart is a pump – working non-stop and so it must be maintained in a proper condition – so that pure blood can be sent to all the parts of the body and impure blood is collected back. Now, in the case of a weak heart, if such impure blood cannot be collected properly, the remaining impure blood in the legs and thighs turn into blue varicose veins. And so to cure them, one must take the treatment for the heart.

Pace-maker and improper heart beats :

Now for the working of a pump, electricity is required. In our body, electricity is produced in human atomic reactor of brain. This bioelectricity activates all the organs of the body and also all the endocrine glands and the heart. So long as the heart gets this electricity, it will function properly. We are well aware that in the case of irregular beats of the heart – denoting heart trouble, a pacemaker is placed under the skin near the heart. Such pacemaker, through its installed battery, sends electric current to the heart and keeps it functioning normally. Now in Acupressure, you get the same effect of a pacemaker when you press on the point no. 36 of Heart. Thus, when you make a practice of pressing your both palms daily and thus also pressing the point of heart, you can avoid any problems about the heart.

Enlarged Heart :

Sometimes, the doctors inform the patients that their hearts are enlarged. Nothing to worry about the same. The heart is like a rubber balloon. If it is pressed from the bottom, it will look like being enlarged. In the same way, if the Solar Plexus has shifted upwards, it lifts the diaphragm upwards and that will lift the heart upwards. In such cases, just correct the Solar

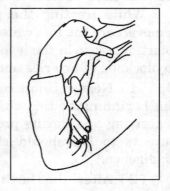

Fig. 80

Plexus and the heart will come to its normal position.

Palpitation or pain in the chest :

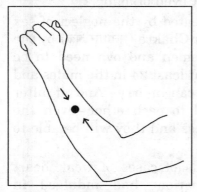

Fig. 81

Such signs denote that the heart requires rest. So, take complete bed rest for 72 to 96 hours. Take the treatment for the Heart. Also press on the back of the arm as shown in the fig. for 1 minute three times a day and the heart will start functioning normally.

Improper circulation of blood :

This is due to less working of Adrenal and Thyroid/Parathyroid glands. These glands can be easily activated through Acupressure. I have observed in many cases about the problems of the heart, the root cause is less functioning of Thyroid/Parathyroid, Sex glands and Adrenal glands, and when corrected, the heart starts functioning normally. It is, therefore, most necessary that the heart functions soundly and properly, these vital endocrine glands should function properly.

Root causes of heart Problems :

While treating the problems of the heart, one must remove/cure the root causes that lead to the weakening of the heart, increase in the level of cholesterol–which in turn leads to blockade of arteries and clotting in the blood.

(1) Neglect before conceiving and during pregnancy : In the beginning of this chapter, care about the heart before conceiving and during pregnancy is already mentioned. The parents to be, should observe such care and avoid any negligence.

(2) After the birth of a child, if proper nutrition, breathing exercises and light physical exercises/outdoor sports and enough rest are taken + Acupressure are taken, the heart will function properly till the last minute of life. There will not be any adverse effect on it even of aging.

(3) The heart problem is created by the neglect of sex glands which are called Mooladhar Chakra (मूलाधार चक्र) by the great Indian Rishis. The vital semen and ova need to be preserved properly till the age of at least 24 in the males and 21 in the females–when they can marry, And if after marriage if both remain faithful to each other–even the frequency of intercourse will be less and they will be able to enjoy happy, blissful marital life.

I have come across hundreds of cases of weak heart problems, because the male patient had indulged in masturbation and female patients had the problem of white discharge. Due to such unnatural ejaculation of vital life enduring substance, excess heat is created in the body. In turn, semen and ova become thin and discharged as nocturnal emission and if at that time proper care is not taken, it develops into uncontrollable discharge of Albumin in the urine. In all such cases, after marriage there is premature ejaculation and so less satisfaction–which in turn leads to increase in the frequency of intercourse–leading to washing out of vital life force. That is why there are more cases of heart attack in the males between the age of 35 to 40 years–this is also confirmed by the WHO. This deficiency can be corrected by taking treatment as mentioned under "Men's Problems" in my book "Health in Your Hands : Volume 1" and restraint in sex.

(4) Improper diet – carelessness – more use of oily-fried eatables and sedentary lifestyle are the main causes of the increase in the level of cholesterol. Today Fast food + ice creams are encouraged + eating between the meals has increased and as such the burden on digestive system – which includes more burden on the liver has increased. Sluggish liver cannot produce enough bile and so enough cholesterol is not consumed by the the liver. This in turn leads to an increase in the level of LDL cholesterol. So, in order to maintain good condition of the heart, balanced diet should be taken. One must also avoid eating/drinking which are harmful to oneself. You can easily find out what eatables/drinks are suitable to you or not – as mentioned in my book "Health in Your Hands : Volume 1, page 120, under "easy way to find out what food/drink its suitable to oneself". Over and above taking a balanced diet, it is necessary to do some light exercise even outdoor sports.

(5) Further, it has been found that improper and excessive use of painkillers leads to the weakening of the heart e. g. Rheumatoid Arthritis. And when such drugs are taken with improper diagnosis, the side effects are quite serious.

(6) In serious diseases like Venereal Diseases, Cancer, HIV/AIDS, impurity of blood or anaemic conditions such as in Thalassemia; Heart is first to be affected. And as such without any negligence, immediate care should be taken to cure these problems. All types of CURES, are possible – Read my book "Health in Your Hands : Volume 1 & 2."

Signal for Heart problem :
When you press on point no. 36 of the Heart and if there is even slight pain, it denotes some developing problems of the heart and so without neglect, immediate care should be taken for the heart and removal of root causes.

In case, there is severe pain on point no. 36 of the heart, it denotes impending heart attack. So immediately take full bed rest for 72 to 96 hours and start Acupressure treatment for Heart.

Treatment for any type of Heart Problems :

(1) Check the Solar Plexus. If it is not in order, correct it. It could be gas trouble. Drink a quarter glass of Soda adding a little of black salt to it.

(2) It can be a muscular pain starting from vertebrae no. 6 to 8 of the spinal column. In such a case, give treatment for 3 to 5 minutes on the point in the middle of the back of the left hand as shown in the fig. 82. Later on, rub eucalyptus oil or pain balm on the chest as well around vertebrae no. 4 to 8 of the spinal column.

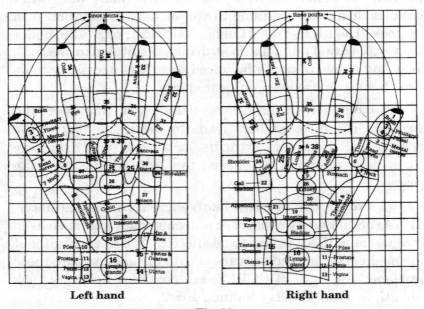

Left hand   Right hand

Fig. 82

If however, there is pain on point no. 36, it means that the cause of the trouble is in the heart. Immediately take bed rest for 72 to 96 hours and start the following treatment.

(a) Give treatment on point no. 36 and point nos. 1 to 5 for two minutes on each point twice a day.

(b) Give treatment on all the other points on each palm for 5 minutes twice a day.

(c) Drink lukewarm concentrated gold/silver/ copper/iron charged water (2 glasses reduced from 8 glasses of water), 2 glasses per day for 1 month. Then daily 2 glasses of such charged water reduced from 4 glasses for further 60 days.

(d) Eat one pomegranate a day. Either eat or drink its juice. Within just 30 days, the level of cholesterol will be normal. For the prevention of any heart problems, you are advised to eat one pomegranate for 30 days every year.

Read history. Even though Mughal Emperors were debaucherous, none got a heart attack; because they had a practice of eating pomegranate or drinking its fresh juice during the season.

(e) Practise Pranayam – breathing exercises as much as possible.

(f) Remove tension – as mentioned in my book "Health in Your Hands."

(g) During the rest, think over your lifestyle. You will be able to trace the root cause. Such a root cause must be removed. Otherwise, there can be another heart attack. Afterwards, lead a normal life, practise Pranayam and do jogging for at least 3 minutes a day. Continue the treatment on point no. 36 once a day.

(h) It has been observed that masturbation in early youth is also one of the root causes of heart attack between the age of 35 to 50 years. With such previous history, please read the chapter for "Men's Problems" and control the sex desire accordingly.

(i) Make a mixture of powders of 100 grams of dried coriander seeds (धनीया) + 100 grams of dried cumin seed (जीरा) Keep it in a bottle. Eat one teaspoon of this powder in the morning and evening for 60 days. This is an anti-oxidant and helps in clearing the blockade, if any. It also controls cholesterol.

(j) Eat a mixture of half a teaspoon of powder of cinnamon + half a teaspoon of pure honey twice a day for 45 to 60 days.

This method was tried on the patients of heart in the hospitals of Canada and England. As this mixture activates liver, the results were surprisingly beneficial. With the treatment taken as per (i) and (j) regularly, one could control the level of cholesterol and thus the heart problem.

(k) Drink at least 2 glasses of green juice (fresh) adding 1 tablespoon of honey in each cup. That can make you EVERGREEN.

(l) Learn Acupressure. That will help you to cure Heart problems anywhere, e. g. My daughter was flying from the U. S. A. to India. She saw the lady sitting beside her feeling very uneasy and heavily perspiring. My daughter immediately pressed on point no. 36 of the heart. She found that point was tender. She started giving lady treatment on point no. 36 of the heart and point no. 1 to 5 of the brain. Just within 5 minutes, the lady got relief and could sleep well and she landed safely in Mumbai to join her doctor husband.

Do not worry or panic even when you find pain in the chest or the heart and are advised angiography and then angioplasty or even Heart's bypass surgery. Try the above treatment for 15 to 30 days and see the wonderful results.

Thus, you will observe that if you just spare 10 minutes a day to press your both palms – each palm for 5 minutes – you will not get the heart problem.

Death is definite and it will come to each one of us some day and at that time the heart will stop. Till then let the heart function properly and give us good health and happiness.

———

CHAPTER 9

THALASSEMIA

This dreaded disease is primarily found in children. When it develops further, and considered to be Thalassemia Major, the blood of the young patients has to be changed every 45 to 30 days. These patients require costly injections. And tragedy is such, that in spite of all these treatments, these patients do not survive long.

The root causes are mainly :

(1) Children of parents who have Thalassemia Minor.

(2) One of the parents is suffering from a venereal disease, or has HIV infection.

(3) The blood group of parents does not match.

(4) In certain communities, there is intermarriage within the family.

On examining these patients, it is found that their digestive organs, stomach, liver, gall bladder are sluggish; their blood producing vital organ of spleen is badly damaged, their endocrine gland of Thyroid/Parathyroid and Sex glands are damaged and so deplete the supply of calcium and phosphorus. Later on, even the Adrenal and Pancreas glands are damaged and so these patients even get diabetes. Under the popular medical therapy there is **No Cure.** The worried unhappy parents have just to watch their children suffer.

Acupressure can play an important role – first in early detection of this disease and then curing it within 60 to 90 days.

Early diagnosis :

When any child looks pale or is not developing satisfactorily, just look into his / her eyes. These eyes will look pale whitish. At that time check for worms and, if necessary, cure it as narrated in Chapter 4, page 181 of "Health in your Hands : Volume 1."

In the case of Thalassemia, check point no. 37 of the spleen, point no. 27 of the stomach, point nos. 22, 23 of the gall bladder and liver and point no. 8 of the Thyroid/Parathyroid. And if these points are painful, it denotes Thalassemia. Thus, even in small children, without exposing them to painful tests, this disease can be easily detected at an early stage.

Cure :

Please read the next chapter about cancer. All the possible treatment mentioned therein for blood cancer is to be given to these patients, i.e.

(a) 4 glasses of gold / silver / copper / iron charged water reduced from 16 glasses. In case of children below 5 years, give about 2 glasses of such water reduced from 8 glasses.

(b) Give 2 to 3 cups of green juice adding in each cup one teaspoonful of health powder + 1 tablespoonful of pure honey.

(c) 1 to 2 glasses of fruit juices.

(d) Plenty of green salad adding therein sprouted *mung* (green Chinese peas), nuts and jaggery (गुड़).

(e) Stop all salts and spices and cooked food wherever possible. Also stop milk, chocolates, biscuits and bread made out of fine flour. If the child cannot remain on this diet, give it well-cooked rice with curd – boiled vegetables and a pinch of rock salt.

(f) Drink the extract of the following first thing in the morning :

21 leaves of bitter neem with stalk.

21 leaves of 'tulsi' with stalk.

21 leaves of 'bilipatra' (7 × 3) with stalk.

Add honey in this juice.

If such leaves are not available, tincture of same in availale at Homoeopathic shops. Take $\frac{1}{2}$ oz. each and mix them in a bottle. Take 5 drops of this mixture in half a cup of lukewarm water in the morning and evening. This is a powerful blood purifier and found very useful in blood cancer.

(g) After 12 to 15 days when the child gets very hungry, give it two to three cups of curds adding crystal sugar, if desired or a pinch of rock salt, whichever is found to be suitable.

(h) Take blue light on the stomach for five minutes and on the back, neck and spine for five minutes twice daily. This will revitalise these organs.

The mixture of powder/pills of the following Biochemic medicines :

Cal flour	$12 \times \frac{1}{2}$ oz.	Kali Phos	$12 \times \frac{1}{2}$ oz.
Cal. Phos	$12 \times \frac{1}{2}$ oz.	Natrum Mur	$12 \times \frac{1}{2}$ oz.
Ferrum Phos	$12 \times \frac{1}{2}$ oz.		

is to be made and $\frac{1}{2}$ gram of powder OR 3 pills of this mixture is to be given thrice a day for 45 days. Stop medicine for 15 days and if necessary, repeat.

If worms are found, give treatment for the same as mentioned on page 183 of "Health in Your Hands : Volume 1". Further to improve digestive system, give Nux Vomica 200 − 4 to 6 pills once a week

Nux Vomica 12 or 30 − 3 pills twice daily.

How to increase haemoglobin :

Moreover, the following treatment is a must for these patients :

Take black dried raisins (काला मनुका) as may be required daily. Soak them in half a cup of water overnight. Eat these black raisins as mentioned below and drink the water.

	Morning	Afternoon	Evening
1st day	1	1	1
2nd day	2	2	2
3rd day	3	3	3
4th day	4	4	4
5th day	4	4	4
6th day	4	4	4
7th day	3	3	3
8th day	2	2	2
9th day	1	1	1

Check the level of haemoglobin in the blood. If necessary repeat as above after nine days and continue in the same manner, till the haemoglobin level is satisfactory. This treatment can also be given to all the patients of cancer, TB, paralysis, arthritis, brain problems and in case of acute anaemia and to all the children, with haemoglobin deficiency.

In case of breastfed infants, the mother has to take the treatment.

Case Study :

In Bangalore, One child suffering from Thalassemia – major had to be given blood every 20 days. Treatment was started. The development was so satisfactory that after just 60 days , further transfusion of blood was not necessary. The child got completely cured in 90 days.

This treatment has been found successful and blood transfusion is stopped within 40/60 days. This treatment may be continued for 120 days, but proper care about the diet should be taken afterwards.

CHAPTER 10

CANCER

Cancer is a dreaded disease. The main point of worry in the case of cancer is that when it is detected, it has already reached an advanced stage and the possibility of complete cure is remote. Moreover, the treatment is so costly that the patient and his relatives get financially and mentally exhausted.

The immediate cause for cancer is the continuous neglect of the organs of the body by the patient. For example, the lungs of a chain-smoker are continuously irritated. The cancer of the mouth or vocal cords is due to the habit of chewing tobacco, drinking hot tea, etc. In the case of cancer of the uterus, negligence about internal hygiene is the root cause. It has been observed that Jewish women who take great care of their internal organs do not normally get cancer of the uterus.

Cancer of the stomach and the intestines is due to overuse of refined flour and rice, coffee, sugar and tea and the habit of excessive drinking of alcohol. It has been observed that labourers in the sugar factory in the West Indies use brown sugar molasses–jaggery and so they are immune to cancer. And cancer of the colon is due to continuous constipation caused by wrong food habits and leading a sedentary life. It has been observed that the people of Gujarat who are vegetarian and consume more milk and milk products like curds, buttermilk, etc. do not generally get this type of cancer.

Another reason is a wrongful approach towards the care of the body. The diseases are nothing but the signals given by the body that there is something wrong in that organ, e.g., tonsils. Instead of removing the root cause of the disease, either the signal, (tonsils) is removed by operation, or the disease (like the common cold) is suppressed with powerful antibiotics. The body is to be treated as a temple, a seat of God and each and every corner of this temple should be kept neat and clean. Instead, the body is treated like a dustbin, wherein useless things are dumped and instead of cleaning out the waste or toxins, they are suppressed so that they become a duct and which after a time results in a malignant growth.

The long-term cause of cancer is the imbalance caused by disturbing the metabolism of our body through (1) eatables grown with the help of inorganic manure and pesticides, (2) more and more use of canned foods, bottled pickles, (3) unwise use of fluoride, (4) working in unhygienic conditions, e.g., working in an asbestos factory, (5) pollution of the environment by the excessive use of diesel, the cutting down of the trees, etc. (6) polluting the water through chemical wastes, etc. (7) going farther and farther away from nature.

Since these root causes of cancer can be removed, cancer can be prevented. You will find that in the animal world this dreaded disease is rarely found. The obvious reason is that they invariably observe the laws of nature.

How cancer develops :

In our body, millions of new cells are formed everyday and they replace the old worn-out cells. This process is carried out by the spleen and it is cleaned and controlled by the lymph glands. When we neglect our body, the process of regeneration of new cells slows down while the process of decaying –destruction of cells–increases, so more toxins gather in the body and the spleen and the lymph glands are overburdened. Slowly but steadily, there is a malignant growth in the body, but it is not easily noticed. Meanwhile, these toxins/wastes are gathering in the body in the part which is most damaged, e.g., for a smoker, these toxins gather in the lungs or in the mouth. When these toxins accumulate in a large quantity, they form a duct and start developing fast. In the meantime, the weak lymph gland is greatly damaged and through it other glands are damaged as well. And a stage is reached when these glands become tired and stop secreting the most vital hormones in the body. This is the time, when malignancy grows at a very fast rate and the final signal is given by nature. There is a change in metabolism, severe headache, loss of weight, change of voice, colour of the spots on the body changes, and there is constant fever. It is only then, that this disease is detected as cancer.

Acupressure plays a great role in the detection, prevention and cure of cancer.

Any minor disturbance of any organ is reflected on the palms or soles. When there is a continued complaint, the first gland to be disturbed is the Thyroid/Parathyroid gland. The second gland to be disturbed in case of problems of degeneration leading towards cancer is the Lymph gland. As mentioned above, this important gland works to remove the toxins and the dead cells from the body. When the process of regeneration of the cells of the body slows down, there is an increase in the activity of clearing the dead cells and preventing pus formation. This gland thus gives the alarm. If you touch on its point no. 16, on hands and feet, these points will be found to be tender and when you press them, you will feel pain.

How to detect cancer in different parts of the body :

Another pointer for the detection is that the organ where cancer is developing is disturbed and there is pain in the corresponding point on the palms and soles. For example, in case of cancer of the breast, there is pain in the middle point on the back of the palm as shown in fig. 86 or in case of cancer in the colon, there is pain in the corresponding point no. 20.

The same way, for cancer in :

Throat	: There is pain on point no. 6
Windpipe Gullet Stomach	: There is pain between point nos. 6 and 27.
	: There is pain on point no. 27
Small Intestine	: There is pain on point no. 19
Large Intestine	: There is pain on point nos. 20 and 10
Liver	: Point nos. 23 and 22

Lungs	: Point no. 30
Brain	: Point nos. 1 to 5 (It is also called tumour.)
Blood	: Point no. 37
Bones	: Point nos. 9 & 37.

Now, if these signals are ignored, the declining process starts disturbing the other glands also and reaches a dangerous point where these endocrine glands become tired and stop secreting hormones. During that time, more and more toxins accumulate forming a duct and start multiplying and thus a fast malignant growth starts in that part of the body damaging the metabolism of the body.

Thus, you will observe that cancer can be detected at a very early stage, and it can be controlled very easily. Moreover, you will observe that if regular Acupressure treatment is taken daily or at least thrice a week, the lethargic spleen or lymph gland can be reactivated, and factors leading to cancer can be checked. **Thus Acupressure can prevent cancer.**

How to detect cancer of the uterus :

The cancer of the uterus is more common in women who do not take proper care of personal hygiene. It is due to continuous irregularity of menstruation, continuous leucorrhoea, etc. This type of cancer can be easily detected. In case of any doubt, press on point nos. 11 to 15 on both the sides of the wrists of both the hands. If there is pain on pressing these points and also on point no. 16 of the lymph gland, it denotes degeneration.

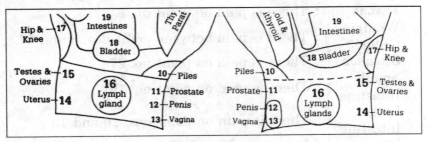

Fig. 83

How to detect cancer of the breasts? Mammography

Just press on the circle in the back of the right palm for the right breast and the left palm for the left breast. If, there is NO PAIN when pressed, it means there is NO CANCER in the breasts. Even if, there is pain on these points, but no pain on point no. 16 of the Lymph gland at that time, it denotes that there is NO CANCER. And just by giving treatment on those points on the back of the palms, the minor

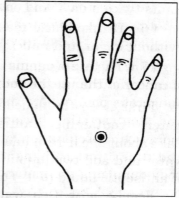

Fig. 84 : Picture showing how to detect cancer of breasts

problem like accumulation of milk in the breast, etc. will be cured. Only pain on the circles on the back of the right palm and also on the point no. 16 of the lymph gland; denotes cancer in the right breast. In the same way cancer in the left breast can be detected by pressing the circle on the back of the left palm and point no. 16 of the lymph gland.

At that time, it is possible that when pressed, there will be pain on point nos. 11 to 15 of the sex glands.

Severe pain on those points on the back side of the palms and on point no. 16 when pressed, denotes that cancer has reached an advanced stage.

EVEN IF CANCER IS DETECTED, DO NOT WORRY. IT IS EASILY CURABLE.

Cure :

Give Acupressure treatment for a 2/2 minutes on each of the following points thrice a day :

(1) On the circles on the back of the palms, for the cancer of the breasts.

(2) On point nos. 11 to 15 on both the sides of the wrists for cancer of the uterus.

(3) On point no. 16 on both the hands.

(4) On points of all the endocrine glands, i.e. point nos. 3, 4, 8, 25 & 28.

(5) Take general Acupressure treatment on all the points twice a day. And on point no. 26 as a last treatment.

(6) Drink 'black tea' one cup in the early morning (without sugar and milk).

(7) The use of vaginal douche is a must for the treatment of cancer of the uterus and the breast.

First clean the douche with water containing antiseptic. Take about one litre of lukewarm water and add two to four drops of antiseptic liquid to it. Then fill the douche with this water by pressing the ball, then keep the plastic part (2 inches) into the vagina and press the ball. Water will flow and clean the inside.

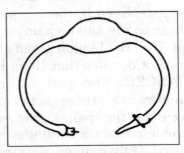

Fig. 85 : Vaginal Douche

Repeat it two to four times. A vaginal douche is also useful when pus cells are found in the urine of a female.

(8) Make the necessary change in diet as mentioned for the treatment of cancer.

(9) In case of more pain on the points on the back of the palms and point no. 16 and also when lumps are found in the breasts, apply north pole of a (low to medium power) magnet on the lumps only for 3/5 minutes two to three times a day.

"A woman of 50 years was found to have cancer in both the breasts and was advised operation. Instead she took the above treatment and was completely cured within 45 days."

"A 40-year-old woman – mother of 4 children, was found to have cancer of the uterus. The cancer was detected even in her left breast. She started the above mentioned Acupressure treatment and continued the same for 60 days. Later on, her husband came and thanked me saying that his wife felt 10 years younger. The same way, several cases have been successfully treated."

Recently, it was observed that in more than a dozen cases of kidney failure where dialysis was being done and when proper improvement was not found, these patients were advised to undergo kidney transplantation. In all these cases, on examination, damage to kidney was not more than 40 to 50% – and the root cause was found to be cancer of the uterus in the females and that of prostate in the males. Within 40 to 60 days of Acupressure treatment, all the patients got cured. It is, therefore, advisable before undergoing dialysis and kidney transplantation to check up about the possibility of cancer.

It has been agreed by the medical world that if cancer is detected at an early stage, it can be cured.

Cure for all types of cancer :

To cure all types of cancer, the whole body is to be treated, the important organs of regeneration, e.g., liver, gall bladder, spleen and kidneys and all the endocrine glands are to be reactivated. Acupressure treatment assists the patient in the process and accelerates recovery by bringing the metabolism of the body in order. The following treatment is suggested :

(1) Check up the solar plexus and put it in order.

(2) Banish salt and spices from the diet. Stop eating cooked food, bread, etc.

(3) Every day take an enema of water boiled with coffee at least two times. That helps to open up the ducts and remove the toxins from the body.

(4) Take vapour treatment on the ducts and cold packs treatment in the case of cancer of the stomach and the uterus. Also apply north pole of a magnet on the ducts for three minutes twice a day. It will dissolve the duct.

(5) Take concentrated lukewarm water of iron, copper, silver and gold, three to four glasses, during the day. Boil 20 glasses of water and reduce it to 4 glasses.

(6) Have 3 to 5 cups of fresh green juice as mentioned on page 25. While preparing such green juice add sprouted cereals, beetroot, carrot, cabbage. Also take plenty of fruits like grapes, apples, pomegranates, papayas, mangoes, etc.

(7) Take Acupressure treatment on all the points twice a day. Also give special extra treatment of two minutes on each point of the endocrine glands – point nos. 3, 4, 8, 14, 15, 16, 25, 28 and 38 (in case of children). After the treatment is taken, take the treatment on point no. 26 of kidneys also.

(8) Practise Pranayam regularly as often as possible.

(9) Take sunbath and if it is not possible, take blue light on the affected part of the body for eight to ten minutes.

(10) In case of the cancer of the mouth, throat or stomach, first cure pyorrhoea if it is there (See page no. 71). If the teeth are in a bad condition, have them extracted.

(11) For the first 10 days, drink pineapple juice as shown below :

Take a ripe pineapple, cut it into two halves vertically, squeeze the juice of the half and drink it first thing in the morning and drink the juice of the balance half in the evening before sunset. If desired, honey can be added to the juice.

(12) Drink the extract of the following the first thing in the morning (even before you take the pineapple juice) :

21 leaves of bitter 'neem' with stalk.

21 leaves of 'tulsi' with stalk.

21 leaves of 'bilipatra' (7×3) with stalk.

This is a MUST in case of cancer of the blood, bones and brain and wherever to be used as blood purifier.

(Only if such leaves are not available, tincture of the same is available at Homoeopathic shops. Mix them in a bottle. Take five drops in half a cup of lukewarm water in the morning and evening.)

(13) After 12 to 15 days or when the patient gets very hungry (it is a good sign of recovery), give the patient three to four ounces of fresh curds, prepared in the following manner. In the boiled warm milk (preferably cow's or goat's milk) add 12/15 leaves of 'tulsi' and prepare the curds. If the patient is of 'pitta prakruti', give him this curds, adding a little powdered crystal sugar. For all other types of patients, this curds can be eaten with little rock salt or black salt in it. Such curds can be had three to four times a day, but before sunset.

(14) Eat roasted bitter gourd 'karela – (करेला)'. Treatment mentioned especially in 11 to 14 has been found effective even in blood cancer.

(15) Give the following combination of biochemic powder / pills :

Calc. Phos.	30×1 oz
Kali Phos.	30×1 oz
Kali Mur	30×1 oz
Ferrum Phos.	30×1 oz
Kali Iodide	30×1 oz

(If Kali Iodide is not available in powder/pills, add its tincture in other pills/powder.) Give 2 grains of powder or 6 pills – thrice a day. After taking this medicine, do not take anything for 10/15 minutes.

In case of severe damage to any of the endocrine glands, e.g. hypothyroid, the same treatment as mentioned above for cancer is to be taken.

(16) We should not forget that cancer is the last warning of nature. Go back to nature and within a short period, you will be able to control and cure this dreaded disease. **It is likely that during the first 8 to 12 days, the patient may have nausea, vomiting or severe headache. He may refuse to take enema, etc. But continue the treatment.** Improvement will be observed within 15 to 20 days, and complete cure is assured within 45 to 90 days depending upon the stage of cancer when this treatment is started. Even if the cancer is in a terminal stage and cannot be cured, this treatment will reduce the unbearable pain the patient is suffering and the pain will subside.

(17) After recovery, take a balanced diet consisting of 50 to 60% whole wheat and cereals, plus vegetables and milk products. Avoid salt. If desired, use rock salt or black salt. It has been noticed that people in Gujarat who have this type of diet do not get cancer of the stomach or intestine.

(18) This dreaded disease results from utter neglect and undue harassment of the body. Accept the result calmly, forgive all, pray to God and take a vow to do only good deeds, to be of some help to others after recovery. **Please note that prayers have more power than drugs.** And last but not least, have self-confidence and be cheerful.

(19) Get rid of bad habits as mentioned in my book, "Health In Your Hands : Volume 1" on page 224.

(20) If Allopathic drugs are taken, take Thuja 200 – 4 pills for 3 days. If rays and chemotherapy are taken, take treatment to remove excess heat as mentioned in Chapter 12.

The following are forbidden :

Processed and canned foods, salted pickles, frozen, jarred, bleached or refined foods, also coffee, black tea, tobacco, alcohol, spices, salt, hair dyes, pain relieving agents and drugs, chlorinated water and toothpaste, and temporarily (till the liver starts functioning well), cheese, eggs, fish, meat and milk.

To eradicate cancer from this world, its root causes namely, pollution of air, pollution of wheat, rice, barley, maize etc., – staple food – through inorganic manure and overuse of insecticides, excessive use of preservatives in canned and bottled fruits and food products, excessive use of tobacco, alcohol, sugar and coffee, meat, etc., must be avoided. People can take care of themselves and prevent these root causes in their own interest, and with the help of Acupressure can give up their bad habits, and thus prevent cancer.

All types of cancer, including that of blood, have been successfully treated. Even patients, considered as incurable, were eventually cured with the above-mentioned treatment, given to them by their relatives in their homes and that too without any costs. Several such cases can be quoted; viz.

(1) Mr. "A" was discharged from hospital as his cancer of throat was considered incurable. He was in such agony that painkiller injections had to be given thrice a day. On the fifth day of treatment, painkiller injections were no more required. On the sixteenth day, he started recovering his appetite and within 45 days, he was totally cured and resumed normal duties.

(2) Mrs. "M", the wife of an M.D., tried several therapies for her loss of weight and failing stamina. At last an acupressurist was consulted. He diagnosed the problems as cancer of the stomach. Treatment was started at home with her husband's permission. Within 60 days, she got cured and gained weight and stamina. Now, she sincerely advocates Acupressure treatment.

(3) A college student, 19 years old, was so much disturbed with his problem that he started thinking of committing suicide. An acupressurist was consulted. He diagnosed it as a case of cancer of the prostate. Without knowledge of any previous history of the case, he told the young man that he was in the practice of masturbation for a long time. With a treatment of only 40 days, the boy was cured. Now, he intends to be a professor. He himself has become an ardent acupressurist and successfully treats patients.

According to this therapy, cancer is one of the easiest diseases to be cured. The patients and their relatives need not worry. They only have to take the above-mentioned treatment.

Even when cancer has spread over 85–90% and the patient is in agony, this treatment will make his condition comfortable. The patient cannot be saved. But he will meet a peaceful death.

CHAPTER 11

BRAIN'S PROBLEMS

In order to understand the root cause of this dreaded disease, one must know the nervous system–the telephone exchange of our body. The afferent nerves from the five senses of touch, hearing, sight, smell and taste take the messages to the brain. The computer in our brain analyses these messages and sends orders through efferent nerves to the muscles and the muscles act accordingly. Sometimes, we find that we receive telephone calls from outside but we cannot make a phone call to others. Sometimes, the telephone instrument becomes dead even though there is no defect in it. The fault is in the telephone exchange. In the same way, the root cause of this disease is in the brain. The power of the battery becomes weak and so the electric current becomes weak and its passing is disturbed by the excitatory nerves fibre due to depolarisation of cell membrane of motor nuclei. That leads to slow and steady degeneration and there is muscular wasting in the affected muscles.

The development of brain and nervous system during pregnancy will be more clear from the pictures on the next page. The different organs of the brain and other parts of the nervous system start developing in the foetus during pregnancy and even up to 9 months after the child's birth. And, therefore, the greatest care should be taken of the foetus and the child during this period. A slight damage develops into a major defect at an advanced stage and then damages the affected part.

As the trouble starts from the brain, it immediately affects the Pituitary and Pineal glands which are situated there. And when these glands are affected, they disturb the working of the Sex glands. Thyroid/Parathyroid glands and also Adrenal glands, leading to hormonal imbalance in the body. So, at the time of this disease, the points of these glands will be found to be tender and will be paining when pressed.

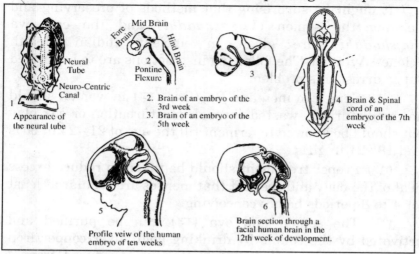

1 Appearance of the neural tube
   Neural Tube
   Neuro-Centric Canal

Fore Brain
Mid Brain
Hind Brain
2 Pontine Flexure

2. Brain of an embryo of the 3rd week
3. Brain of an embryo of the 5th week

4 Brain & Spinal cord of an embryo of the 7th week

5 Profile veiw of the human embryo of ten weeks

6 Brain section through a facial human brain in the 12th week of development.

Fig. 86

In order to prevent this dreaded disease, the root cause — hereditary and the damage to the brain during pregnancy should be controlled. We take great care of the earth-soil by properly ploughing, watering and cleaning it before the best quality of selected seeds are sown in it. We also take great care to see that these seeds are selected in such a way that the plant develops properly and can even resist the diseases. However, when conceiving a human embryo, no such care is taken.

Nowadays, semen is not, preserved properly and allowed to be fermented till the age of 21-24. In the same way, most of the girls have problems of menses which clearly indicates that their ovaries are not functioning satisfactorily. Further, excess drinking of coffee, tea, liquor, smoking and even addiction to drugs have increased, thereby disturbing the metabolism of the hormones. And this imbalance of metabolism of hormones in male and female is one of the prime reasons for the improper development of the nervous system including the brain of the child to be born.

Another reason is the improper care of diet, drinking, smoking and drug addiction during pregnancy.

It might be surprising that methods of preserving and cleaning the semen (*Viryashuddhi*) and the egg–ova (*Rajshuddhi*) are given in ancient Indian Health Sciene–Ayurved. The following instructions are to be carried out to arrest this problem :

(1) Semen in men and Raj/Ova (रज) in women should not be disturbed–wasted through masturbation or sex play but should be allowed to ferment till the age of 21–24 in boys and 18–21 in girls.

(2) Proper treatment should be taken to reduce excess heat of the body and see to it that menses are regular at least for 4 to 8 periods before conceiving.

(3) The semen and ova (रज) can be purified and activated by the couple by drinking gold/silver/copper/iron charged water/one glass out of 2 glasses reduced from 4 glasses and also by taking Acupressure treatment every day.

(4) After conceiving, the expectant mother should drink this water and take acupressure treatment daily. This will ensure proper growth of the foetus.

You have noticed how the brain of the child starts developing from the third month and goes on developing not only till birth, but even up to nine months after the birth. And as such in order to prevent all types of brain's problems, the pregnant mother should take utmost care as under :

(1) Maintain her body in such a way that the brain of the child is not damaged.

(2) She should take care of her body and prevent diseases like severe cold, fever for a long period, mumps, acidity, excess heat in the body etc. e.g. mumps and severe cold during pregnanacy leads to deafness and dumbness of the body.

(a) Damage to the optic nerve of the foetus leads to blindness.

(b) Insufficient circulation to the brain of the foetus leads to retardation–a child may become a Mongolian.

(c) Even sex after six months of pregnancy could damage the brain of the foetus. So, in India, to prevent such a mishap, pregnant women are advised to go in the fifth month of pregnancy to parents, where she can remain in a happy mood – fulfill her new desires to eat and drink, have full rest and avoid sex.

(3) In order that the brain of the child develops properly and possibility of hereditary diseases could be minimised, pregnant woman should drink at least 1 glass of gold/silver/copper/iron charged water reduced from 2 glasses of water. Such a practice will greatly reduce the possibility of deafness – dumbness, blindness and retardation, even polio. May be it may even prevent Muscular Dystrophy. Moreover, such a practice will be able to prevent Juvenile Diabetes.

As the brain goes on developing after the birth till nine months, proper care should be taken so that there is no damage to the developing brain of the child. Wherever possible, the child/its head should not be exposed to extreme cold/wind and even heat.

With intensive research in China, it is found that if the expectant mother refrains from other vices of drinking too much tea and coffee, drinks and smoking, the child to be born does not have desire for sweets – chocolates and biscuits and thus can refrain from sugar for more than a year. In that case, American Dental Association has a firm conviction that if a child can refrain from sugar for a year, the teeth of the child will remain good throughout life unless damaged by wrongful habits and neglect.

It should be noted that Nature has given extra responsibility to women. They only can become MOTHER. We observe in Nature about the care a mother takes for her offspring before birth and after birth. Then, if we call ourselves advanced, we must take extra care. Women should not try to compete with Men in smoking, drinking alcohol, heavy manual work. They are SUPERIOR and MOTHER of Man. As such knowing full well about the bad effects of tobacco and alcohol on the foetus, the expectant mother should avoid bad habits of smoking and drinking. Let them try its effects on the energy of the body as per fig. no. 68 on page 120 of "Health in Your Hands : Volume 1."

Thus, if such precautions are taken before and during pregnancy, possibility of brain's problem can be removed to a great extent.

Treatment :

One must note that we can reach the inside of the brain only through blood and so to correct any problems of brain; one has to take a long term treatment of 4 to 6 months. Surgery of brain is not advisable for children or even adults.

Muscular Dystrophy and similar other diseases of Brain/Neuro disorders/Multiple Sceleriosis/Retardation :

These diseases are noticed at the end of the 3rd year or afterwards, when there is difficulty in walking, climbing staircases or when the patient may start losing control of leg muscles and may fall down frequently. Later on, it affects the shoulder muscles and once the patient is confined to a wheel chair, these diseases progressively paralyse the functioning of different organs of the body. Later on, the brain stops functioning and the patient dies. These diseases have developed in a vast proportion causing great worry. In spite of spending millions of dollars every year, the diseases have not been controlled so far. However, Acupressure can play a great role in preventing and curing these diseases.

The root causes of these diseases are :

(1) Hereditary – familial.

(2) Sometimes, when a woman has sex relations with more than one male, there is hormonal imbalance, which often affects her children.

(3) In families having Red – Green colour blindness.

(4) Disorder of the female organs. In such cases, proper care should be taken at the time of childbirth.

(5) Damage to the foetus during pregnancy, and

(6) Damage to the brain of the child of less than nine months old.

(7) In those families where these diseases are found in the boys, their sisters have a 50/50 chance of being the carriers of these diseases and therefore should be put to the following tests :

(a) Serum creatine kinase estimation (b) quantitative electromyography and (c) muscles biopsy.

And in case they are found to be carriers, they must be sterilised so that they cannot have child. They can adopt child.

For those patients who are already affected by this disease, the following treatment will greatly assist them to control these and similar other diseases of the brain and the nervous system, i.e. retardation/multiple sceleriosis, etc.

Cure of Muscular Dystrophy – Polio, Multiple Sclerosis, Retardation – etc. i.e. all types of BRAIN's Problems :

(1) High powered-concentrated gold/silver/copper/iron charged water to be given as under :

$\frac{1}{2}$ glass reduced from 8 glasses for 8 days.

1 glass reduced from 8 glasses for 8 days.

2 glasses reduced from 8 glasses for 8 days. and then

2 glasses reduced from 8 glasses to be given till recovery and 60 days thereafter.

After 6 months, 1 glass reduced from 2 glasses of water to be given for a period of two years. This treatment has been proved to give push to the brain and its motor nuclei and start the functions of all endocrine glands and all the organs of the body.

(2) Acupressure treatment of 2 minutes 3 times a day to be given to point nos. 1 to 6, 11 to 15, 25, 28 and 38.

(3) Treatment on the webs and back of palms twice a day will be useful to relieve any nervous tension and correct any impairment to them, also to tone them up.

(4) Health drink/powder to be given twice a day.

(5) Green juices of leafy vegetables and honey to be freely given 2 to 4 cups a day.

(6) Fresh fruit juices – 2 to 3 glasses to be given daily.

(7) Blue light to be given for 5 to 7 minutes each on head and spine twice a day.

(8) Give brainwash powder on the 1st day, 5th day and 10th day only. More use of this powder can damage the delicate cells of the brain –

(9) Pranayam – see Chapter 2, page 146.

(10) Kapalbhati and Bhastrika – see page 152.

(11) Rub the soles of the patient for 5/5 minutes in the morning and evening till the soles are warmer than the head.

Polio :

This is due to virus infection in the motor nuclei of the brain stem and in the gray matter of the spinal cord and paralysis of the connected muscles.

(a) Give treatment as mentioned above for the Brain's problems.

(b) Give vapour treatment or hot pack treatment on the affected part for one month.

(c) Afterwards, give hot and cold packs alternately for 10 minutes, twice a day.

(d) After this, dry up the affected parts and rub oil on them as mentioned on page 201 of "Health In Your Hands : Volume 1."

(e) Give blue and red light for 10 minutes each on the spinal cord/head and the affected parts.

(f) Practise Sun Pranayam, Kapal Bhati and Bhastrika as much as possible.

If the treatment is given within 3 months, it is totally cured. Even if the treatment is tried later, it gives good result and reduces the defect.

Meningitis :

This is due to congestion of water in the brain and could even lead to fever – sometimes high fever.

(1) Please give full bed rest to the patient.

(2) All treatment including that of Brainwash as mentioned above for brain's problem should be given.

Caution :

In hospitals, fluid is extracted from the top of head to do the test of this fluid. Many times, this damages the Pineal gland and thereby Pituitary and other endocrine glands, which leads to malfunctioning of some organs for life and leads to early awakening of sex desire, leading to juvenile delinquency.

How to prepare brain's wash/powder :

This is not snuff—no tobacco—it is a powder of a fruit called KAYFAL—N.O.MYRICACAE. First remove the outer thick/hardened shell. Take the inside pulp. Dry it in the sun. Make fine powder of 300 mesh.

Take 80% of such powder.
+ 15% of fine powder of Cardamom. (एलायची)
+ 5% of fine powder of pure Saffron
  (if not available add 5% of
  fine powder of Black pepper)

How to use it :

Close one nostril. Keep a pinch of this brain's wash/powder under the other nostril and inhale forcibly. Do the same way with the other nostril. In case of a child, do it forcibly.

Within a minute or two, there will be heavy sneezing—15 to 30 times and water and air will come out from the head—eyes and nose may be watering. This water may be pinkish in colour. Do not worry.

Repeat the same way on the 5th day and the 10th day only. Do not continue. It can damage the delicate cells inside the brain.

This powder is also useful in sinusitis but in that case use ONLY on the 1st day and the 5th day.

The paste of this powder is also useful for cough/congestion of children. Apply lukewarm paste on the forehead and the chest overnight.

Parkinson's Disease :

(shivering of any part of the body – generally fingers and hands) : This is due to hypertension and excess heat in the body. That damages the nerve endings in the brain,leading to shivering of any part of the body.

Treatment :

The same treatment as mentioned above for brain's problem + treatment shown on page 219 of "Health In Your Hands : Volume 1" for nervous tension. Drinking of charged water + green juice at least 2 cups + Blue Light on head for 5 to 7 minutes twice a day is a MUST.

Case study :

A leading paediatrician of Mumbai got this problem. He had to stop performing operations. I was consulted. He started taking treatment at home and within 60 days, he started his practice again.

Mental breakdown/severe depression/even madness :

The root cause of all the problems is damage in the brain. As such the treatment mentioned above is found to be very useful. Along with that treatment , do treatment mentioned for nervous tension on page 219 of "Health In Your Hands : Volume 1" Results are just astounding.

Case study :

(1) A professor came to our centre. He was so much depressed that he wanted to commit suicide. He was advised the above treatment. Within just 10 days, the change was so dramatic that he came to our centre only to inform that he is confident to live for hundred years and that too very happily.

(2) A lady came with a complaint that her brother was insane. He had become mad at the age of fifteen – and during the last 10 years no treatment has been effective – At present he does not care to wear even clothes. So she could not bring him to the centre. She was given proper guidance. When awake, Blue light could not be given to the patient. So Blue Light was

given on his head and spine when he was asleep. There was slow but steady progress. And within 6 months that gentleman started living a normal life.

Similarly, several cases can be cited.

Coma :

When there is a serious damage to Central Nervous system, the supply of cerebrospinal fluid to the brain becomes so low that the motor nuclei does not function and the patient goes into a Coma–DO NOT PANIC.

Treatment :

Give the patient through mouth or tube, 1 oz–30 mililitre of concentrated gold charged water-reduced from 1 litre of water–during the day+give treatment on point nos. 1 to 5, 8,11 to 15, 25–28 & 36 twice a day for 1-1 minute on each point+Rub both the soles for 5 minutes each twice a day+give Blue light for 5 minutes on the head, twice a day.

In most cases, the patient will regain consciousness within a week.

If the patient does not regain consciousness within a week, add 2 carats of pure diamonds (not 1 diamond of 2 carats–but it can be 20 to 40 diamonds)–while preparing the abovementioned concentrated gold charged water. Diamond is a pure carbon, a negative element, Gold is a positive element.

Thus, by giving such water to drink, positive and negative elements, points of the brain cells get recharged and the patient gains consciousness at the earliest. Please note that the patient will not die in a Coma. Once he regains consciousness, give him treatment as mentioned under brain's problems.

Several patients, even in hospitals, are given the abovementioned treatment and patients have recovered–even after remaining in a Coma for 3 months–even when doctors had lost hopes.

In all the cases of serious and chronic diseases, combine the treatment shown in chapters 6, 7, 8 and 9 of "Health In Your Hands : Volume 1" for a faster recovery.

The cure achieved as a result of this treatment is not temporary but of lasting nature. The organ starts functioning normally and will continue to do so until the laws of nature are broken. You will also note that Mother Nature helps us to cure the diseases if we give her time to cure us. And Acupressure treatment helps Nature – our body – to get rid of the disease faster. And thereafter with regular Acupressure treatment, health could be maintained.

In the case of contagious diseases, it is advisable to keep the patient isolated. At least keep the children away from the patient. Wash his/her clothes and utensils separately and maintain cleanliness.

Please note that all the diseases, whatever may be their different names, are related to the functioning of the organs of the body. Therefore, for treating any disease, not named here, the root cause and the organ affected must be found and treatment should be given on the point corresponding to that particular organ.

You will observe that Acupressure can create miracles. We need not worry about dreaded diseases – they have not been understood properly and wrongly labelled as Dreaded Dragons. In reality, all these dreaded diseases are only Paper Dragons and can be defeated – all the dreaded diseases can be CURED – except DEATH.

Please note that any disease except Death is curable. And Death is a MUST for every living being. Do not be afraid of Death. It is the door through which everybody has to pass to enter a new world. Death is like a kind mother who takes away this old body and gives us a new body – a new life.

It should be noted that all the serious illnesses are the results of bad deeds done in the past lives. Accept the results and offer prayers from the Heart not only for the Cure – but to give you enough strength to bear the sufferings – Forgive all – beg friendship of all the living beings and make a vow to be useful to others, when cured. All nights always lead to DAWN.

CHAPTER 12

HIV / AIDS

Acquired Immune Deficiency Syndrome is popularly known as AIDS. It is the most serious stage after one gets HIV infection. However, that stage does not come overnight. It has been found that after one gets HIV infection, it takes 2 to 12 years before this stage is reached – when rare illness of opportunistic diseases like Pneumocystis Carinii pneumonia – called PCP and Kaposi's sarcoma, etc. occur in the body. If untreated, or if the symptoms of the diseases are not diagnosed in time, these diseases prove fatal in 10 to 30 % of the cases.

As AIDS is not cured by antibiotics and other drugs available to the present medical science, the doctors are baffled and so the world is terrorized by this dreaded epidemic. According to the statistics, in 1993, 1.5 million people in the U.S.A. we afflicted by AIDS, plus 1 to 2 million people were feared to have HIV infection which is the causative agent.

	HIV	AIDS
U.S.A.	14,95,000	53,400
West Europe	11,96,000	27,900
East Europe	44,000	9,000
Latin America	14,07,000	4,17,000
Africa	91,49,000	32,77,000
Asia	13,00,000	2,56,000

This disease is spreading to the other countries of the world.

The spread of this disease has created another big problem of how to provide medical care to the increasing number of infected people. Many doctors refuse to treat such patients. Thus, AIDS has become a big dilemma and threat to mankind.

It is surprising to note that like cancer, AIDS has not been understood properly and so proper treatment is not being given. It is accepted that this disease develops after getting Human Immunodeficiency Virus (HIV) infection, which attacks the white cells of the blood, and in the fight against HIV, more and more white cells are destroyed, thus damaging the immune system of the body. When such white cells become less than 200, AIDS is confirmed and no cure for the same has been found so far. At this stage, the patient gets infectious illness of Pneumocystis Carinii pneumonia (PCP) and Kaposi's sarcoma, etc. Slowly and steadily, it becomes fatal.

How does one get HIV Infection?

In order to understand this problem, one must study how one gets HIV infection and how such infection develops into AIDS. It is now accepted that one gets such HIV infection through the body liquids of the affected person, i.e. blood, semen and saliva. It is not contagious and so one does not get it, by shaking hands or kissing the patient. And so there is no chance of being infected by HIV, while treating these patients affected with HIV infection and AIDS. One gets such HIV infection through :

Blood Transfusion :

(1) All the blood collecting agencies of the world must take precaution to test the donor's blood.

(2) Only in emergency cases and when all other treatments have failed, should surgery be resorted to. This will minimise the need for blood transfusion.

(3) **Use of needles** : (i) All medical practitioners using needles for giving injections MUST ensure the use of disposable needles. They should sterilise the needle before reuse. (ii) Because drug addicts often use the same needle, HIV is widely prevalent among them.

Cure for drug addiction, as mentioned below has been found effective and should be widely propagated.

How to stop Drug Addiction?

(1) Continue the treatment for two minutes three times a day on the point shown 3″ above ear lobes in the figure on both the sides of the head. See fig. 88.

(2) Give general treatment together with two minutes treatment each on endocrine glands at least thrice a day.

(3) Give two glasses of gold / silver / copper / iron charged water reduced from six glasses for one month. Then give two glasses of this water reduced from four glasses for a further two months.

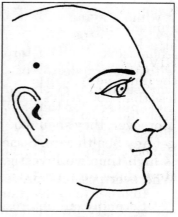

Fig. 88

(4) The craving for drugs will be greatly reduced within 15/20 days. Only then can the patient be asked to stop the drugs. Meanwhile, the quantity of drug intake may be reduced progressively.

(5) Give the patient two to three cups of green juices and one to two glasses of fruit juices daily.

(6) During the three months treatment, give blue light on the head and the spinal cord for five minutes each twice a day (See fig. 33).

"One young man, aged 22, had been taking drugs for about six years. He also had the habit of masturbation. He started the Acupressure treatment. After 20 days, he stopped taking drugs. Within 45 days, not only he became free from addiction, but his masturbating habit had considerably decreased. He became an ardent follower of Acupressure.

Strict warning must be given to drug addicts that they will not be given any health care, if they get HIV infection.

All the governments should agree to severely punish all the persons found to be dealing in drugs. The very root cause has to be eliminated.

Thus, one of the main causes of AIDS can be controlled.

Sex Abuse :

Another cause of HIV infection is **Sex Abuse.** It must be noted that sex is a fragile toy. If the child does not take care of it while playing with it, the toy will break and the child will cry to escape the punishment. Society of gay people – homosexuals and heterosexuals behave like children playing with this fragile toy of sex. These people should be strictly warned, that they should change their sexplay – stop oral sex and anal sex – so that HIV infection does not spread any more. Moreover, they should be given a warning that they would not get any health care. Society cannot pay for their sex abuse. It is high time we investigated why one becomes homosexual. Wherever possible, preventive measures should be taken.

Secondly, all heterosexuals with HIV infection should be sterilised, so that they do not spread this disease to their children through their wives. These people should get the HIV Test done periodically and MUST have safe sex till they are declared negative. Wives of these heterosexuals must be given rights to get (a) immediate divorce and (b) proper compensation, if it is found that they got the HIV from their husbands. Any pregnant lady, suspecting HIV should get the HIV Test done and terminate pregnancy, if found to be positive. The couple suffering from HIV can adopt children – but should not be allowed to produce children with HIV.

Understanding AIDS :

To understand this disease more easily, let us consider our body as a fort – a castle – with seven gates – which are the endocrine glands. Blood and saliva are the pipelines. Now, the HIV infection is an unknown enemy. It gets into the blood stream damaging the supply line of nutrition and the central power house (the brain). By the time the enemy is known, the damage is too much, but not beyond cure. At this stage, under the popular treatment, bombardment of antibiotics and heavy drugs is made inside the fort. Consequently, there are fires (ulcers in stomach, mouth, etc.). Even the pipelines are damaged and so the necessary supply of nutrition starts getting depleted. Consequently, the defence immune system of the body becomes weak. A vicious cycle starts. The first gate to be damaged is of the Thyroid/Parathyroid (depleting the supply of calcium), the second one will be Sex-Gonads/glands, in the case of sex abuse–(affecting phosphorus supply); the third gate to be damaged will be the Lymph gland, as it is taxed from two fronts, on the one hand it has to fight the toxin of HIV infection, on the other hand, it has to work more to remove excess dead cells dying daily. Thus the immune system becomes weak.

But as the vicious cycle continues with more and more bombardment of heavier, powerful antibiotic drugs that are administered–which only damages more and more houses inside the fort–(more organs are damaged, setting in of more and more infectious diseases) slowly and steadily, the other gates become weak. Even the people in the fort get annoyed with such bombardment and may stop their cooperation, i.e. internal immune system stops functioning. It is a well-known fact of science that when the internal force is reduced–like air from a tin box–the outside force (air) will crush it. The same way, infectious diseases attack the body from all the gates. The weakened defence force cannot fight on all gates. One by one, the gates are lost and eventually the battle is lost–as the vital pipelines are cut off, most people with *Kaff* (कफ) temperament get infected with PCP and some people with *Pitta* (पित्त) temperament get infected with Kaposi's sarcoma.

The best way to win this battle against HIV infection and prevent the development of AIDS is to empower the gates–(activate the endocrine glands) and protect the pipelines (purify the blood), activate the defence immune system and proper lights to be arranged in all the dark corners (activate all the organs) of the fort, so that this enemy cannot hide. It has to run away.

Development of AIDS from HIV Infection :

Here such patients can be divided into two categories :

(1) **HIV Infection due to sex abuse :** In this case the Thyroid/Parathyroid, Sex glands (Gonads), may be Adrenal gland and Lymph glands and liver are already damaged.

Moreover, these patients do not change their lifestyle and so, when drugs are administered blindly, excess heat is created. This leads to ulcers, more damage to the liver, reducing its capacity to create more bile to control acidity and the bacteria and a vicious cycle develops in such a way that with every extra dose of more powerful drugs and antibiotics, more and more infectious diseases develop and within two years or less, AIDS stage is reached.

(2) **HIV Infection is the result of casual, unsafe sex or blood transfusion in a normally healthy person :** Here it takes from three years to twelve years before AIDS stage is reached.

Now let us see how AIDS develops. When one gets HIV infection, the immune system of the body puts up a spirited fight. The first gland to be affected is Thyroid/Parathyroid, which leads to the deficiency of calcium and iodine in the body.

As all the endocrine glands are interconnected, the next gland to be damaged is the Sex gland/Gonad, which controls the digestion of phosphorous in the body. When these two glands do not function properly, the internal heat of the body is reduced, reducing the hunger which leads to the creation of excess water in the body – leading to frequent colds and sinus for which antibiotics/drugs are administered. This consequently leads to the production of more H^+ in the body. Consequently the liver is damaged. This leads to **Candidiasis.** The mouth and oesophagus are the most common sites in such HIV patient. This leads to ulcers in the mouth and rectum leading to chronic mucocutaneous or disseminated herpes or complex virus infection.

Sometimes, the body tries to remove excess heat by creating loose motions which is considered as chronic **Cryptosporidiosis**, an intestinal infection. And as the body is not supplemented with proper nutrition, the vital supply of nutrition is damaged.

Later on, Adrenal gland is damaged, and it damages proper oxygenisation in the body. Together with this, sinus-cold affects the lungs, and this leads to cytomegalovirus (CMV) infection, causing more severe effects. As the lungs are damaged, proper supply of purified blood to the brain is affected and damages the vital –

(a) Pineal gland – which leads to **Cryptococcosis,** a fungal infection attacking the lungs, which may spread to the brains leading to **Meningitis.**

(b) And damage to Pituitary gland – leading to the damage to optic nerve – **Taxoplasmosis**, damaging eye sight.

Meanwhile, the lifestyle is not changed, nor the endocrine glands (which create hormones – which work as antibiotics) are activated, lymph gland has to overwork; it has to work to remove the daily dead cells and also to remove more and more white cells dying in the fight against HIV infection. As the Lymph gland is tired and functions less, more and more toxins gather in the body damaging the kidneys.

During this process, a period of three to twelve years, as the drugs/antibiotics are not effective, not only does the body not create resistance against them, but also it helps the infection to flourish.

Consequently, the tired endocrine glands stop functioning, and the whole immune system stops functioning. Thus, AIDS starts and most of the patients – 80% PCP owing to gathering of more mucus in the lungs and the rest are infected by Kaposi's sarcoma – eruption of excess heat from the body. And even at this stage as no effective medicines are given, the rare infectious diseases become fatal.

It's a fact that HIV/AIDS is not properly understood. Even though the vital endocrine glands play an important role in the immune defence system of our body, it is a pity that their functioning is not properly understood and so it has not been possible to control them. Moreover, as this HIV infection affects the white cells in the blood, and therefore, necessary steps should be taken to detoxify and purify the blood, but unfortunately this is not done. And so, more and more unwise use of powerful drugs (steroids) and antibiotics, acts only to lead the HIV patient to become the victim of AIDS.

One must know that heavy dosages of antibiotics or other drugs have not been effective so far and it is high time that alternative medicines were tried. Even the experts on AIDS have admitted that in some cases, the treatment of alternative medicines has been found effective. There are several instances, around California where the patients who after trying the popular allopathic treatment unsuccessfully, have tried alternative medicines, nature cure and Chinese drugs, etc. and the positive HIV Test has become negative.

Surprisingly, Acupressure can play a great role in the early detection and then prevention of HIV infection to develop into AIDS by curing it within eight to twelve weeks; and then CURING even 50 to 70 % of patients of AIDS.

Diagnosis :

Acupressure can play an important role in the early detection of HIV infection. In blood cancer, the degeneration of the blood is a slow process and only after the other digestive organs and endocrine glands are damaged, the spleen – the producer of blood – is affected. So there is a pain on its point no. 37 on the left palm or sole, along with pain on point nos. 27, 28, 22, 23, 8 and 11 to 15 also.

Now, in the case of HIV infection, it affects the blood – so even when a person looks healthy, one would find pain – hurting on point of spleen no. 37 and may be on the point of lymph gland which has to overwork to fight out infection. Thus, when there is hurting – uneasy pain point of spleen (point no. 37), and Thyroid/Parathyroid (point no. 8) it can be an indication of HIV infection. In cases where HIV has advanced, there will be pain even on point no. 16 of the lymph gland. In case of doubt, check the family-husband-wife and all children below 20 years of age.

In the case of HIV patients with sex abuse, there would be pain even on point nos. 11 to 15 of (Gonads), Sex glands and on point of Adrenal (showing excess heat in the body) no. 28. In case, these patients have diabetes, the disease develops rapidly.

Cure :

Once HIV infection is located, the treatment must be started immediately. The whole body has to be treated and not the symptoms. One important thing the patient MUST follow is to stop the root causes by which one gets HIV infection. For example, when a plane is ready for take off, all other systems are closed, till it is airborne, in the same way one must stop all the activities which would burden the organs, especially the digestive organs and endocrine glands. Treatment will be as follows :

(1) Stop taking all cooked foods, also milk, tea, coffee and tobacco, thus preventing toxins coming into the body. Also stop taking salt, meat, fats and liquor.

(2) To empower the life battery and functioning of all organs of the body, drink four glasses of gold/silver/copper/iron charged water, reduced from 16 glasses of water. (Method to prepare such water is given in Chapter 2, page 156 of this book.)

This water works as an antibiotic–(without any side effect) and peps up all the organs.

(3) To detoxify the body, a change in the diet is utmost necessary.

(a) Give two to three glasses of fresh fruit juice. (pineapple juice is found to be very effective.)

(b) Give three to four cups of green juice–extract of leafy vegetables–sprouted Chinese greenpeas (मूंग), etc. cereals, raddish–carrots+ginger+Amla (concentrated Vitamin C). In one cup of such juice add 1 tablespoonful of pure honey.

(c) Patient can eat as much green salad and as many fruits as he may desire.

(d) Give daily enema of lukewarm water adding to it 2 teaspoonfuls of coffee powder and castor oil for 15/20 days. This will purify the anus and the large intestines.

(e) Give an extract of

21 leaves of bitter neem tree with stem.

21 leaves with stem of holy basil (Tulsi).

21 leaves of Bilipatra (Eagle Mar)

daily with honey, first thing in the morning.

This has been found very effective in purifying the blood. Where fresh leaves are not available, one can take five drops of extract (tincture) of these three types of leaves (a Homoeopathic medicine) twice a day.

(f) Stimulating all the organs and endocrine glands by giving 5+5 minute pressure on points of both the palms and then one to two minutes pressure on all the points which are painful and on all the points of all the endocrine glands – thrice a day.

(g) In case of female patient, vaginal douche has to be given twice for the first 15 days and then once a day (See fig. 87).

(h) Abstinence from sex for 60 days.

(i) The body can be supplemented with biochemic salts of (mixture of) pills/powder

Cal. Phos   30×(1 oz)

Kali Phos   30×(1 oz)

Kali Mur   30×(1 oz)

Ferrum Phos   30×(1 oz)

Kali Iodide   30×(1 oz)

(If Kali Iodide is not available in powder/pill form, add its tincture in other pill/powder. Give two grains of powder or six pills – thrice daily). No eatables for 15 minutes before and after taking this medicine.

In the case of patients who have already developed AIDS, treatment to remove excess heat as mentioned below is to be given :

First treatment for 15 days should be given then the treatment should be stopped for 10 days and then again the treatment be given for 15 days. This will control fever, if any. In the case of fever, give as much warm water to drink and for treatment as shown in Chapter 2 for fever.

Deep breathing – Pranayam, with Linga Mudra and Pran Mudra for PCP. (Refer Chapter 2)

Sheetli and Varuna Mudra for patients of Kaposi's sarcoma.

Blue light on the whole body + urine therapy should also be tried for quicker results.

Thus, within eight to twelve weeks, the HIV infection will come under control and ELISA TEST will become negative. **Thus HIV can be prevented from turning into AIDS.**

Moreover, the same treatment could be more effective, even, on the patients of AIDS.

Treatment for AIDS :

Now AIDS patients have two main diseases : PCP and Kaposi's sarcoma.

PCP :

The above treatment is very effective.

(1) To remove Eosinophilia from the blood, they should take the following for 15 to 20 days.

After sunrise, take half a teaspoon of half ground Bishops seeds (अजवाईन), soak them in lemon drops for at least two hours and eat the same before sunset.

(2) Lie down on the back. Ask someone to pour one or two tablespoonfuls of honey in the mouth in such a way that it goes directly into the throat.

(3) They should first take red/orange light for two to four minutes on the chest – both lungs and back. Then blue light should be given for five to ten minutes twice a day. Stop taking light, when heat is felt.

(4) They should do Sun Mudra, Linga (Shiv) Mudra and the Pran Mudra. (Refer to Chapter 2)

(5) Do the following twice a day when under an attack of breathlessness :

Press hard on the back, on the points shown in the fig. 87 for ten seconds and pause. Repeat for a few minutes.

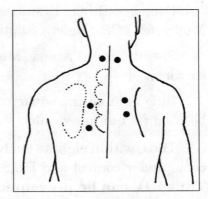

Fig. 87

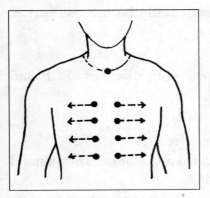

Fig. 88

At the same time, ask the patient to rub from the middle of the chest to the sides for two to five minutes. Also give treatment for one minute on the point shown below the neck. (See fig. 88)

This pressing and rubbing on the chest is also very useful and effective at the time of attack of asthma.

It may be noted that during this treatment, cold will increase. That is a positive sign of recovery. In that case, drink hot/lukewarm water, reduce food/take more of fruits/green juices enabling the body to throw out the excess water and toxins from the system.

Breathlessness :

Press on the points on the back and rub on the chest as shown above fig. 87 & 88. Also do Sun Pranayam.

Kaposi's sarcoma :

(1) Remove heat as mentioned below :

For removing the excess heat from the body :

(a) Take one teaspoonful of Haritki Churna (Harde Powder – Powder of Terminalia Chebula Retz) +1/2 teaspoonful of sugar first thing in the morning for eight to ten days continuously, then twice a week. This will also keep the bowels clean.

(b) Take the powder of 15 black pepper (काली मिर्च) + 2 teaspoonfuls of crystal sugar. Soak them in $1\frac{1}{2}$ glass of water overnight. Blend it and drink it all as first thing in the morning for 15 days. After 15 days, add 5 almonds in blending and drink for further 10 days. This is very useful even in jaundice, psoriasis, sunstroke, etc.

After 25 days :

(c) Take five black peppers (काली मिर्च) + 10/12 black raisins (काला मनुका) + 1 teaspoonful of Saunf. Soak them in one glass of water in the evening. The next day, blend them and drink it in the afternoon. It's a useful drink in summer.

(d) Take equal quantity of cumin seed powder (जीरा), black pepper (काली मिर्च), saunf, amla powder, crystal sugar (मिसरी), ginger powder (सुंठ). Grind them together and keep it in a bottle. Take one teaspoonful of this powder with water in the morning and evening.

(2) Apply green juice and pulp of vegetables on the skin and give blue light on the same for five to ten minutes twice a day.

During this treatment drugs are to be stopped gradually in four to six days, and four pills of Thuja 200 – (a Homoeopathic medicine) is to be taken once a day for three days. This will counter the side effects of the drugs taken previously.

It may be noted that this treatment is harmless (no side effects), does not cost much and could be easily taken by the patient or can be given to the patient by his/her relatives at home. I have heard of wonderful results in all types of cancer/HIV and has found that this treatment is effective in at least 60 to 75% patients of AIDS.

Prevention :

The first cause of HIV infection, i.e. through blood can be prevented by the medical people. And the patients of drug addiction can be given treatment and warning. Thus, this cause can be also eliminated.

Another cause is sex abuse :

It may be possible to treat the homosexuals and heterosexuals as patients. And if proper treatment is given to them, they may become normal.

Safe Sex :

When a male is aroused of sex desire, he is not able to use his discretion to use condoms and have safe sex. The following treatment will enable the person to have self control and so safe sex.

Control :

Take a rubber ball of about 2″ diameter – like a tennis ball. Place it under the seat between the anus and testicles when loose clothes are worn. Sit on the ball for 5 to 10 minutes twice a day. This method can be tried by women also and is very effective in leucorrhoea. See fig. 89.

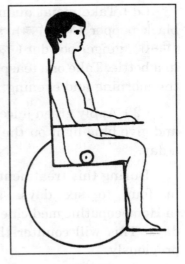

Fig. 89

How to increase spermatozoa in the semen?

(a) Abstain from sex.

(b) Keep control as mentioned above.

(c) Drink two glasses of gold/silver/copper/iron charged water reduced from four glasses.

(d) After 15 days of the above treatment, take one dry fig and one dry date. Cut them into small pieces and soak them in one cup of water. Next day morning, drink this water, chew the small pieces of fig and date. And drink one cup of hot milk with one teaspoonful of crystal sugar and one cardamom. Within three to six months, the sperms will increase to normal level.

The above treatment can also be taken by childless couples. After four to six months of treatment and in more than 75% cases, they will be blessed with a child.

If the growing youths are taught the treatment of acupressure from the age of ten to twelve, they will be able to control themselves and refrain from sex and drug delinquency. Moreover, they can be taught the above method of self control.

It is high time to pause and think. Sex is a great pleasure, but care should be taken in its indulgence. In nature, it comes in a natural way. Animals have self sex control. In our world, on one hand, sex is exploited and then a complaint is made of sex abuse. In the case of diabetes, self control is advised. Excessive use of sugar/sweets for diabetic patients is dangerous. Then, why not there be self restraint for sex?

It may be noted that popular medical treatment has failed to prevent the cause of diabetes, cancer and AIDS. Let's go back to mother nature and try natural therapies. Results will be wonderful and there will be health and happiness in the world.

If the mankind desires to survive from the dreaded diseases, one *must* go back to nature and accept its health sciences.

Man must realise, reconsider the whole aspect and make amends to wife and children who have been forcibly made victims of HIV infection and AIDS. It should be accepted that sex abuse is a disease like drug addiction and proper treatment for the same must be started at once on a war footing.

It may be noted that in the underdeveloped countries, sex is one of the major attractions for pleasure. And sex is being provoked more and more through cinema, magazines and TV. It is possible that if all the people are medically examined, it may be found that HIV has reached alarming levels. And if proper steps are not taken at the earliest, it would spread like a wildfire and can become a great danger to life on the earth.

I, therefore, suggest the following :

1. A team of young volunteers of students of university + trained nurses + dedicated social workers + retired professors and teachers is to be created and trained in Acupressure. Such a training can be completed in 12/16 hours by reading my books "Health in Your Hands : Volume 1 & 2" at least twice and making note of what they have not understood. Such training camps can be arranged at few important centres in each country.

2. After training in Acupressure is completed, free health camps should be arranged in the maximum number of centres and it must be made compulsory for all the families to come forward for a check-up. They will be checked up thoroughly and proper guidance about the treatment will be given to them for not only HIV, but also for all types of diseases.

3. A small booklet about HIV should be prepared in local languages and given to each family.

4. All the females engaged in commercial sex should be checked up and proper treatment should be suggested. They should be taught how to use vaginal douche everyday.

5. All the females found to have such infection should be given treatment and shown the use of vaginal douche.

6. All the youths should be made aware of the dangers of free sex and its adverse consequences. They should be taught to control the sex desire which is possible. After the age of 21 condoms should be made freely available.

7. The volunteers should visit each family in pairs and examine all the members and teach them how to take Acupressure treatment at home.

8. In this work, the help of local nurses should be taken. They will be able to show and teach the use of vaginal douche to women.

9. The affected patients should be convinced and persuaded to come to the health centres every 15 days. At this health centres, provision should be made to supply charged water.

10. All the positive patients of HIV must be strictly warned about the grave consequences and be given a thorough treatment for two/three months till their infection is cured.

11. The affected children should be given treatment for three months. State should provide them fresh fruits and black raisin (काला मनुका) which are a must to combat their Thalassemia.

12. Retired professors and teachers should be included in the training camp and later on they should be given the charge of health centres where training can be imparted.

Thus, if such action is taken on a war footing, not only HIV but even cancer, cataract, asthma, diabetes and other diseases will be cured and controlled. In short, within a period of only 24/45 months, health can be guaranteed to all.

13. The cost involved is very negligible. Benevolent organisations and social organisations like Rotary, Lions, Giants International clubs can assist. Even the health department of all the Governments can contribute.

On my part, I am willing to train 300 to 1000 volunteers at each centre, to supervise such health camps and give them expert guidance whenever necessary, free of charge.

In this prestigious project, the local newspapers and magazines can play an important role. Wherever possible, the use of the powerful medium of TV, seminars and demonstrations should be made. Video cassettes can be prepared for the laymen.

How to prevent disaster after marriage :

The physical aspect of a marriage is (A) Satisfaction in sex (B) to have healthy children.

Now certificates about the physical fitness and that the boy or girl has NO HIV are not possible. After marriage, one comes to know about any deficiency and as regards HIV, one comes to know of it after they have children and these children are having problem. Only then if the couple goes only to an Acupressurist, he/she may be able to find about HIV, while going through the root cause. Meanwhile, the couple may have more than one child.

Even when they come to know about the deficiency of semen or come to know about HIV, it is very difficult to abstain from sex, which is very necessary for the cure of these problems. I have been very much perturbed to observe that every week, I come across more than 100 cases of problems in children and women; where these problems are related to V. D., deficiency in semen and HIV. It is a pity that society has not paid any attention to this growing problem. Even I have found HIV among the college going boys and girls.

Acupressure can prevent such problems. One must have knowledge about this Health Science, at least those youths who would be going for marriage. First, they should use this therapy and cure their health problem if any. Before engagement and marriage, one should take the following precautions :

Check point nos. 11 to 15 and also point no. 37. Also see the nails of both the boy and the girl.

Now if the half-moons as shown in Fig. 41 are not visible in any of the fingers except the thumb or the first finger called index finger, OR these white moons are not milky white but look dull like water in the nails of the boy, then it denotes that he may have some sex deficiency due to masturbation. In the case white spots are coming out of these white moons, it denotes that still masturbation is continued.

Now if the same thing is observed in the girl, it denotes that she may have the problem of white discharge, known as Leucorrhoea. She may have problem in conceiving or the children to be born would weak and she may not be able to satisfy her husband and be able to accept the extra liability of the marriage.

Pain on point no. 37 of the Spleen :

Press on point no. 37 on the left palm. one would find pain on this point if :

(1) One has Malaria for more than 20 days. There will be doctor's certificate and moreover this fact would be known to neighbours and could be easily verified.

(2) If one has got Cancer in the blood – which is obvious and therefore, one should not consider about this proposal.

(3) One may have Thalassemmia – Here medical certificate is available. This disease is curable and so if otherwise desirable, treatment for the same should be taken before marriage and proper care should be taken before planning for a child and also during pregnancy.

(4) Otherwise it could be due to HIV infection. And it is not detected in ordinary blood Test or even in ELISA Test. Only in Western Block Test, it can be detected. Cure for this dreaded problem has been given before. Engagement or marriage can be entered into only after one is satisfied that this disease is totally cured.

So, do not hurry for engagement or marriage. In case the engagement is already entered into, and otherwise then, marriage should be postponed for a year and proper treatment should be started at once.

Moreover, nowadays, many youths who have gone abroad for studies and settled there, come back to home country with a desire to get a bride. As there is sexual freedom and easy life in these foreign countries, it is possible that these youths may have acquired HIV. Please take proper care in such cases.

This HIV is a silent killer. After marriage, the other partner is likely to acquire HIV in the first intercourse and then the children born thereafter will be having HIV.

During the last three years, I have come across hundreds of such cases, where just after a year or two, the wife came to her parents with a child and both are found to be infected with HIV. Of course, such a woman can get a divorce. But even though she may cure her HIV, she would find it extremely difficult to get a husband; as the society knows that she had HIV. And what about the innocent child?

It is high time, the medical world, the social workers and the Governments of all the countries of the world paid proper attention to this grave problem, which is getting bigger and bigger every day. If we desire that our future generation should be HEALTHY and HAPPY, we must take immediate remedial steps on a war footing against HIV/AIDS.

———

CHAPTER 13

CONSULTATION THROUGH POST/PHONE

For readers :

First read my books, "Health in Your Hands : Volume 1 & 2" thoroughly. Find out the root cause and start treatment accordingly. For example, in the case of Kidney problem, try to find out why the kidney is damaged. May be there is pain on point nos. 11 to 15 + 16 & OR 37. And so you are supposed to take the treatment not only for Kidney, i. e., "PYELITIS" but also for Cancer as mentioned in the books.

Even then, if you desire to consult me or any Acupressurist by post/telephone then first press on the two palms as shown in fig. 39 (a) and (b) in Volume 1; and fig. 16 (a) & (b) of Volume 2. Find out which points are painful and then inform accordingly. Also give a brief note about your present problem. **There is no necessity to narrate your history or send the Medical Reports.**

For Practitioners :

Consider the points and the brief note given to you by the patient. Find out the root cause and guide the patient accordingly.

It may be noted that only in Acupressure, such consultation is possible even without examining the patient, through post/phone. It is, therefore, most necessary for the patient to read my books, "Health in Your Hands : Volume 1 and 2."

CHAPTER 14

CONCLUSION

Dear Readers,

During the last thirty months, I have been able to locate HIV in about six thousand families, i.e. about 25,000 persons. With proper treatment, this disease comes under control.

The Acupressure treatment has benefited not only about 2,00,000 patients who have visited our free Acupressure centre but more than 40 million people in India. Moreover, this therapy has been tested by more than 2500 medical practitioners for their own problems. Many of these medical practitioners have ordered my book for reference and practice. This itself proves the efficacy of this 'Do It Yourself' therapy of Acupressure.

This health science of nature – Acupressure is the only therapy which gives protection against almost all the diseases. Its diagnosis is equal to that of MRI (Magnetic Resonance Imaging) tests and that too instantly and totally costless. It is able to cure all types of diseases.

It is high time the mankind reconsidered this fact. If they desire to survive from these fast spreading diseases, they have no alternative but to surrender to nature and accept its therapies.

This Nature's 'Do It Yourself' Acupressure therapy itself is a science and not a matter of belief.

Dear reader, you know that this treatment does not cost you any money. Moreover, it is harmless. It has no side-effects. Therefore, as a sensible person desiring good health try this therapy sincerely and regularly for at least 15 days and observe its wonderful and amazing results. **Health is the birth right of mankind and it can be achieved very easily. Very shortly you will become your own doctor and a firm** believer of "Your Health Is In Your Hands". At the time of pressing your palms or soles, please thank the Great Supreme Power, GOD, who has installed this wonderful system of self-cure in your body.

Clarification for all foreigners – Non-Indians

Rishis	= Ancient Yogis – saints
Injection	= shot
Peg	= short
Gram flour	= flour of a pulse called gram
Sudarshan Powder (सुदर्शन चुर्ण)	= A bitter Ayurvedic Powder
Harde/Haritki (हरडे / हरितकी चुर्ण)	= Powder of Terminalia chebula Retz- an Ayurvedic medicine.
Kayfal (कायफल)	= N. O. Myricacae
Bilipatra (बिलीपत्र)	= Eagle Mar
Neem (नीम)	= Azadiracta Indica.
Tulsi (श्वामतूलसी)	= Ocimum centum
Amla (आमला)	= Embalica – an Indian nut (having concentrated vitamin C)

Nux Vomica
Thuja ⎫ = Homoeopathic medicines

Cal. Phos + Cal. Fl. + Kali
Phos + Nat. Mur + Kali
Iodide etc. ⎫ = Biochemic medicines

(All Homoeopathic and Biochemic medicines are available at any Homoeopathic Drug Store/Pharmacy.)

DO THIS DAILY

1. Press your two palms each for 5 minutes – on front and back.
2. If, over 40 years, press for 2 minutes the middle of the right arm. See figure below.

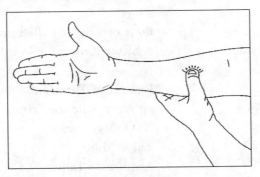

3. Then press on all the points where it pains, i.e. give treatment 3 times a day for 2 minutes on each point like pumping.
4. In the evening, while sitting in a chair, roll your soles of the legs on a roller. See figure below.

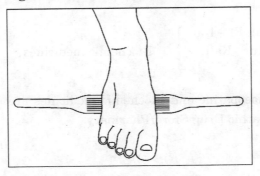

5. Make a habit of drinking :
   (a) One glass of hot water – preferably charged water as first thing in the morning.
   (b) Drinking one glass of green juice adding 1 tablespoonful of honey.
   (c) Drink one glass of fresh fruit juice.
6. Correct the Solar Plexus and avoid constipation.

BEFORE STARTING TREATMENT
PROPER DIAGNOSIS
IS A MUST

NOW YOU CAN
DO SUCH DIAGNOSIS
in your Home without
TESTS & COST

Read this Important Book

HEALTH IN YOUR HANDS : VOLUME 2

**based on the experience of
2,00,000 Patients for : over twenty
years**

by
World Renowned Acupressurist
Dr. Devendra Vora

*A MUST for every HOME &
all the Medical Practitioners*

Total **MEDICAL INSURANCE**
only
For less than Ten Dollars
Handbook of
ACUPRESSURE
by
World Renowned Acupressurist
Dr. Devendra Vora

HEALTH IN
YOUR HANDS : VOLUME 1

Read this unique book and learn this
"DO IT YOURSELF THERAPY"
and treat all types of diseases
What the Medical Practitioners say about this book :
"Most ideal book to give as a gift to
friends and relatives."
Dr. Jagdish Bhat, Ex-Dean of B. Y. L. Nair and
L. T. M. G. Sion Hospitals, Mumbai.

"It is an excellent book" *– Hanna Blumenfield,*
Leading Acupressurist of U.S.A.

"This is one of the finest books,
I have read on Reflexology."
Dr. S. Isseri, F.R.C.S., Durban, S. Africa.

"Your book enabled me to cure my twenty-year old
constipation within just 2 Days."
Dr. Sat Paul Singh, Professor of Punjab University.

गाला की आरोग्यविषयक श्रेष्ठ पुस्तकें

ये पुस्तकें अँग्रेजी, मराठी और गुजराती भाषा में भी सभी पुस्तक–विक्रेता के पास से मिल सकती है।

Knowledge is wealth

H 1